791.43
.013
sto
2013

# stolen glimpses
# captive shadows

# stolenglimpses

WRITING ON FILM 2002–2012

# captiveshadows

## GEOFFREY O'BRIEN

COUNTERPOINT | BERKELEY

Stolen Glimpses, Captive Shadows:
Writing on Film, 2002–2012
Copyright © Geoffrey O'Brien 2013

Library of Congress Cataloging-in-Publication Data

O'Brien, Geoffrey, 1948-
  [Essays. Selections]
  Stolen glimpses, captive shadows : writing on film, 2002-2012 / Geoffrey O'Brien.
      pages cm
  ISBN 978-1-61902-170-9
1. Motion pictures. I. Title.
  PN1994.O28 2013
  791.43—dc23
  2013002370

Cover design by Michael Kellner
Interior design by Neuwirth & Associates

COUNTERPOINT
1919 Fifth Street
Berkeley, CA 94710
www.counterpointpress.com

Printed in the United States of America
Distributed by Publishers Group West

10 9 8 7 6 5 4 3 2 1

*for Robert Silvers*

# contents

# preface

MOVIES WERE A RECENT INVENTION, and now they are mutating into some further, indeterminable identity: a transient episode in what is after all nothing but the history of transience. The machinery for preserving moments, a triumph of nineteenth-century scientific ambition, was itself to be only of a certain moment. It is impossible to foresee in what form its archive will be preserved, if at all, or whether most of it will join the eroded cave paintings, shredded tapestries, and burnt icons in the great museum of oblivion.

Before the machinery was movies it took other forms: daguerreotypes, flickering mobile toys, or stereoscopic projections like those that Ralph Waldo Emerson saw in Concord, Massachusetts, on November 14, 1860, taking them as an almost unsurpassable display of technical advancement: "Yesterday eve I attended at the Lyceum in the Town Hall the Exhibition of Stereoscopic views magnified on the wall, which seems to me the last & most important application of this wonderful art: for here was London, Paris, Switzerland, Spain, &, at last, Egypt, brought visibly & accurately to Concord, for authentic examination by women & children, who had never left their state." Emerson ends his account with a sentence that I take as an early and prescient instance of American film writing: "And the lovely manner in which one picture was changed for another beat the faculty of dreaming." A little over half a century later the world would indeed be dotted with dream palaces.

And less than a century after that the visions that filled those palaces would shrink to the size of a screen held in the palm of the hand. It's as if the cities themselves had disappeared into those miniature screens.

It is easy to lose sight of how strange it all is, a breaching of barriers so thoroughly assimilated that those who came before—the earlier generations who managed to live without photography or sound recording or simultaneous broadcast—seem stunted beings who lacked a fundamental part of their sensory apparatus. But cinema, just for having been around a while, doesn't get any less strange, or any less powerful. To remember the strangeness is perhaps a way of keeping the power under some sort of manageable control, lest we be altogether overwhelmed by shadows.

The mere fact that a movie can exist is a more astonishing fact than the qualities of any given movie, just as the existence of language is more astonishing than any poem. There was always something so implausible about this invention as to fall necessarily under suspicion. This was smuggler's booty. The heavy metal cans contained stolen glimpses of other worlds. To hang suspended in air, see through walls, fly over cities and peer unseen at their inhabitants, go back in time: these must be in some sense illicit pleasures. Movies are the banal miracle, an achieved magic to which we have almost become inured.

What interests and unsettles is that "almost": that troubling margin of unease with what takes place when I watch an old film. Have we really internalized once and for all the fact that we can do this? Forget for a moment about "art" or "history" or "distraction" or other such alibis. There are other names for the temptation to which I have so often yielded. I possess a machine that permits time travel.

There are limits to its capacities. I can move backward but never forward. My role does not go beyond spying on the inhabitants of other moments and surveying as much as I can of their domain. But it's as easy as pushing open an unlatched screen door. I want to go there not because it's imaginary but because it's real. Odysseus and Aeneas had to cross the River Styx to gaze on the dead, I can do it as much as I please to the point of indifference: watch them walk, laugh at their jokes, perk up at the rhythms of their dancing.

A CAVE PAINTING, it might be argued, is no less strange, or an alphabet. It is unnervingly odd, at bottom, to inhabit ancient sentences. The mere sight of a black stone cup that quenched neolithic thirst might well set off tremors of alarm about the time through which we so heedlessly pass. Yet every form, every image, every sentence ever made was made to tamp down any such alarm by marking a point in time to which one could return at will. A physical object was not even required. From memory alone the shape or phrase could be reconstituted just as it was.

But still it was not enough. Emerson and his friend William Ellery Channing advanced through the Concord woods observing their constantly changing surfaces, their sudden shifts of light and quivers of startled life: "But we say, where is he who is to save the present moment, & cause that this beauty not be lost?"

Science took that as a challenge and invented the mechanism that seemed to answer Emerson's question. Movies were a device to stop time in its tracks—trap it like a genie in a bottle—and keep it from ever escaping. Film seemed close to being the perfect trap, a sticky dangling strip for moments to get stuck on. And so in the towns and cities of the twentieth century the spectators marched like entranced sleepwalkers into the sealed palaces, processing the universal newsreel of the shared dream life.

What drug could be more powerful than the permission to cross over into that world? If there were from the start so many movies about drugs—about opium, about whiskey, about cigarettes, about gambling, about mad and feverish dancing, about hypnotism, about irresistible love-magic—it was because movies were themselves the drug that permitted the most profound escape from world and self. The movie theaters were always dream palaces, even when they consisted of nothing but miniature peepholes.

The escape was so well planned that we may need to begin plotting how to escape from our escape, now that our library of images forms the very walls within which we live. We are sufficiently possessed by our time machines that we use them to travel to the present moment,

a destination ever more remote. The environment becomes dream palace, as movies continue to evolve into the nameless thing well on its
way to becoming the only form—the all-encompassing all-enveloping
around-the-clock interactive simulacrum of what used to be known as
the real world, a slithering clutter that is undoubtedly (as in the futurological visions marketed as cheap paperback thrills half a century
ago) learning not only to read but to anticipate our thoughts.

From the time this invention emerged into human life, our world
became the planet whose inhabitants, most curiously from some imagined Martian perspective, filmed themselves so that they might over
and over again watch themselves. You can see them, for example, in
a home movie from the late silent era miraculously preserved in an
archive, getting on and off trains, splashing in pools of water, admiring natural wonders, looking at themselves being there amid roller
coasters and miniature golf courses and celebrated rock formations.
Perhaps they did not grasp at first that the imprint of such movements,
such glances, would become emblems capable of infesting a lifetime's
worth of dreams. Replayed in memory those filmed gestures and locations seem almost part of the body, an internalized heraldic history of
the life of feeling. We cannot quite make our peace with the fundamental mysteriousness of what has been captured. Departed life splashes
on us.


WE WATCH WHAT is moving fast from a platform that is also moving
fast. The angles and distances change with nerve-wracking suddenness. What was intimately familiar becomes grotesquely strange. What
was fuzzily quaint becomes, with equal suddenness, a visit from a lost
loved one. The past is splendidly restored only to disappear again more
thoroughly than before. The startling new thing becomes material for
retrospectives. The glimpses that cinema stole from life we steal again
from cinema. Obliquely, on the rebound, by way of a reflection, life
looks at life.

# popcorn park

ON HALCYON AFTERNOONS BACK IN the Age of Pop, around 1966 or so, college students and other idlers—mostly male, as was and is the tendency—liked to use the latest stack of Marvel Comics as text for a free-floating commentary. The vantage point hardly mattered: aesthetics, Jungian psychology, the dynamics of American social life, the sexual implications of superhero costuming. Marvel's creations were grist for any kind of rumination, high or low. They provided a shorthand for categorizing personalities and situations (an analogy for almost anything could be found somewhere within the rapidly expanding Marvel Universe), and, most satisfying of all, could be taken as frivolously or as seriously as you wanted. In those days it was not unusual to hear Stan Lee (then still at least the credited writer of almost all the company's dozen or so titles) praised as a protean intelligence of near-Shakespearean dimensions, while the distinctive styles of Marvel's artists—Jack Kirby, Steve Ditko, Jim Steranko, and many others—fueled hours of discussion about the nature of the line and the employment of space.

Here, many felt, was the real Pop Art, not the appropriation of mass culture by the likes of Lichtenstein and Warhol but a sophisticated reinvention of that culture by longtime veterans of its lowliest reaches. The simplistic charms of old-style superhero comics, with their infantile motivations and threadbare fantasy worlds, had been revamped by

Stan Lee and his colleagues into an elaborate playing-out of the genre's possibilities. Marvel's superheroes were self-conscious, plagued by doubts, subject to irrational obsessions, and the increasingly complicated narratives in which they interacted were a knowing encyclopedia of all the elements of adventure serial and soap opera. The main characters—the Fantastic Four, the Incredible Hulk, Dr. Strange (Master of the Mystic Arts), Iron Man, Thor, Sub-Mariner, and, most popular of all, Spider-Man—each had his own emotional shadings and fetishistic peculiarities. Best of all, the proceedings were bathed in a humor which, if not deathlessly witty, gave the proceedings a reliably jaunty cadence: "Though there be many writers, none but Stan Lee could have penned this tale! Though there be many artists, none but Steve Ditko could have drawn this tale! Though there be many letterers, none but Artie Simek was available when we needed him!"

Marvel Comics were overtly formulistic, drawing attention to their visual and narrative devices, and interlarding even the most portentous scenes with wisecracks from the sidelines. The reader was constantly reminded that the story was being invented from one frame to the next, and the result was a sense of complicity between reader and artist. At least at the outset, before they too evolved into a gigantic corporate enterprise, Marvel Comics were perceived as an antidote to the squareness and predictability of mass entertainment. At once good-natured and anti-heroic, they preserved the spirit of seat-of-the-pants inspiration associated with pulp magazines and B-movies; they had something of the free-flowing comic invention of the early days of *Mad* magazine, coupled with a serious absorption in the evolving mythology of their characters. If not homemade, they seemed at least made in a very small, congenially noisy workplace, full of jokes, kibitzing, and sudden bursts of collective enthusiasm. (In fact, the myth of such a workplace, as conveyed in the asides and intros of the episodes, may have been Stan Lee's most convincing creation.)

And then there was the art. The stories were good for one go-round, but the graphics often became permanent points of reference. A comic book was like a movie you could hold in your hand, contemplating the action as a series of immobilized moments of tension: in some ways it was better than a movie, because of the scope it offered to expand imaginatively on what the page offered. Even aside from the difficulties of staging the fanciful combats and intergalactic confrontations of the comics (now solved after a fashion by the advent of computerized special effects), it seemed unlikely that any movie could ever capture the way the best comics felt lightweight and monumental in the same instant, while remaining the direct handwritten evidence of a human touch. What movies gained in virtual presence they lost in the jauntiness of a world made with pen and ink.

Sam Raimi's *Spider-Man*, which became the latest warm-weather blockbuster to break all previous first-weekend attendance records, adheres rather faithfully to the letter of the original comic book. Much of it is a straightforward recapitulation of the origin of Spider-Man, as recounted on his first appearance in *Amazing Fantasy* in August 1962: the transformation of serious, socially awkward science major Peter Parker by the bite of a radioactive (in the movie, genetically altered) spider into a superhero capable of climbing walls, swinging from building to building on webs, and sensing the approach of danger with his "spider sense." The catch was that he was never quite able to make his peace with that transformation. At the time the idea of a teenage superhero was a novelty, and the idea of a neurotic teenage superhero, troubled by recurrent feelings of guilt and inadequacy, seemed positively revolutionary.

The crucial plot point in the original episode was that Peter Parker's initial burst of unwonted arrogance on receiving his spider powers led through a sequence of ineluctable coincidences to the death of his beloved Uncle Ben. The notion of a moral lapse (his momentary hubris) that could never really be atoned for gave the comic book its air of perpetual dissatisfaction; being Spider-Man was not only a burden in itself but a perpetual reminder to the hero of his own shortcomings, a kind of penance. There was always the possibility that he would fail again, and so he was condemned to a vigilant monitoring of his own reactions and impulses. In such a situation an unqualified sense of triumph was by definition impossible. In its own goofy way, *The Amazing Spider-Man* acknowledged the tragic sense of life.

Raimi is finely attuned to those nuances, but what once were unanticipated tweaks of characterization have over time become nearly solemn. It was amusing in the mid-sixties to juxtapose Stan Lee with Shakespeare, to find an analogy between Shakespeare's multifariousness and Lee's populous mythology, and contrariwise between Lee's sure instinct for entertainment and Shakespeare's unwavering theatricality. But that doesn't mean that Spider-Man can assume the gravitas of Lear or Hamlet, even with Danny Elfman's somber theme music stirring up a mood of troubled pensiveness. The problem is partly one of scale. If you compare Steve Ditko's art for that first Spider-Man episode with the visual look of Raimi's film, it's like putting the drawing on a 1950s matchbox next to one of the huge digital displays that now define the landscape of Times Square. Ditko's boxy little frames, however, have a quirky vigor and caricatural grace that let us know a live hand is tracing them, and when those scrawny miniature figures are forced to contend with moral dilemmas they acquire a quixotic stature. Such is the odd intimacy that comics can command.

Raimi's film, on the other hand—and the same could be said of most such contemporary films—looks like what it is, a work of large-scale industry. If you admire it, it's in the same way you might admire a World's Fair or a suspension bridge. *The Amazing Spider-Man* came up from the bottom; not many people were looking for original invention in ten-cent comic books in 1962. *Spider-Man*, the movie, descends from above, trailing clouds of magazine covers and licensed toys, and thus has a ponderousness its model altogether lacked. The scenes of digitally simulated combat—like most scenes of digitally simulated combat—have little more life to them than the rapidly shifting arrangements of numbers on the screen of an electronic calculator. Not for one moment do we believe that any entity is colliding with any other entity. The heft of actual being and actual contact is replaced by a terminally weightless play of microdots. The action scenes certainly lack the humorous inventiveness of the whirling and careening body parts in

Sam Raimi's breakthrough feature, the low-budget horror picture *The Evil Dead* (1983), a movie whose nonstop carnival of demonic possession in a haunted cabin was much closer in its freewheeling spirit, if not its gruesome content, to Marvel Comics at their best.

It must also be said that the enactments of aerial assault—for instance in the protracted scene where the Green Goblin, Spider-Man's psychotic nemesis, massacres the board of directors of a technology corporation in the midst of a public festival—have a brutality of tone that nearly sinks the mood of fantasy. Perhaps it is only because I watched the film in a recently reopened movie theater directly overlooking Ground Zero that such evocations of urban structures demolished by flying objects felt less than diverting. At any rate I did not feel alone in an audience that seemed clearly unexhilarated by the numbing digitized intimations of bludgeoning impact.

The paradox of digital effects is that the more real they look the less real they feel. The most primitive models and painted backdrops of the early silent era convey far more the sense of events occurring in actual space, and thus far more the possibility of emotional consequence. Like the digital Rome of *Gladiator*, which never looked like anything other than an architect's blueprint, the aerial ballets of *Spider-Man* lack a crucial element: air. Raimi's film is something of an epic of New York, but despite all the elaborate (and elaborately altered) location work, it can't help feeling like a mere simulacrum.

Marvel's original *Spider-Man* by contrast got much of its edge from the intersection of comic-book absurdity with the commonplaces of New York in the Lindsay years. No-nonsense cab drivers, hot dog stands, *The Ed Sullivan Show*: it was amid such familiar cultural markers that Spider-Man waged his annihilating battles against the Vulture or the Kingpin or Doctor Octopus. It hardly mattered that New York was depicted in a thoroughly stylized fashion; the fact that it was indicated at all was as bracing a blast of reality as the steam from a Con Ed work site. J. Jonah Jameson, the short-tempered, cigar-chewing newspaper publisher (who gets sadly short shrift in the movie version), embodied something of the ambience of those unventilated back rooms where you could imagine the old-time comic books being cranked out.

Raimi is on much surer ground with the soap opera elements—Peter Parker's invalid aunt, his girlfriend troubles, his simmering jealousies and resentments—that were probably the secret reason for the comic's special appeal. There are even moments when Raimi seems to be evoking the mood of curdled domesticity that he cultivated to such ominous effect in the underrated thriller *A Simple Plan*, as if to defy the inevitable moment of heartwarming emotional outpouring which all American movies now require. *The Amazing Spider-Man* was essentially a romance comic disguised as a superhero comic, a secret feminization of the man-of-steel tradition, and Tobey Maguire's incarnation of Peter Parker has a cuddly charm that will doubtless lead to many sequels, even if his performance lacks the quality of nerdy anguish so well expressed by Steve Ditko's primitively expressive artwork. Maguire looks a little too capable of enjoying himself, with the result that it's hard to believe the final act of romantic renunciation, when he chooses to give up the girl of his dreams to follow a more ascetic path of lonely heroism. Willem Dafoe's fire-eating performance as the Green Goblin is on the other hand almost too fully achieved; he makes everybody else look as if they're just rehearsing.

Raimi has done the sort of unimpeachably professional job that means we are probably witnessing the birth of another highly profitable franchise. As an entertainment *Spider-Man* has pretty much everything it needs. It lacks only that factor of eccentricity, that wild card of random improvisation that made the comics so much fun in the first place. That would of course be too much to expect. If *Spider-Man* had been filmed back in the sixties, we might have gotten something like Joseph Losey's *Modesty Blaise* (1966) or Mario Bava's *Danger: Diabolik* (1968), obtrusive exercises in applying primary-colored Pop Art style to every frame, with results that were eye-popping if not necessarily moving or even absorbing. If it had been filmed in the seventies or eighties, it would probably have been a tacky production filmed on location in a developing country and jazzed up with a little gratuitous nudity or a bit of martial arts. What we get now is *Spider-Man* as narrative theme park, cautious, respectful, planned down to the last dangling coil of webbing, realized by the usual coordinated teams of disciplined professionals, and pre-sold with the skill that is an art in itself to a global audience that will wake up to find that this is what it was waiting for all along.

*The New York Review of Books*, 2002

# learning to argue with
# pauline kael

IN HIGH SCHOOL AND COLLEGE, on the days when Pauline Kael's reviews appeared in *The New Yorker,* I would read them through (often to the exclusion of anything else in the magazine) with rapt attention and frequent amusement. Having done so, I would proceed to quarrel with them at length, either inwardly or to anyone who would listen. As an enthusiast of Westerns, gangster movies, and lurid horror of the Hammer and Cinecittà schools, a devoted supporter of Samuel Fuller and Sergio Leone, I was aware of belonging to a tribe of youthful auteurists she characterized in tones ranging from contempt to pitying bemusement. Reading her was sometimes like being scolded at a distance by an instructor with a flair for mocking exactitude. I was not to be persuaded out of my tastes even by Kael's finely tuned wit, yet she did raise the uncomfortable question of whether I could mount a defense as articulate, as cunningly modulated, as worldly and self-confident as her attacks. It was one thing to admire *Curse of the Demon* or *Hercules Conquers Atlantis* or *The Rise and Fall of Legs Diamond,* and quite another thing to find language adequate to explaining such admiration.

Of course I continued to read and reread Kael because of the pleasure she was constantly affording in the most unexpected ways: in her quick sketches of actors or scenes, her aphoristic encapsulations (even when they were infuriating) of the American cultural scene and sixties youth culture, the splashes of color and line that enlivened reviews of some of the deadliest movies imaginable, her relentless prodding of anything she found false or inadequate—a misbegotten movie like *The Shoes of the Fisherman* or *The Night of the Following Day*—until it seemed to break apart on the page, a wreckage consisting of elegantly turned sentences. She was such great company that it was always a pleasure to anticipate renewed quarrels.

Her faculty of sheer humorous invention keeps her reviews of even the most minor pictures alive. Who else would have described Sandy Dennis in *Sweet November* as "an icky little rabbit Babbit" or suggested, in discussing the star quality of Candice Bergen and Omar Sharif: "Perhaps stars like these could be bred, like broad-backed circus horses, or minks." Her disenchantment with the self-deceptions of "youthful" late-sixties film culture would surge up eloquently, as in her review of *Joanna*:

> We are getting the howling banalities of the past brought back in creamy Panavision and fruity DeLuxe color and enough Mod clothes to choke a clotheshorse, and they're brought back not with irony but with moronic solemnity. There's a less publicized side of the generation gap: we remember this stuff from the last time around. Mod filmmakers, it appears, have just discovered the Rubáiyát and are working their way toward *The Razor's Edge.*

Each review was a graph of energy, charted in prose whose rhythms were inexorable. Yet—and she insisted on the point—it was experience in the real world that she was writing about, even if only the experience of watching a movie: an act that she rendered with a novelistic density that made most other film criticism seem random or wanly generalizing.

Returning to her writing after so many years, I'm still puzzled by a central ambivalence in her judgments that seems to gravitate around the notions of "art" and "trash." In her famous essay "Trash, Art, and the

Movies" (*Harper's*, February 1969)—the closest she came to a general statement of intentions—she wants to celebrate the gaudy pleasures of cinematic vulgarity: "I don't trust anyone who doesn't admit having at some time in his life enjoyed trashy American movies . . . Why should pleasure need justification?" She directs withering scorn at those stuffed-shirt humanists who admire *Judgment at Nuremberg* or *Wild Strawberries* but can't appreciate *The Thomas Crown Affair* (1969). But she's equally at odds with anyone who likes trash a little bit too much, likes it enough to think that "trash" is perhaps a term of doubtful use: "If an older generation was persuaded to *dismiss* trash, now a younger generation, with the press and schools in hot pursuit, has begun to talk about trash as if it were really very serious art." It doesn't help that her examples of yesterday's kitsch now mistaken for art are *Shanghai Express* and—amazingly for someone who would go on to wildly praise the Hitchcock homages of Brian de Palma—*Notorious*. She goes in circles on this theme, churning up perplexities about pleasure and puritanism, bourgeois complacency and radical transgression, without ever coming to a comfortable resting point. What is clear is that there is no party of which she wishes to be a member. If she has to declare for anything, it will be the sovereignty of her own taste.

Kael defined her own responses with such thoroughness that little room was left for the possibility of anyone responding differently. It was a little like being at the table with the sort of voluble, entertaining, and supremely informed dinner companion who annihilates your counterarguments before you even get a chance to express them. If this was irritating to the opinionated young cinephile that I was in 1968, it later proved to be her greatest gift to anyone writing about film. There was all the room in the world for different responses—but only on condition that they were treated with something approaching the same level of detail and forthrightness, the same faithfulness to moment-by-moment experience, the same refusal to deny that movies exist in a world that keeps forcing its way into even the most hermetic of viewing experiences.

*Artforum*, 2002

# this is how it happens

THAT ERIC ROHMER, NOW EIGHTY-TWO, should embark on a technically innovative film set during the French Revolution underscores the quiet experimentalism of his filmmaking, an experimentalism sometimes indistinguishable from a return to the earliest cinematic sources. Anyone might have adapted the 1801 memoirs of British aristocrat Grace Dalrymple Elliott, with their account of her troubled friendship with her former lover the duke of Orléans—she a fervent monarchist, he a radicalized aristocrat—and the dangers she experienced during the Revolution; the story, with its escapes and deceptions, trials and imprisonments, does not lack intrinsic excitement. The result in most cases could be predicted: the sort of subtly modernized emotional drama that indulges the touristic delights of ancient luxuries while carefully flattering contemporary ideas about psychology and political motivation. Rohmer has instead chosen fidelity to his text, relying on Elliott for as much of the dialogue as possible, and a filmic approach that emulates the static setups of D.W. Griffith's own French-revolutionary epic of 1921, *Orphans of the Storm*.

*The Lady and the Duke* (*L'Anglaise et le Duc*) stirred up considerable resentment among some French critics troubled at its apparent sympathy for monarchism and its depiction of the French Revolution almost exclusively in terms of uncontrolled mob violence and petty tyranny exercised by Jacobin apparatchiks. (While Anglophone spectators reared on *A Tale of Two Cities* will find little to surprise them in such a characterization, the intricacies of post-Bastille maneuvering—from the ambiguous stance of "Égalité" Orléans to the defection to England of General Dumouriez—may seem slightly opaque, despite Rohmer's lucid exposition.) Yet it would be a pity to see *The Lady and the Duke* primarily as a history film, or as part of a debate on political ideas— ideas that Rohmer, perhaps with a degree of irony, is happy to attribute solely to Grace Elliott, although he did remark to the Parisian daily *Libération* that "I do think [she] was mostly right about the Revolution: It was the end of a world, of a refined civilization."

Deeply interested in historical reconstruction, Rohmer nonetheless rejects the "pseudo-fidelity" of documentary-style restagings. He has chosen (and not, as he has insisted, for reasons of economy) to use painted backdrops and digital techniques for the exterior sequences, most of them depicting scenes of massacre, flight, revolutionary mobi- lization. These scenes, more true than real, are both beautiful and terrifying. The most horrible events take place in the perspective of a child's theater or stereoscopic toy. Far from aestheticizing violence, these exterior episodes have the impact of events that one doesn't dare to look at too closely but cannot purge from memory. If the move- ment of bodies and the depth of space seem unreal, they embody all the more effectively the wooziness of public trauma. A sense of repose is absent because in every case the point for the characters is to pass through, hide, get away.

The interiors, which predominate, are by contrast filmed on a single studio set varied by backdrops and sliding walls to serve as eight dif- ferent locations. The use of a single set isn't especially noticeable, but it does mean that Rohmer is not going to spend a lot of time moving the camera to show off the furniture and the architecture. The spaces are just spaces, and in this film that means they are essentially ref- uges. Danger is outside—seen through a telescope from a balcony or heard as distant shouts and howls—until it intrudes in the form of a midnight visit from the local constabulary. Mostly people wait: for the militiamen to be satisfied and leave, for a chance to slip a fugitive over a wall. A scene in which Grace and her friends await the results of the crucial vote on the king's execution could pass for a fairly pleasant dinner party on election night; that disparity between polite surface and imminent violence acutely conveys the condition of people trying very hard not to surrender to their own anxiety. "Perhaps this is how it happens," Rohmer has remarked, "when History overturns the lives of individuals."

*The Lady and the Duke* rejoins Rohmer's more familiar romantic comedies by presenting a series of intimate conversations between a couple who cannot quite find a point of agreement. Here the question is not whether they will be lovers but whether, having been lovers and friends, they can continue to be allies. With inspired casting Rohmer has pitted Jean-Claude Dreyfus, a traditional actor in the grand French manner—all gestures and winks and elaborate articulation—as the duke, against a relatively inexperienced English actress, Lucy Russell, whose performance is little short of sublime.

Russell's very body language and accent—from the moment she utters the phrase "*Je suis une étrangère*"—distinguish her from the rest of the cast. She is, preeminently, an Englishwoman, an outsider, refusing to become part of the appalling spectacle around her: the element that won't blend, a figure of pure defiance whose political convictions are ultimately less interesting than her refusal to modify her tone in order to placate either friends or enemies. Between them Dreyfus and Russell achieve the tone of comedy in the midst of deepening catastrophe, and without in any way mitigating that catastrophe. For its surfaces and its inner equilibrium alike, *The Lady and the Duke* may be the most beautiful of Rohmer's films.

*Artforum*, 2002

# prospero on the run

PHILIP K. DICK'S SHORT STORY "The Minority Report," which
was first published in the magazine *Fantastic Universe* in 1956, posits
a future America in which crime has been virtually abolished through
the employment of mentally retarded people—"gibbering, fumbling
creatures, with . . . enlarged heads and wasted bodies"—who possess
the wild talent of seeing crimes before they happen. Wired to a network of computers, the "pre-cogs" transmit visions of future events, on
the basis of which future criminals are arrested and incarcerated in a
vast detention camp.

The story's tricky but oddly perfunctory narrative hook—the director
of the Precrime program is himself fingered by the pre-cogs as a future
murderer—provides the occasion for a run-through of paradoxes associated with prediction, particularly the notion that knowledge of how
things will turn out makes it possible to change the outcome. The "minority report" of the title refers to a dissenting pre-cog's variant vision of the
future, proven wrong by the concurrence of two majority reports, a situation which is likened to the use of multiple computers to verify a solution.
Of the story's relevance to actual problems of cybernetics or to the laws
of probability I am not competent to speak; to a lay reader it has more the
effect of a discussion of mathematical theory overheard in a dream.

With its background of postwar devastation and a murky, top-secret
contention between military and civilian branches of government,

its concern for the fate of thought criminals, and its troubling link-age (under federal auspices) of brain damage and computer science, "The Minority Report" is a dream—a bad dream—straight out of the 1950s. Written relatively early in Dick's prolific career, it offers only rudimentary traces of those virtual realities and industrially marketed simulacra characteristic of his remarkably influential later fiction. Also suggestive of the 1950s is its no-frills prose style, which evokes a per-fectly dull future devoid of exoticism or poetic resonance: "Cold, light rain beat against the pavement, as the car moved through the dark streets of New York City toward the police building. . . . Helplessly, Anderton watched pedestrians hurrying along the rain-swept side-walks. He felt no strong emotion." We might have stumbled into the middle of *The Pre-Cog in the Gray Flannel Suit.*

*Minority Report,* the movie that Steven Spielberg has made from this by now somewhat distant source, is couched in a style far removed from Dick's flatly functional prose. Its first reel is as bravura a display of style as Spielberg has ever offered, as we watch a movie-within-a-movie of adultery, jealousy, and homicidal rage being assembled from the visions of the pre-cogs by Tom Cruise and his team of Precrime techies who must race against time to find within these images clues to the location of a murder before it is committed. The rapid cutting between the "real" events, the stylized, fragmentary visions of the pre-cogs (a trio of semi-dormant prophets lying on their backs in a glassed-in pool), and the zooms and enlargements effected by Cruise with a mere wave of his hands to the tune of Schubert's "Unfinished Symphony," each image interlarded with billowing layers of reflections and superimpositions, is a relentless display of the futuristic technol-ogy on which it comments: even the smoke and mirrors have smoke and mirrors. Spielberg seems to want to make a catalog of his own devices, to lay bare the inventory of tricks available to him, in a mood compounded of exhilaration and dread.

If I can do this, he appears to imply, then the future that the film is about has already arrived. Unlike the other Dick-derived films of recent decades—notably Ridley Scott's *Blade Runner* and Paul Verhoeven's

*Total Recall—Minority Report* is not so much a work of elegiac or satiric anticipation as it is an acknowledgment that it is already too late to turn back. Even if the screenplay raises moral issues about free will and advance knowledge, insisting somewhat stridently that one can always choose a better course of action, the dazzling and enveloping stylistic maneuvers imply that such independent renunciation is henceforth likely to occur only in the movies. The technology is too powerful for the characters to assert an existence apart from it. The very notion of background and foreground is obliterated by a visual field in which the people are little more than swirls of information oscillating among other analogous swirls. If Spielberg's last film, the much underrated *A.I.*, culminated in a tragic apprehension of human limitation, *Minority Report* charts a more self-contradictory path. At its strongest it unleashes mythic forces, and then tries to contain them with flimsy last-reel fix-ups. It's as if the Cumaean Sibyl were uneasily cast in a remake of *The Fugitive*.

Dick's story plays with the idea of multiple future time-paths, something like Borges's garden of forking paths. In its early stages *Minority Report*, with its casual interaction of present-tense humans with three-dimensional talking archival holograms and live-action prophetic visions, suggests the idea of a movie in which past, present, and future can unfold simultaneously. Tom Cruise's Precrime "theater of operations" could be seen as the ultimate film studio, capable not merely of imitating but of intervening in reality, and getting its inspired script concepts not from a bunch of contract screenwriters but from a captive team of seers, throwbacks to the most ancient oracles, who soak in a high-tech aquarium (called, appropriately, the Temple) complete with an infatuated, half-mad scientist-companion. These early scenes of the lab at work have a charm that must be autobiographical, since they amount to a metaphorical description of Spielberg's daily routine making movies. In that light, it is easy to imagine that considerable personal anxiety underlies the notion (suggested by Cruise's fate after the pre-cogs identify him as a murderer-to-be) of the director shut out from his own studio—barred from using the equipment that he has so incomparably mastered, accused, as it were, by his own creation.

Prospero on the run: except that Prospero in this version is a damaged man in perpetual mourning for his mysteriously vanished six-year-old son, separated from his wife, and addicted to a drug that he buys from a drug dealer with empty eye sockets. The revelation of those dreadful holes is part of an elaborate pattern of eye-related motifs summed up in the female pre-cog's repetitive question: "Can you see?" In the world of *Minority Report*, public security is maintained by random eye-scans, and criminals have their eyes replaced in order to elude the scanners; crime is suppressed by the transmutation of the pre-cogs' inner visions into electronically reproducible form; the memories of past anticipations are downloaded electronically from the brains of the pre-cog seers. The symbolism looms portentously—was it to invoke the totemic presence of Ingmar Bergman that Max von Sydow was cast in the picture?—but with undeniable effectiveness.

By the time Tom Cruise is having his eyes surgically removed by a grotesque doctor-and-nurse pair holed up in a generically sleazy tenement apartment, the symbolism has veered into the realm of a horror-movie creepiness that Spielberg has never—or at least not since *Jaws*—explored with quite such enthusiasm. Like the best horror movies, this segment derives its effect more from what we don't see than from what we do, but the power of suggestion is sufficient to conjure up a mood of deep unpleasantness from which the rest of the film wants in some sense to escape, just as the spectator wants unquestionably to escape from the clamps that pin Cruise's eyes open in preparation for his operation. The film seems to gain a cumulative power—laced with grotesque humor—the deeper it drives its protagonist into darkness.

While the blindfolded hero (he must wait twelve hours for his replaced eyes to heal) submits to uncontrollable inward visions—like home-movie playbacks—of his son's disappearance, police investigators unleash small electronic eye-scanning spiders into the tenement where he's hiding out. We are given an aerial view as the spiders swarm through the building, "reading" the eyes of tenants as they quarrel, make love, or sit on the toilet, their activities scarcely interrupted by the incursion.

The whole episode is a kind of giddy parody of a thirties movie in the *Street Scene* or *Dead End* mode (complete with camera angles worthy of Busby Berkeley). The tenement itself is a retrograde reminder of a vanished pre-techno world of milk bottles and peeling wallpaper, while the electronic spiders—like all those symbolic eyes—evoke nothing so much as the made-for-Hollywood surrealism of Dalí's designs for Hitchcock's *Spellbound*. (In a similar way the slimy and cynical eye doctor and his aging peroxide-blonde companion seem to have crawled out from an obscure Graham Greene novel adapted into a Bela Lugosi movie.) This ought to be indigestible but it's exuberantly sustained, as if to show just how many moods and cultural references and potential plot turns Spielberg can telegraph from one shot to the next. Like much of *Minority Report*, the sequence has an air of willful gaudiness seeking constantly to surpass itself.

"Put the camera down," a hologram of Cruise's estranged wife tells him only half-jokingly in an early scene, in a three-dimensional home movie retrieved from happier days, to be replayed in his moments of drugged, anguished leisure. The voyeuristic nastiness of, say, the camera-obsessed killer in Michael Powell's *Peeping Tom* is not so far away, and a good deal of the fascination of the movie's early scenes lies in wondering just how far the director is willing to push things. One so wants Cruise to live up to the seediness of these first scenes, to be less of a hero than he must finally become to satisfy the requirements of the chase thriller into which the movie gradually evolves.

The tone shifts with a needlessly protracted flight-and-pursuit sequence—all soaring and swooping and dragging through the mud, sliding through burning tunnels and crashing through floorboards—that seems designed chiefly to wake up anyone who might be dozing over his popcorn. The computer-game wizardry continues with an elaborate but empty scene in a car factory, with Cruise and his pursuers fighting it out on the assembly line to the point where Cruise ends up built into the car and driving it off the line, a variation on an unrealized Alfred Hitchcock gag intended for *North by Northwest*, realized in the manner of a James Bond punchline. But then changes of emotional register seem almost the point here: each episode resembles a movie in itself—the suspense plot, the marriage plot, the technology and ethics plot, the mystical wonder plot—so that the cynicism of one scene is contradicted but not annulled by the hopefulness of another.

IF FILM NOIR was the Jacobean drama of America in the forties, since the eighties the large-scale futurological melodrama—*Blade Runner, Total Recall, Strange Days, Twelve Monkeys, The Matrix*—has taken its place as the genre where style for its own sake, carried off with a Renaissance swagger, is as a matter of course wedded to the most extreme psychological and political situations. (By contrast the *Flash Gordon*–derived space adventures in the *Star Wars* mold might be likened to the allegorical masques, more celebratory than sensational, favored for more ceremonial Jacobean occasions.)

To this genre Fritz Lang's *Metropolis* (1927) stands in somewhat the same relation as Thomas Kyd's *The Spanish Tragedy* to its ever more baroque and bloody successors: the initiating statement that can be reworked, reversed, echoed, expanded, burlesqued. What the sensibility associated with Philip K. Dick added to the mix was the self-consciousness that makes every identity a possible mask or simulacrum, every parallel world potentially a drug-induced delusion or politically motivated fun park. The brute fact of technological power is undermined by the queasy, spiraling what-ifs of a self-doubt so severe that it ends by doubting the world. The more material it gets, the more subtly decorporealized the whole enterprise becomes: a world of smeared light and oddly weightless transportation, hovering on the brink of realizing that it has become a mirror image of something that wasn't there to begin with, a parody of its own advertising campaign. The hall of advertising holograms that Tom Cruise strolls through in *Minority Report*—each ad calling him by name as he comes near—is at once the triumph of product placement and a vision of a peculiarly painless hell.

The beauty of the form is precisely that it permits the contemplation of the direst possibilities under conditions of optimum lightheadedness. End of the world? Disappearance of the individual? Appropriation of memory itself by machines or by sinister corporate forces controlling the machines? The emptying out of whatever seemed real? All nothing more than the daydream of a summer afternoon, the soothing delight of a session at the multiplex, no more troubling than a dead king's curse or a courtier's revenge, especially if broken up with wisecracks and flights of humorous invention. (The futuristic product design with which the movie teems is the contemporary form of quibbling wit.)

Comedy, rough stuff, ingenious puzzles, and the most tearful personal drama can be mixed together without a hint of inappropriateness: in fact such a contradictory mix is required to give the full flavor of a well-rounded future, neither too apocalyptic nor too transparently wish-fulfilling. A movie like *Minority Report* can fulfill many functions at once: mall-of-the-future consumer preview, brainteaser for the computer whizzes, action picture where in comic-book style absolutely anything can happen, forum for provocatively reframing big questions about sex roles or environmentalism or personal privacy, kaleidoscopic fun fair made of speed and glitter.

Spielberg being Spielberg, he adds to the mix his clearly unavoidable drama of familial devotion and familial loss, a drama hinging here on not one but two brutal crimes, one involving the loss of a child and one the murder of a parent, one forever unsolvable and the other the plot's Key to All Keys, the secret crime that (it turns out) made Precrime possible in the first place. In its latter reaches the narrative must race a little too breathlessly to ensure that by solving a crime the hero will also save himself from his own despair and be given a shot at reintegrating himself into domestic life. In that process, the screenplay must gesture a little too heavily to make sure that everybody still has some notion of what the movie is supposed to be about. (When Cruise has the chance to exact vengeance for the loss of his son, a pre-cog tells him, "You still have a choice!") The multi-track possibilities begin to narrow into the considerably more well-worn grooves of a thriller seen many times before, all so we can get to the other side of what we've been caught up in.

The problems with which the plot concerns itself—of predicting the future, of preventing crime in advance, of guarding against the abuse of oracles—are in some sense false problems, since no such foolproof oracles exist or are likely to, although they make possible some fleeting what-if speculations on the nature of time and probability. Spielberg doesn't seem particularly interested in exploring the philosophical possibilities of the setup, such as they are. His approach is fundamentally emotional, and he gets more juice out of the mysteriousness of the pre-cogs, the notion of cops as servants in the temple of the oracles, the architecture of a Precrime lab where the upper high-technology region is adjacent to—and entirely dependent upon—a chthonic lower region of mist-draped waters and vatic pre-cog utterances. The possibility of a high-tech archaism, a direct link of the most deeply buried human impulses to the most advanced and by now almost autonomous machinery, is the kind of magic to which Spielberg responds. That he responds with an increasingly evident ambivalence is what makes his last two movies so interesting.

When the female pre-cog Agatha announces that she's tired of the future, it's a plateau marking the movie's farthest limit of exploration. Unfortunately, when Agatha (for plot reasons too complicated to summarize) is taken out of her amniotic pool and brought into the outside world, she loses a good deal of her aura. The moment she begins to talk something like a regular, if somewhat spaced-out human, the mythic power of the persona dissipates rapidly; she could be a troubled teen coming to grips with her problems at a rehab center or a New Age channeler making a house call. A chase through a futuristic mall, to the tune of "Moon River," has its diverting aspects, but by the time Tom Cruise has spirited Agatha away to his wife's tasteful country house the whole situation comes dangerously close to comedy—what do you offer an oracle for lunch?—just as the script wants it to approach tragedy. At that point, as it happens, the intrigue is already collapsing under its own weight.

In the pool-bound Agatha, Spielberg has found a mythic image for the unknowable sources of his inspiration; and he makes us believe in that inspiration because of the remarkable beauty of so much that he has realized here. In a recent interview in *Wired*, Spielberg has little of note to say about the future or about pre-cogs, but he becomes eloquent in talking about the beauty of film as opposed to the digital technology which will replace it: "The screen is alive. The screen is always alive with chaos and excitement, and that will certainly be gone when we convert to a digital camera and a digital projector." The densely imagined frames of *Minority Report* are indeed often "alive with chaos and excitement," and the effect of that passionate formalism far outweighs any deficiencies of script or concept, and any disappointment with the way the film is forced to resolve itself.

To humanize Agatha is inevitably to trivialize her. She's a force that the film can't really contain, because its own narrative power comes from soaking, so to speak, in her pool. Enlist her as a sort of secret weapon that can be carted from place to place and the power of the image is lost. Spielberg is unable adequately to answer the question of what becomes of oracles after their services are no longer required, and this makes the film's last sequence profoundly unsatisfactory: the pre-cogs are more or less put out to pasture, sent to live out their days in a wilderness cabin well stocked with comfortable old furniture and ample reading material. The idea of a future built on a visionary gift is traded in for a future much like what we already have, and so the visionaries must be stashed away somewhere. It feels a bit like sending the oracle of Delphi to a retirement home, and it doesn't sit right. What was wanted—wanted above all because of the suggestiveness of the world that Spielberg has set up from the beginning—was something more appropriate to such an uncanny being, a fate perhaps more like that of the Sibyl in Petronius, suspended in a cage for children to gawk at, muttering, "I want to die." In effect the movie works hard, in the end, to erase the future that it has so carefully, and brilliantly, built up. It wants to go home.

*The New York Review of Books*, 2002

# minister of fear

THE IMAGES IN FRITZ LANG'S films exist on a permanent borderline. Are they something we dreamt or something we glimpsed, unwillingly, out the window? Did we desire them, or did we want above all else to keep them at bay? The stairs of a high-rise clogged with evacuated workers, a factory complex exploding in the middle of the night, a nightclub audience mesmerized by the dance of a sexy automaton, a city subjected to a block-by-block search for a child-murderer: this is the language of crisis, yet it's a crisis without any obvious exit or solution, a crisis whose patterns are teased out by an aesthete of catastrophe. What most disturbs about Lang's movies is our continuing perplexity about what they are for. From the global criminal conspiracy of *The Spiders* to the two-way mirrors of *The Thousand Eyes of Dr. Mabuse*, from the archaic conflagrations of *Kriemhild's Revenge* to the apocalyptic gangsterism of *The Big Heat*, Lang leads us over and over again into the heart of a permanent emergency—whether it's the outbreak of war or the strangling of a showgirl—without telling us why. All we know is that we aren't allowed to look away.

We can't look away, that is, if we are able to look in the first place. Seeing Lang's movies in decent prints and at full length hasn't always been easy; the German classics have been seen in the U.S. almost exclusively in drastically cut versions, and American films like *House by the River* and *Human Desire* have been hard to find in any form at all. While waiting for a stateside retrospective on the order of the one held recently at the Filmmuseum Berlin, we can at least savor the immense catalogue published in conjunction with it. It is a curious dossier, despite its title (*Fritz Lang: His Life and Work, Photographs and Documents*) neither biography nor critical survey, but rather an assemblage of evidence, with text in German, French, and a sometimes mangled English. It's as if Lang were, if not a criminal, at least someone under grave suspicion, whose activities needed to be examined piece by piece with an eye for the detail that doesn't fit. One pictures Inspector Lohmann, the avuncular police chief of *M* and *The Testament of Dr. Mabuse*, spreading these letters and notebooks and photographs over his desk and muttering: "*Na ja*, it is a complex case, we must look for the pattern."

Readers of Patrick McGilligan's *Fritz Lang: The Nature of the Beast* (1997)—still the only full-scale biography—will recall a portrait that, despite a swirl of contradictions, resolved itself into a figure of monstrous vanity and ambition, servile to superiors and tyrannical to underlings, someone who might well be suspected of unspeakable crimes and vices, always with the proviso that nothing could be firmly stated due to insufficient evidence. McGilligan's loss of empathy toward his subject was so marked that a reader might wonder whether the director was being given an altogether fair shake.

The present compendium (the volume's physical heft makes the word singularly appropriate) seems in part designed to put forward, in deliberately neutral fashion, some counterarguments in Lang's favor. Where McGilligan drew, out of necessity, on a good deal of speculation and gossip, this catalogue sticks to what can be documented, the more official the better. Thus we have birth certificates, enrollment certificates, passports; Lang's receipt book as a much-decorated combatant in World War I; a certificate of good conduct issued at the request of French authorities by the police chief of Berlin in 1934, after Lang's emigration to Paris; FBI files noting Lang's connection with such doubtful characters as Bertolt Brecht and Hanns Eisler (including a 1951 notation that Lang was "a talented director but politically a child, a 'sucker' for organization sponsor and donor lists").

The paperwork, far from bringing Lang into focus, makes him harder to read. The most nagging controversies surrounding his life remain where they were. Existing documents relating to the fate of Lang's first wife, who died in 1920 as a result of a "shot in the chest, accident" as noted by the doctor called to the scene, fail to clarify the circumstances of what may have been accident, suicide, or (according to certain slanderous rumors) murder. Lang's alleged participation in a Nazi film organization, hinging on a single item in a 1933 trade paper, can neither be confirmed nor denied; and while his account of precipitately leaving Germany the day after being courted by Goebbels to head the German film industry has been discredited, what really went down remains unclear. (We do, however, have Goebbels's diary entry after seeing *M*: "Fantastic! Counters all that sentimental humanitarianism. For the death penalty! Well done. One day, Lang will be our director.")

A major concern of the book is to absolve Lang of any ambiguity in his opposition to the Nazis, and here at least the evidence is compelling. His financial generosity to refugees and to anti-Nazi organizations is plentifully recorded, and the tenor of his private correspondence does not point toward opportunism or clouded motives. To Eleanor Rosé, a close friend of his youth, he wrote in 1945: "I hate Germany so much that I don't want to see anything of this country in my life again. I have become an American citizen six years ago and try . . . to forget that I belong to a race which brought so much misfortune upon this earth of ours." His social world in America remained very German; a snapshot from a Hollywood living room in 1936 shows him in apparently jovial conclave with G.W. Pabst, Joseph Schildkraut, Peter Lorre, and Erich von Stroheim. Subsequently, as this book clarifies, he formed a close friendship with Theodor Adorno, but by many of the émigrés he was not so well loved. His falling-out with Brecht is well known, and Kurt Weill complains in a letter to Lotte Lenya of his collaboration with "this pompous guy Lang" (*mit diesem aufgeblasenen Lang*); Lang's former lover Marlene Dietrich later wrote of his "Teutonic arrogance" and called him a member of "Sadist Incorporated." Even the sympathetic

Eleanor Rosé could offer only this by way of eulogy: "I hope that he was able to get away from this hypocritical world without a struggle. He had had enough—or rather, he had always had enough, even at twenty-two—but his desire for power drove him on endlessly."

That desire for power encompassed, at the very least, a desire to shape his photographic representation, from a 1923 spread of Lang and his wife Thea von Harbou sprawled in a Berlin apartment overflowing with pedigreed pets, satin pillows, and artwork ranging from Asian tapestries to erotic drawings by Klimt and Schiele, to a 1960 portrait of the director in Germany, his thin smile, monocle, and cigarette holder reinforcing an impression of sardonic dignity. The interiors of Lang's homes in Germany and America could pass for settings in his films—the disposition of objects and spaces has the same elegant yet ultimately cold exactness—and the portraits and production stills (was any director ever photographed so frequently on the job?) convey an unrelenting attention to surface and gesture. The warmest and most unguarded portraits, interestingly enough, show him with his stuffed monkey, Peter, a toy that became a cherished companion whom he would dress up and put to bed.

Interspersed among the documents are images from the films, reproduced on a scale that makes the book constantly pleasurable to leaf through: a hieratic scene of Margarete Schön as Kriemhild keeping vigil with her maidens over the tomb of Siegfried; Peter Lorre as the child-murderer studying his face in the mirror; an anonymous assassin in *The Testament of Dr. Mabuse* taking aim through a limousine window; an enraged woman, part of the lynch mob in *Fury*, hurling a kerosene-soaked rag; the adulterous lovers Glenn Ford and Gloria Grahame embracing in a train compartment framed by bare walls in *Human Desire*, a shot whose minimalism is as oppressive in its tensions as the elaborate decorative patterns of *Die Nibelungen*.

In such images we come to grips with the main paradox of Lang's work: that his films at their most pulpish seem real, and at their most real seem pulpish. *Dr. Mabuse, der Spieler* was received in 1922 as an authentic depiction of the present moment: "a concentrate of all the excessive stimulation, decadence, sensation and speculation which have befallen us over the past few years." *M* was controversial for drawing on a serial murder case still in the courts; *The Testament of Dr. Mabuse* was banned by the Nazis as "a veritable textbook on how to prepare and commit terrorist acts." Two decades later, *The Big Heat* came under attack from the administrators of the Production Code for its "portrayal of crime and corruption in a large American city, in which it is shown that the Mayor, Chief of Police, and City Council are all under complete domination of a master criminal." (It was François Truffaut who pointed out at the time that—even allowing for the happy ending in which Glenn Ford cleanses the police department of corruption—no such film could possibly have been made in France in 1953.) Yet no director was more capable of creating an atmosphere of deliberate fakeness, hollowness, somnambulistic otherness.

Lang's films test the limits of what can be conveyed cinematically. How could a body of work so explicit—to the point of humorlessness—in its development of signs remain so mysteriously opaque? The more they show us the more they seal their essential muteness. We keep looking because we still don't know what we are being shown. Nor, perhaps, did Lang. We find him, in the 1960s, beguiling himself with slam-bang detective novels by John Creasey (*Terror by Day, Death from Below, Give Me Murder*) while contemplating the news as if it were one of his own movies: "The very justified Negro revolution, then earthquakes, countless murders, etc., well, all the ingredients of a F.L. film." In old age he acknowledges his astonishment at "the instinctive assurance with which I made my films." The most detailed of dossiers can only circle around an activity as concentrated and implacable as it was obscure in its ends.

*Bookforum*, 2002

# an artisan of the unseen

JACQUES TOURNEUR COULD FIGURE AS a test-case for auteurism. A director who said that he never turned down a screenplay—"I
did my best with whatever they gave me"—Tourneur produced a succession of films of which almost every one belongs to a clearly defined,
often formulaic genre: the Western, the horror movie, the noir thriller,
the pirate movie, the spy movie, the medieval adventure movie, the jungle movie, all the way down (as the studio system collapses around him)
to *Timbuktu,* with Victor Mature lending able-bodied support to French
colonialism in a backlot Sahara, and *The Giant of Marathon,* with Steve
Reeves fending off hordes of invading Persians. His filmography suggests the workaday artisan, an identity Tourneur was happy to claim for
himself. When a French critic asked him what place he thought his films
would occupy in the history of cinema, he replied: "None."

To find profundity among the frames of *Appointment in Honduras*
and *Great Day in the Morning* might strike some as the ultimate
expression of auteurism as mystical cult, perceiving revelation in what
to the unreceptive looks very much like standard industrial product,
more or less pleasing but singularly devoid of any obvious ambition.
The spectator's question becomes: Is there really something there at
all, or am I imagining this? That question, as it happens, leads directly
into the heart of a life work that, however unassuming, has over time
surrendered none of its power to fascinate. Can there be a durable

will-o'-the-wisp, a monumental glimmer? Maybe only in the movies, and most particularly in the movies of Jacques Tourneur.

If the classical Hollywood film can embody a science of manipulation, Tourneur's films stand out by their refusal to dictate a reading. This is not to be confused with vagueness, even if Tourneur's films elicit the same words over and over from a range of commentators: hypnotic, elusive, enigmatic, uncertain, mysterious, ambiguous, ambivalent. His French admirer Louis Skorecki wrote an essay entitled "Tourneur Does Not Exist." Sometimes it's possible to feel that his films don't exist, especially when they've eluded you for years. I can remember seeing *The Fearmakers* for the first time on late-night television in the mid-sixties, and hanging on to the memory of its unaccountable strangeness for decades until a second chance came along. That second exposure only deepened the mystery of how this little movie got its hooks into me in the first place.

*The Fearmakers*, in the light of retrospect, turned out to be an extremely low-budget late-fifties anticommunist melodrama based on a forties antifascist novel, full of wooden speeches about subversive forces trying to influence public opinion, taking place (mostly) on a couple of office sets that would not have been out of place in an Ed Wood movie and filmed in a style verging much of the time on TV-perfunctory, with a cast of almost indigestible oddity (a brainwashed Dana Andrews doing battle against sinister Red agents Dick Foran, Mel Tormé, and Veda Ann Borg). By the standards of *Out of the Past* or *I Walked with a Zombie*, it wasn't much to look at. Yet once again the movie began to work its effect: there was that crucial encounter with a stranger sitting next to Dana Andrews on an airplane, with its grungily accurate evocation of the claustrophobia of plane travel; that ominous boarding house where Andrews spends a sleepless night; that persistent mood of insomnia and restlessness—all so many points of incursion into the ordinary, until even the banal desks and corridors took on the quality of a distracted reverie.

Was this the movie I had remembered seeing, or had my imagination in the interim between viewings created a sort of dematerialized

*Fearmakers,* like those Tibetan gods that the devotee sees come to life amid the abstractions of a mandala? There is often a sense, with Tourneur's films, that space is being created for precisely such an alternate movie; where other directors close in on an explicit point, Tourneur makes room for an indeterminate openness. The collaborations with Val Lewton that established him as a director—*Cat People, I Walked with a Zombie, The Leopard Man*—were built around the notion that what you don't see is scarier than what you do, an idea sufficiently high-concept that it even found its way into the screenplay of Vincente Minnelli's *The Bad and the Beautiful,* as the gimmick of genius that launches Kirk Douglas's career: a rare instance of film theory becoming a plot point in a Hollywood movie.

Yet to speak of openness is not to imply mistiness. The effects, moment by moment, are exactly defined, so much so that at times Tourneur's cinema seems nothing but a flow of etched surfaces, to be savored in somewhat the same spirit as cloud-drift at dusk, or ebb tide on the shingle. The technical mastery is obvious, the deeper question being toward what end it is deployed. His films leave a tantalizing sense that the next time you see them they will have changed; and, indeed, years of returning to them have convinced me that their apparent resistance to the jadedness of overfamiliarity is not an optical illusion. The best of his work remains curiously unfixed in the mind even after many viewings. Their precise details fade from memory more than those of other directors; you remember an effect but have trouble recalling precisely how it was achieved. If with other directors you can mentally call up compositions, assertive camera movements, shock cuts, moments of emotional crisis or sudden revelation or jazzy byplay, with Tourneur you cling in memory to a vivid but uncapturable sense of place and mood, like a scene from early childhood or from a dream that even though only half-remembered lingers stubbornly in mind. They come in, so to speak, under the radar, carrying a suggestion of infiltration and concealment, a pervasion of unseen forces, and this is as true of an upbeat, wholesomely spiritual story like *Stars in My Crown* as of *Curse of the Demon.* Happiness and faith are no less mysterious, in fact

no less troubling, than the outer reaches of anxiety and occult possession. The directorial touch is exact but disconcertingly light. He makes
everybody else look overemphatic. As Chris Fujiwara points out in his
superb study *Jacques Tourneur: The Cinema of Nightfall*, Tourneur's
films have a way of beginning in the middle, with characters making
obscure references to previous events. With many of his movies—for
instance *I Walked with a Zombie, Out of the Past, Canyon Passage*—you
sense that no matter how many times you see them, you can never
altogether untangle the story line. Crucial things happen offscreen or
before the movie starts; motivations and backstory don't ever become
entirely clear; minor characters turn out to have complicated stories of
their own that we never quite learn about.

He makes time mysterious. We move backward (the return to childhood in *Stars in My Crown*) or find ourselves seemingly stalled in a fro-
zen moment (the trek through the jungle in *Appointment in Honduras*)
or forget who is supposed to be telling the story (the shifting viewpoints of *I Walked with a Zombie*) or lose track of sequence (the disorienting narrative turns of *Out of the Past* and *Nightfall*). To find out all
we want to know we would have to break through the screen, entering
that space that we can perceive only as a stream of two-dimensional
configurations. If the movies perpetually enact a crossing of boundaries, the ultimate boundary is the uncrossable one closing the spectator
off from what he watches.

Tourneur gives you the drama and at the same time a distance
from the drama, establishing a strange calm in the heart of violent or
unnerving circumstances. This has nothing to do with an aestheticiza-
tion of violence or horror. *Anne of the Indies*, for all its scenes of plank-
walking and seafaring mayhem, must be the gentlest pirate movie ever
made, and certainly the only one where you find yourself seriously
wondering about the quality of the pirates' emotional life. A scene like
the murder of the gold miner McIver in *Canyon Passage*—or rather the
prelude to it, the murder itself taking place offscreen—is marked by a
detachment that makes it possible to feel equal pity for the victim and
for the murderer, a sympathetic weakling about to seal his own doom.

The emphases in such sequences can be so gently placed—the compositions so free, seemingly, of any imposed viewpoint—that you watch a film over and over simply to feel out its dramatic rhythms. A first viewing of *Canyon Passage* (certainly one of Tourneur's four or five best films) might be merely puzzling: it seems to be a Western in which none of the characters has a clearly defined goal, but each is full of hidden and often contradictory feelings toward the others, and in which the scenes of lull and mild anticipation weigh as much as the occasional bursts of violence.

Tourneur's pleasures are in some sense obvious; you can think of *Canyon Passage* as an exercise in the contemplation of appearances, a sheer appreciation of space and color, of live glances and movement flickering in the corner of the frame, all the mysterious random choreographies of everyday life. Returning to the film to indulge again in those appearances, you find on closer look a world apart, a place with its own peculiar rhythms and modes of behavior. Yet it's a world that in its way seems more real than that of other movies, as if the characters didn't know they were characters or that anyone was looking, a world—and this is what makes Tourneur's B-pictures so unusual— without histrionics. As many have remarked, vocal delivery in his films is unusually low-pitched, approximating the level of ordinary conversation, and he is thus able to create an air of unlikely verisimilitude even in the context of backlot adventure movies. You might call it a sort of neorealism of the imaginary. Perhaps that's why, in *Berlin Express*, the cutting between staged scenes of noirish intrigue (complete with a scary clown to rival Lang's *Spione*) and documentary footage of war-ruined German cities is far less jarring than it ought to be.

TOURNEUR'S LIFE APPEARS to have been almost as understated as his art. The major determining aspect of his biography precedes his birth: he was the son of the silent film director Maurice Tourneur, and thereby had the inestimable advantage of learning all about movie technique as a matter of course and at a very early age, working as bit player, script clerk, cutter, assistant director. Tourneur *père* (he had changed his name from Maurice Thomas because, according to Fujiwara, the latter sounded "too English") was an evidently flamboyant character who had been an illustrator and designer, an assistant to Rodin and Puvis de Chavannes, an artillery officer, a stage actor, and ultimately a successful filmmaker who by 1914 had emigrated to America. He declared to *Motion Picture Magazine* in 1917: "We are not photographers, but artists . . . We must present the effect such a scene has upon the artist-director's mind, so that an audience will catch the mental reaction."

In one of his rare interviews Jacques states simply, "I learned everything with my father." He also suggested in more ways than one that his father's character was marked by coldness and cruelty, and it's possible to read his own approach to direction as a mix of emulation and criticism. He disparages the notion—which his father seems to have embodied—of director as dictator, expressing a particular aversion for the bullying of actors. Indeed, Tourneur speaks more often about the problems of actors than his own problems as a director. Actors must be treated gently, he insists; the director must understand how traumatic their job is. He emphasizes matters of gentleness and delicacy, whether in handling actors or handling light sources.

He likes to speak of himself as lazy, spoiled, born with a silver spoon in his mouth. Indeed, he credits whatever success he has had to a sublime passivity: "All my life, everything has come to me by itself, and I think it's because I made no effort to bring things to me; if I'd made an effort, maybe I would have harmed myself; everything came by itself." It isn't clear whether by "everything" he means the yachts and Cadillacs and fine wines on which he spent the money that finally wasn't there anymore, or rather the professional career about which he is not in the least apologetic: "I'm a director, it's my profession. I believe it's a profession that takes all your time; you can't be producer and director and writer all at once. To be an honest director, you have to devote all your time and all your energy to it." He was there on the set from seven in the morning until eight in the evening, he tells us; he gave the cameramen a hard time because the lighting had to be exactly the way he wanted it; he did everything he could to make the actors feel free and relaxed. "You have to like what you do, because a person who likes his work makes life pleasant, and if a person doesn't like his work it's painful." If most of those who master directing come to it from the outside, as a castle to be stormed, Tourneur was the odd case who stayed in the place where he started out, for whom filmmaking was simply the only thing he had ever learned how to do.

The son's legacy is a comfortable technical command, further polished in the second unit work with Val Lewton on *A Tale of Two Cities* (1935) and in a long series of MGM shorts on everything from harness racing to the discovery of radium, with a special emphasis on strange tales of uncanny prediction and unaccountable coincidence. By the time he gets to *Cat People* (1942), he's a technician who can afford to be calm and to obey his dictum that "it's bad to think too much, everything should be instinctive." For a range of studios and with widely varying budgets, and despite that the fact he almost never had much say about scripts or casting, Tourneur would continue to exercise a remarkable degree of control over the feel of his films. He complained about a few instances (most famously the close-ups of the slavering monster in *Curse of the Demon*) where producers interfered with his conception, but for the most part his accommodating approach seems to have enabled him to preserve an enviable freedom in the matters that concerned him most.

His best films—and it should be said that, until the misbegotten final features for American-International, none is without interest—have a quality like *fin de siècle* symbolist painting, and are effective, like the best of such paintings, to the extent that the symbols resist final interpretation. *Out of the Past*, long since accepted as perhaps the paradigm of film noir, looks more and more like the supreme visual poem of an extraordinarily rich period of American filmmaking: a supernatural film so uncanny that it doesn't even need the supernatural, and an American vernacular work so un-American that sometimes it feels like the greatest film that Jean Cocteau never made. They couldn't all be sustained on that level—not all actors were Robert Mitchum, not all cameramen Nicholas Musuraca, and few scripts so full of opportunities—but as you watch them unreel you are constantly being surprised.

We might take as a kind of self-portrait the alcoholic ship's doctor so sensitively played by Herbert Marshall in *Anne of the Indies*, philosophical advisor to Jean Peters (magnificent in the title role), who tells her: "Long ago, my dear, I gave up all beliefs." Tourneur, sybarite and aesthete though he may have been, did apparently cherish a few beliefs. In more than one interview he spoke of parallel worlds, sources of signals that we would pick up on if only we were on the same wavelength: "There is another world, and if only we could. . . ." If only we could, what then? The enduring charm (and I mean the word in its more ancient and forceful sense) of his films is to suggest an answer—not quite visible yet, but almost perceptible beyond the next frame—to a question that cannot even be formulated.

*Film Comment*, 2002

# devotional furies

IF THE VIDEO RENTAL STORE is a pharmacy of desires, the video clerk is the obscure scientist who has tested all the potions on himself, poisons and elixirs alike. Has he grown strong in the process, or terminally jaded, or perhaps fatally attached to the objects of his vision? Imagine that he goes home and dreams a dream in which the videos mingle and mate with one another: a cast of Japanese gangsters in wraparound shades, women held captive by sadistic South American prison wardens, female vampires and maimed martial artists, Mexican wrestlers and Italian serial killers, avengers of the Western plains accompanied by pan flutes and a chorus of whistlers, swarming multitudes escaped from *Suspiria* and *Shogun Assassin* and *The Streetfighter's Last Revenge*, all of them asserting the ferocious tenacity of ghosts, demons, and tutelary spirits. He wakes to find himself transformed. The unknown that was imbued with dread and strangeness is now irredeemably part of him, a language without which he can barely state who he is.

Quentin Tarantino's *Kill Bill* is a movie conceived in such a language. If the superb *Jackie Brown* seemed to move in the direction of real worn-out spaces and real elegiac feelings, *Kill Bill*—or at least the first half of it, just released in a most curious marketing ploy as *Kill Bill: Vol. 1*—marks the return with a literal vengeance of Tarantino the demonic video store clerk, enamored of the grainy unattainable epiphanies of lost drive-ins and Chinatown movie theaters and all-night gore fests. It's a love poem, but the kind of love poem that makes you wonder if you want to go out with the person who wrote it, or that at least makes you wonder if by responding to it you won't become complicit in a liaison that will leave deep scars. Scars are everywhere here, and blood, much blood, blood dripping or splattering or geysering or congealing or turning a pool of water bright red, elicited often by dismemberment and decapitation, and invoked almost often enough to become ornamental, a floral decoration on the envelope of the love letter.

And to whom is the love letter addressed? To Uma Thurman, the battered bleeding bride transformed into an avenging swordswoman who dominates the screen at almost every instant, hurling imprecations in English and Japanese and lunging to deliver one more savage slice with an impressive air of conviction? (Thurman deserves a prize, if not for acting then for endurance.) Or are we in the realm of allegory, where the splendid isolated figures of women (Daryl Hannah, Vivica Fox, Lucy Liu) represent not, as in the middle ages, Prudence or Charity or Wisdom, but rather Kung Fu or American International or Chambara or Blaxploitation, those eternal categories of the mind? From the opening frame (the old ShawScope logo of beloved memory), the genre formulas that Tarantino lovingly reenacts and enlarges upon are not so much in-jokes as traces of sacred ritual, complete with requisite vestments and liturgy. The jokey obscenities and pop culture hipsterisms can hardly disguise the fundamentally solemn aura of this entertainment.

It's a solemnity that threatens to reveal at its center nothing at all. The mass slaughter that Uma Thurman executes in the middle of a lavishly postmodern Tokyo nightclub takes place on a glass floor overlooking a recreation of a Zen rock garden, scarcely visible among the cascade of severed limbs. That moment, occurring just about at the midpoint of the two-part film, might I suppose be its pivot point: the symbolic opposition of bloodshed and nothingness, turbulent mayhem and tranquilizing abstraction. Or would the center be, more appropriately, the Japanese all-girl punk band that a few moments earlier belts out a version of the Ikettes' "I'm Blue (The Gong-Gong Song)," just before a simpering uniformed schoolgirl steps out swinging a jagged-pointed mace?

To turn a penny arcade into a Zen monastery, or a Zen monastery into a penny arcade: it isn't that *Kill Bill* can't make up its mind but rather that (in what might be a triumph of mystical insight) it no longer has a mind to make up. It has gone beyond all that, leaving only a few martial arts movie aphorisms to denote the point where meaning vanished once and for all. It is, then, a vision of Hell, if Hell were imagined as a live-action cartoon (or, in the extended anime flashback, a literal cartoon) full of deft parodies, superbly apposite music, bracing color schemes, and dazzling compositions, a cartoon teaching that those who do not assault must resign themselves to being assaulted.

What holds it all together is formalism. The air of flagrant artifice must be sustained, in the first place, to prevent any apprehension that the violence is real. If it were real, then one might begin to wonder why it was really necessary to make—or to see—a movie in which during most of its running time women are verbally abused, raped (albeit off-camera), slapped, beaten, stabbed, and dismembered. Most of the suffering is inflicted by women, as well, of course (although in the background there is always the nefarious Bill, in this installment represented only as the offscreen voice of David Carradine). Keep telling yourself that it's only a pastiche. Remind yourself that all the images were already there, in the thousand movies that Tarantino has drawn on; remember how much Chu Yuan had already surpassed him, as regards woman-on-woman mayhem, in the last reel of *Intimate Confessions of a Chinese Courtesan*. All the same, the director's relentless enthusiasm for his own private bloodbath can begin to feel like a hobbyist's mind-numbing guided tour of his collection of rare trading cards.

Tarantino also needs the formalism because this time around he has had to sacrifice a good many of the elements that he's relied on in the past. The martial arts genre is, to put it mildly, not primarily reliant on words, and Tarantino signals his adherence to the genre's requirements in the first scene with an abrupt and nasty set-to between Uma Thurman and Vivica Fox in the dining room of Fox's comfortably appointed Pasadena home. There is little occasion in *Kill Bill* for the extended verbal riffing of the earlier films, and much of what he comes up with seems thin. The sight of Thurman and Fox yelling "bitch" at each other comes close to dissolving the movie into silliness right from the start, while some outbursts of colorful misogynistic filth from a Texas sheriff and a depraved hospital orderly seem almost desperate attempts to give the fans the anticipated quota of shockers to memorize. There is little real humor except for a wonderful scene between Thurman and Sonny Chiba as a master swordsman masquerading as a sushi chef, in which Chiba hauls out every tired compliment familiar to tourists in Japan ("You say exactly like Japanese") as if the pointed deployment of such clichés were a species of martial art.

The mere presence of Sonny Chiba is sufficient to summon up a whole world of East Asian filmmaking in relation to which *Kill Bill* figures as a rogue disciple, like Toshiro Mifune in *Seven Samurai*. Some elements of the homage kick in early on, especially on the soundtrack during the fight scenes, with their old-time high-definition bone-crunching sound effects. But from the minute Thurman, having woken from her four-year coma in a Texas hospital (recalled to life by a mosquito piercing her skin in extreme close-up), heads off to Okinawa to begin her systematic vengeance on her would-be killers (an animated map shows the plane's trajectory), the movie becomes elated: it is going where it wants to go.

It wants to go to Heaven, Heaven being the aesthetic formalism that can take the form of a brutal murder in exquisite anime stylization, a jetliner flying impossibly low over Tokyo so that Uma Thurman can study the streets from her window seat, a yakuza gang sprung from the demented world of some early Seijun Suzuki film, a water dipper clacking down in the foreground of a garden scene to frame the death duel taking place in the background, the streak of blood making calligraphy on the snowy ground. Above all it takes the form of prolonged murderous sword fights, or rather of a single sword fight that engulfs some hundred combatants in a death struggle with Thurman. Here Tarantino gets in his little joke by showing us, after the seemingly interminable fight is over, the shot that other movies never show: a wide floor space completely covered with groaning mutilated yakuza crawling out over the bodies of their fallen comrades.

It's hard to imagine where Tarantino can go from there in *Vol. 2*, but then a certain monotony is to be expected and even welcomed in this genre. Martial arts movies are not finally about surprise but about the steady sustaining drone of action that unfolds as if it were a natural phenomenon that when observed with the proper detachment can be both invigorating and beautiful. Much as he might want to be, though, Tarantino is not King Hu or Chang Cheh or Chu Yuan, Kenji Misumi or Kinji Fukasaku. Not that he lacks their gifts—*Kill Bill* confirms him as a filmmaker of astonishing invention and aplomb—but that he lacks their context. A director peculiarly inspired by place, whether the hideout in *Reservoir Dogs* or the shopping mall in *Jackie Brown* or the cavernous nightclub in *Kill Bill*, Tarantino finally has to invent a cultural space in which his movies can exist. Here he has woven it out of strips of old celluloid, a sort of carnival tent hoisted up in a void: a haunted funhouse for resurrected swordswomen, where they can eternally enact the same unfinished and unfinishable revenge drama.

*Film Comment*, 2003

# getting medieval at
# the multiplex

IN MEDIEVAL ENGLISH PASSION PLAYS, a bladder filled with blood, discreetly fastened to the actor playing the Savior, was sometimes used to simulate with gory realism the piercing of Christ's side; on at least one occasion, the actor in the role of Christ was killed when the fellow player wielding the spear missed his target. At a later date, in a reflection of drastically changed views and sensibilities, theatrical representations of any biblical characters at all were prohibited in England, a statute that remained in force into the twentieth century. A similar uneasiness prevailed in nineteenth-century America. When a dramatization of the life of Christ played in San Francisco in 1879 (it starred James O'Neill, the playwright's father), all the episodes following the surrender of Jesus into Pontius Pilate's custody were omitted following protests from religious groups.

The invention of movies, and the rapid proliferation of cinematic treatments of Jesus, stirred up contention about the potential sacrilege involved in any attempt to film the sacred narrative. There were any number of issues. For some, the mere fact of an actor portraying Jesus was an impediment, although others felt that it was only sacrilegious if the actor was paid, thereby turning authentic religious ritual (the Oberammergau Passion Play, for instance, of which filmed versions both real and fraudulent were circulated) into commercial exploitation. As late as 1912, the feature-length *From the Manger to the Cross* (filmed in the Holy Land) sparked debates about whether showing such a film in the secular atmosphere of a movie theater was not in itself a form of desecration, compounded by the charging of admission.

What is most striking in early films about Jesus is the care taken not to offend through any kind of excess or overemphasis. The actors playing Jesus remain as expressionless as possible, and events are depicted with ceremonial restraint, as if the slightest hint of lively or unexpected movement might distract from the required mood of solemnity. The resulting films tend to be somewhat detached in their effect. Ferdinand Zecca's very early and quite lovely *The Life and Passion of Jesus Christ* (1905) has the quality of a wonder book of sacred images sprung into toylike movement, magical but divorced from any sense that these scenes have anything to do with life as we know it. Cecil B. De Mille's *King of Kings* (1927) was a more sophisticated version of the same kind of thing, with the director reining in his flair for pandering showmanship (although he did permit himself a garish interlude in Mary Magdalene's parlor) so as not to mar the reverential tone. It was important for movies about Christ to demonstrate that they were not to be confused with the mass of ordinary, vulgar movies. This lingering sense of decorum was still in evidence in the 1950s, when a biblical epic like *The Robe* discreetly avoided direct depiction of Jesus, "out of respect," as disappointed younger viewers who had hoped for a more direct vision were assured.

How far we have come: or else how far we have come full circle. Mel Gibson's *The Passion of the Christ* cuts through any such decorum with an unflinching violence that breaks with precedent in genuinely radical fashion. In its intended function it may be closer to those earlier Jesus films, designed for use by churches and missionary groups, rather than to such latter-day revisionist efforts as Nicholas Ray's *King of Kings*, Pier Paolo Pasolini's *The Gospel According to St. Matthew*, and Martin Scorsese's *The Last Temptation of Christ* (not to mention the interlude of musicalized flower-bedecked evangelism embodied in *Godspell* and *Jesus Christ Superstar*); but Gibson has studied attentively all the ways in which movies have explored transgression. For the tasteful ponderousness of George Stevens's *The Greatest Story Ever Told*—a sort of souvenir gospel careful to offend no one—he substitutes a deliberately unsettling, in fact scary tone, a tone that is mere prelude to the prolonged unblinking stare at human torture and sacrifice that is to follow.

Gibson's film is bound to instill a sense of dread for believers and non-believers alike, although clearly not always for the same reasons. By "believers" I mean those viewers prepared to accept the film more or less on its own inspirational terms. Many religious persons have taken care to distance themselves from Gibson's methods and to reject in detail what they take as his interpolated messages. In any case the dread is tangible from the start, elicited with a visual shorthand adapted from horror movies: the menacing murky light of Gethsemane, the slithering snake, the androgynous Satan out of an Aubrey Beardsley drawing, the creepy New Age slasher-film music, the spooky mutterings and flashes of demonic faces that surface at unexpected moments.

Under those flourishes lurks a more basic and real-world fear: a man, unarmed and unprotected, is going to be taken into custody by authorities who will show him no mercy. The singular effectiveness of *The Passion of the Christ* comes from its relentless commitment to the fate of that man, a fate that in the terms available to film can only be presented as the fate of his body. The movie forces a contemplation of the desire to avoid pain; the desire to look away; perhaps even the unacknowledged desire to inflict pain; and that extended contemplation turns out to be the movie itself, in total. In a different movie the authorities to whose will he is given over might be the Gestapo, or the KGB, or a team of Mafia enforcers, and whether the man would live or die might depend on whether he was the star or merely a supporting character. Here they are agents of the Sanhedrin, the Jewish ruling council, and consequently the film enlists itself as part of a history of representation whose sinister consequences can hardly be ignored.

As Jesus is dragged off to be interrogated by Caiaphas and the priests of the temple, we are swept up in an atmosphere of casual pitiless violence and hard-edged political manipulation that would be at

home in the world of a spaghetti Western, some spinoff of *Django*—
or for that matter in *The Road Warrior*. (It would also be at home in
a cinematic recreation of the toxic political landscapes symbolized
by Srebrenica or Kosovo.) Caiaphas and his associates embody, in
movie terms, an untempered malevolence. Arrogant, grinning with
self-satisfaction, wily in dissimulation, incapable of compassion, the
temple priests as presented here might be icons in full regalia emerging from some sixteenth-century engraving designed to illustrate the
wickedness of the Jews. They are able effortlessly to manipulate Roman
authority as embodied by a Pontius Pilate who is essentially a tough
but not altogether unsympathetic military bureaucrat a bit too worried
about hanging on to his job, with a wife whose intuitive empathy for
Jesus seems to foreshadow the converted imperium of Constantine.
Almost irrelevant to questions of real power, in this context, is an epi-
cene Herod who might be a coked-up record producer on the wrong
end of a three-day binge.

All of this, it can be argued, is nothing more than the articulating
of a tradition, the same tradition—almost the same gestures—that can
be traced in the episodes of those English miracle plays. Since we do
not in fact live in the Middle Ages (except perhaps metaphorically),
the precise use Gibson has made of those acts and gestures, and what
he intends by that use, will be questioned, as they ought to be. For one
small instance: in his apparent eagerness to let the Roman commanders
morally off the hook, Gibson allows the Roman foot soldiers displays
of insubordination that seem quite remarkable in an army renowned
for its discipline; they are constantly exceeding their instructions when
it comes to brutalizing their prisoner. Gibson's good faith, or lack of it,
in stirring up historical subtexts through a deft orchestration of visual
cues is almost beside the point. The dread many feel is not of the film's
overt content but of the well of ancient antipathies it taps into. It is a
dread of what exists in the world beyond the screen.

Such misgivings are a backhanded acknowledgment of the very real
skill and artfulness of *The Passion of the Christ*. If it were laughably
inept, few would worry about its possible side effects. In fact Gibson

has achieved a stunning act of translation, recasting the matter of a medieval passion play in the cinematic language of the multiplex without altering its fundamental nature. Speaking of languages, Gibson's decision to play the film in Aramaic and Latin was for his purposes a brilliant one, not because of its supposed historical accuracy, which has in any case been questioned, but because the fact that all the dialogue is spoken in languages incomprehensible to any living audience reinforces the notion of a fallen world not yet redeemed by the Word. The film will be subtitled no matter where it is exhibited, and the subtitles figure not as interpretation but as Truth existing in a different sphere above and beyond the wreckage of mortal life. In the 1960s and 1970s, in Ray's *King of Kings* and Norman Jewison's *Jesus Christ Superstar*, filmmakers looked for ways to make Jesus our contemporary. Gibson's goal is to make us the contemporaries of Jesus. The up-to-the-minute trappings of the film are there simply to make it legible, to provide a point of reentry into ancient events which, from the religious point of view, are eternally and constantly continuing to unfold. Any available stylistic elements, whether borrowed from *Exorcist II: The Heretic, Conan the Barbarian,* or *Mad Max Beyond Thunderdome,* can be brought into play, but without in any way diluting or distracting from the rigor (not to say fanaticism) of the intent: the inculcation of an unyielding and unambiguous religious conviction.

With Scorsese's *The Last Temptation of Christ*—which got around the constrictions of reverence by taking not the Gospels but Nikos Kazantzakis's Dostoyevskyan novel as its source—there was a liberating sense of the imagination set free. Going beyond Ray and Pasolini, Scorsese improvised a set of variations on the sacred narrative, exploring it not as a series of fixed, detached images but as a world that you could move around in, whose characters had lives and not merely ceremonial exits and entrances. The film's set pieces—among them the baptism by John, the expulsion of the money changers, the entry into Jerusalem, the scourging—were a re-visioning that changed the possibilities for anyone coming after. The movie also established, by the firestorm that accompanied its production and release, that henceforth any film dealing with this subject might expect to encounter intense and pervasive pressures.

*The Passion of the Christ* has been embraced by many of the same people likely to have protested *The Last Temptation*, yet I would be very surprised if Gibson did not make a careful study of Scorsese's treatment of these materials. (The forensic realism of Steven Spielberg's *Saving Private Ryan*, not to mention Spielberg's audacity in bringing the Holocaust to the multiplex in *Schindler's List*, must also have been significant for him.) Scorsese's handling of the scourging, for example, was brief but genuinely shocking in its evocation of bloody brutality. Gibson has seized hold of that effect and prolonged it into what seems about ten bludgeoning minutes. There is of course a wide gap between the "what if" of Scorsese and Gibson's "thus it is," but both films convey (no matter if toward very different ends) a sense of the breaching of the permissible: a breaching that exacerbates the violence—however implicit, however contained—in the very notion of yoking human and divine in a single body.

The rotting carcass of a scapegoat, by which Judas hangs himself, provides an ideogrammic synopsis of the *Passion*'s scenario. The theme is sacrifice, and divinity attained through sacrifice. Movie violence, which ultimately tends to be wielded by good guys upon the persons of bad guys, is here inflicted on the embodiment of goodness itself, and the movie itself is nothing but a procession, a gauntlet, through the heart of malicious violence. The sheer difficulty of dying is finally almost the only object of our gaze. Where in ordinary movies the protagonist seeks not to be killed, here he seeks not to die too soon. In purely spectatorial terms, a kind of perverse suspense operates around the question of whether he will survive long enough to make it to the cross. Many have objected that the extent of the violence visited here on Jesus would have killed him much sooner, but—aside from the fact that we are in any case in the realm of the miraculous—this excessive prolongation might also be construed as a way of counteracting the affectless video-game kills of most popular entertainment.

The act of dying is here an act of making. "Behold, I make all things new" is uttered here from a body barely alive, to assert that this is not passive but active suffering, the willing submission to physical torture and destruction as a means to a necessary end. It asserts also that this act is the crucial one, of which all earlier preachings and healings (of which we catch only faint glimpses in flashbacks that, cast against the visceral bloodshed of the principal event, have the disconcerting quality of Kodak moments) were in the nature of signs and portents. Dying is not disappearance but metamorphosis, and I am sure I detected, in the voice of the dying Jesus as he utters "It is accomplished," an undertone of souped-up electronica designed to convey—again, in the precise lingua franca of the multiplex—the emergence of another and more powerful being from within, man fully transmuted into god.

The shock effect of *The Passion of the Christ* is its resort, in order to convey a sacred event that is by definition unfilmable, not to transcendent beauty but to a vocabulary of violence most often associated with the basest of horror movies. (But, of course, of all genres it is in horror movies that buried religious ideas most abound.) From the start we are dropped down in a degraded world consisting chiefly of human faces either cruel or terrified or grief-stricken, a world revolving around pain. The murderous brutality at the center of the fallen world is also the pivot on which it will turn, the precise means by which its condition will be fundamentally changed.

Gibson wants to take us through the needle's eye of violently inflicted death and to experience that as a kind of birth, and he will use every trick in the action-movie book to accomplish that aim. Small wonder that this movie has terrified as many as it has uplifted. To encounter, at the movies, a vision of revealed religion in its savage state—the world literally split open in the very body of the revealer—is to be reminded of the many diverse ends toward which the potency of film can be, but so rarely is, channeled. In the altered world we have lived in since September 11, Gibson's movie can easily be taken as an omen—or an encouragement—of a cultural shift toward a fierce religious absolutism all too much in sync with some of the most destructive forces at large in the world.

Writing a review of *The Passion of the Christ* is quite different from writing a review of all the potential responses this movie may well instill, and all the acts and attitudes those responses might inspire. Considered in a vacuum, it's a fascinating object. Potentially it might even be an incitement to sincere meditation on the horror of torture and judicial murder. It's also a useful occasion to think about all the other events, and other belief systems, and other interpretations of the universe that have not yet been translated to film. Many such potential films flashed across my consciousness while undergoing Gibson's filmic ritual—in fact a whole counter-history of religion and religious persecution—and I am grateful for such provocation wherever found. Finally, however, *The Passion of the Christ* is likely to be judged in light of the uses that others will make of it, out there in the world—a world in which, all signs indicate, this movie is going to be circulating for a long, long time.

*Film Comment*, 2004

# was it all just a dream?

MICHAEL MOORE DOESN'T SO MUCH make documentaries as make movies with documents: if, that is, the term "documentary" has any more descriptive precision than, say, "nonfiction." In his first film, *Roger & Me* (1989), Moore invented for himself the genre in which he has continued to work: call it first-person polemic, or expressionist bulletin board, or theatricalized Op-Ed piece. *Roger & Me* tells the story of how General Motors cut its losses in Flint, Michigan, without any regard for the fate of the workers left behind, and turns it into a whimsical quest by Moore for an interview with GM's chairman, Roger Smith. Along the way, an assortment of found footage—home movies, promotional films, TV newscasts, performance clips featuring celebrities on the order of Anita Bryant and Pat Boone, scenes from old Hollywood pictures—are interwoven with the staged encounters that have become Moore's trademark, in which various spokespersons and security officers are enlisted as bit players in a comically timed confrontation with authority.

Points are made through shamelessly broad devices—the Beach Boys sing "Wouldn't It Be Nice" over relentless tracking shots of wrecked and abandoned housing in Flint, Roger Smith delivers an unctuous Christmas oration, complete with a reading from Charles Dickens, while a sheriff's deputy in Flint evicts a family put out of work by the GM plant closings—and somehow, through all this comical and at times blatantly theatrical business, a story does get told about the very real effects of an economic catastrophe, and about the apparent indifference to its human consequences on the part of those who made the managerial decisions. It has been told not so much through Moore's tendentious voice-overs as through the dozens of people, from unemployed auto workers to the receptionist at Roger Smith's health club, whose gazes and vocal inflections and gestures Moore so artfully and deliberately juxtaposes.

Substituting the administration of George W. Bush for General Motors, Moore's new film, *Fahrenheit 9/11*, could almost be a remake of *Roger & Me*. While operating on a larger scale, it draws on the same formal gimmicks and leads to the same broad and simple conclusion, a conclusion toward which Charles Dickens might well have had some empathy: that the big shots do things for their own self-serving reasons and don't give a damn about you or me or all the others who maneuver for temporary advantage in a situation not of their choosing. Indeed, in *Fahrenheit*, as in his previous film, the anti-NRA tract *Bowling for Columbine* (2002), Moore eventually brings the movie back to Flint, as if to reaffirm a core of personal experience as his center even when contemplating the most far-flung events. This stubborn subjectivity, grounded in local knowledge and reinforced by habitual gestures and comic tics, is strained in his new movie almost to the breaking point as he incorporates as much as he can of the history of the past four years, but it is something he can't afford to lose. If he isn't the hometown guy from Flint, with the skeptical eye and the deceptively laid-back manner, then who is he?

Moore's persona has by now taken on a somewhat stylized quality, but at the same time it has receded into the position of a mere structural device, a functionally effective way of getting the tale told. The effectiveness of the telling is in a sense what *Fahrenheit 9/11* is about. Its fiction is that one man—not a lecturer or the representative of a political party, but somebody you might meet at a party or in a bar—is telling you according to his own lights what's been going on in the world lately. He's funny, stridently opinionated, occasionally eloquent, and on top of that he has a fund of anecdotes and visual aids to back up his story; from time to time, without interrupting the thread of his discourse, he changes the music on the sound system to produce some startling and amusing effects. What makes it all the more persuasive is that, at every step, he reminds you in devastating detail how ineptly or deceptively others have told their versions of this same story. The proof of their ineptitude or deception is that he's telling you things you haven't heard before, and showing you pictures that seem to speak for themselves. It's not a story about a well-hidden conspiracy: all you have to do, he implies, is look around. You could step outside the room where you're sitting and pick up the trail anywhere, right on the street.

His version of the story begins with how George W. Bush was elected to the presidency under dubious circumstances and settled into what promised to be a single mediocre term until he was jolted awake by the attacks of September 11; how his response to those attacks was muddied by, among other factors, long-standing business ties to the Saudi royal family; how the Bush administration used the War on Terror as a means to instill fear in the American public and erode civil liberties through the Patriot Act while failing actually to protect homeland security; and, finally, how (for reasons having much to do with oil profits, and nothing to do with the horrific nature of Saddam Hussein's regime) an invasion of Iraq was mounted after deliberately misleading the public about Saddam's weaponry and links to al-Qaeda. The upshot is that poor people who have joined the military for lack of other employment end up dead and wounded in the service of a lie. A final quotation from Orwell's *1984* is used to plant the notion that the Iraq war is part of a wider and inherently unfinishable global war whose real purpose is to keep power in the hands of America's economic elite.

THIS BALD SYNOPSIS, admittedly the further simplification of a simplification, entirely fails to convey the film's very real power. It does not unfold like a lecture but like the tour of a fun house, a fun house whose mirrors and skewed angles turn out to be a place all too easy to recognize as home. Strangely for so overtly polemical a work, *Fahrenheit 9/11* can be seen as a triumph of form over content. What is least persuasive about it is the specifics of its arguments; what is exhilarating and often moving about it has to do above all with the materials, many of them archival and many not seen before, which are enlisted in support of those arguments, materials that linger and expand in the mind in ways that go far beyond the sometimes casually deployed debating points. We may never know just why the name of James Bath (a fellow National Guardsman with whom George W. Bush trained in Texas, and who later participated in a business deal involving both Bush and a member of the bin Laden family) was expunged from the officially released transcript of Bush's military records, or whether or not the desire of certain business interests to build a natural gas pipeline through Afghanistan significantly impeded American response to the Taliban and al-Qaeda; and in any event Moore as a rule only conveys enough information to arouse suspicion, not nearly enough to begin to make a case.

But then making a case, well reasoned or not, is not really what the movie, or Moore as a filmmaker, is about. *Fahrenheit 9/11* can be regarded as more or less the movie version of his book *Dude, Where's My Country?*, which lays out in a fairly slapdash style many of the same charges: about undue Saudi influence on the Bush family, about the proposed Unocal pipeline as a determinant of American policy in Afghanistan, and about the administration's deliberate fearmongering since September 11. Like many another movie version of a potentially controversial book, *Fahrenheit 9/11* tones down some of the material. The book, for instance, explicitly "throw[s] out a possibility" of direct Saudi responsibility for the September 11 attacks, suggesting that it might have been "not a 'terrorist' attack, but, rather, a military attack against the United States," and goes so far as to state, "There is no terrorist threat"—or rather, to give the full flavor of Moore's prose, "THERE . . . IS . . . NO . . . TERRORIST . . . THREAT!" (He quickly, if not very convincingly, qualifies this: "Now, when I say there is no terrorist threat, I am not saying that there are no terrorists, or that there are no terrorist incidents, or that there won't be other terrorist incidents in the future. . . . But just because there are a few terrorists does not mean we are all in some exaggerated state of danger"—except, that is, from "our own multi-millionaire, corporate terrorists.")

It must be said that Moore is a good deal less persuasive when he doesn't have his audiovisual displays at his disposal. On the bare page he is the artist stripped of his tools, however strange a statement that may be to make about an author whose books sell in the millions of copies. Funny as he sometimes is in print, Moore finally cannot resist bludgeoning the reader into submission with his reductive prose:

> Everyone—except those who die in it—loves a good war, especially one you can win quickly. We, good. Them, bad. Them, dead. We win! Cue the cameras, the victorious POTUS is landing on the aircarrier.

In *Fahrenheit 9/11* the gist of this passage is conveyed, to quite different effect, by a clip from the early days of the Iraq war of TV anchorwoman Katie Couric chirping, "I just want you to know I think Navy SEALs rock!" and by actual footage of Bush on that aircraft carrier, beneath the now notorious MISSION ACCOMPLISHED banner, the scene underscored by the maddeningly buoyant theme of the early Eighties TV show *The Greatest American Hero* ("Suddenly I'm up on top of the world, / Shoulda been somebody else. / Believe it or not I'm walking on air, / I never thought I could feel so free"). Rather than a series of slogans and one-liners that become tiresome even if you agree with them, the film offers signs captured from the air, little pieces of the environment we inhabit. An overt connoisseurship of sources comes into play. The fun that Moore has mixing his materials—including the fairly cheap fun of the *Dragnet* clips, the *Bonanza* bit with Bush and Company riding off to Afghanistan, the music video effect of REM's "Shiny Happy People" as backdrop to scenes of Bushes and Saudis socializing together, the World Wrestling Federation–style roll call of the Coalition of the Willing—is meant to be shared by an audience sufficiently at home with all forms of sampling and downloading to take a virtually professional interest in the fine points of Moore's mix tape.

The movie constantly reinforces the audience's expectation that it will be shown unexpected things: things that are merely amusing, whether the amateurish enthusiasm of John Ashcroft singing his own composition "Let the Eagle Soar" or the exquisite lip-glossed vacuousness of Britney Spears expressing her unquestioning support for the president; things you've forgotten or never caught the first time around, like Prince Bandar reminiscing on *Larry King Live* about his single meeting with Osama bin Laden; and things you've never seen at all, like the slightly pained expression on Colin Powell's face as he endures a photo op with a Saudi dignitary, or Bush humorously addressing a group of ultrarich campaign supporters ("Some people call you the elite; I call you my base"); footage that was never shown, or that was truncated when shown, or that was shown only in other countries and would not have been allowed on American TV. There are Moore's signature stunts, although fewer than usual—like accosting congressmen and asking them to encourage their children to join the military—and the confrontations that fall into place so neatly they appear to be setups, like Moore being questioned by Secret Service agents for standing across the street from the Saudi embassy.

The movie works by appealing to the primal curiosity that lured people into nickelodeons, the desire to see what comes next in the string of attractions, and unlike some of those nickelodeon operators, Moore makes good on the promise. The blankly stunned face of George W. Bush, already informed about the Trade Center attacks, as he continues to sit in a Florida elementary school classroom reading "The Pet Goat" with the kids—regardless of how you read it and regardless of Moore's intrusive voice-over—is what most viewers of *Fahrenheit 9/11* will take away with them, and it isn't something you could have stayed home and watched on TV.

It is curious that many people will go to see this movie simply to get a closer look at the president. There is a gap between any chief executive and his public image, but the mysteriously absent presence of Bush the Second—the sense that he is being perpetually displayed yet fundamentally withheld from view—still seems singular, and in consequence Moore is able to get mileage out of moments that are not in themselves shocking revelations: Bush flexing his mouth in what looks like a weird grin before announcing that the Iraq war had started, or hopelessly fumbling the old "Fool me once, shame on you" line, or segueing from talk of terrorism to a demonstration of his golf swing, moments that will probably have more subtly destructive impact than all the mustering of information about Saudi investments or the greed of Halliburton.

We are invited to contemplate the evolution of George W. Bush's physiognomy over time—or rather the persistence of certain traits that become odder the longer one looks at them: the cracked, side-of-the-mouth smile, the withdrawn gaze, the equal capacity to express haplessness and guile. Eventually Bush becomes a kind of punctuation mark, his remarks seeming increasingly off-key or unfeeling when placed against scenes of gathering horror and grief. This might of course be taken as a belated tribute to the Russian director Lev Kuleshov's famous demonstration of how the expression of a filmed face appears to change depending on what other footage it is juxtaposed with. On the other hand, it's hard to imagine a more piercing quick sketch than the August 1992 interview in which Bush brags almost naively about the enviable "access to power" he enjoys, his father being the president, a moment topped only by the footage of Bush delivering his famous "I'm a war president" remark with a spasmodic detachment that has to be seen to be believed.

You can argue with the use to which these separate pieces are being put, but they fascinate in themselves. They have a built-in complexity that teases out contradictions and grace notes from the broad strokes of Moore's narrative. Like an obsessed collector, Moore brings you things to look at. He says, "Let me show you what I mean," and what he shows ends up suggesting meanings beyond his point, meanings that persist as a cloud of potentialities. It's not that Moore's materials get away from him, quite the contrary; the hallmark of his films is the way every element has been lovingly handpicked. His evident fascination for what he works with gives his movies their sense of independent life. Dozens of people who emerge, sometimes only for a few seconds, in the course of *Fahrenheit 9/11*—soldiers and civilians, business reps and state troopers, politicians and people on the street—cling to memory as characters in their own right, beyond whatever polemical point is being made. His greatest gift may be as a casting director.

As a filmmaker Moore displays an imaginative sympathy inseparable from a predilection for the unprogrammed and the unpredictable. That flair for irrational whimsy cuts deeper than his own more predictable arguments, and where it reaches its limits, gaping holes become manifest. The personalized, "my world and welcome to it" tone can go only so far. *Fahrenheit 9/11* sometimes feels like a tour on which the guide conspicuously steers you away from certain rooms. Some of the things that Moore leaves out are merely puzzling, since they would have strengthened the case against the war: he does nothing with Guantánamo and the "enemy combatant" issue, the flap over the identification of Joseph Wilson's wife as a CIA agent, the negligence with regard to protecting cultural sites and much else in Baghdad, the general lack of planning for the occupation of Iraq. Lack of sufficiently gripping footage may have been a problem for some of these matters. It does, however, seem especially odd that he makes so little of the failure to find weapons of mass destruction.

But perhaps to have raised these issues at all would have drawn attention to other and more troubling omissions. This is a film about the September 11 attacks and the War on Terror that omits any discussion of al-Qaeda and Islamist radicalism, while drastically fudging its account of the Afghanistan war, and a film on the Iraq war that avoids any discussion of the nature of Saddam Hussein's regime (Saddam figures exclusively, and fleetingly, as a client of the United States during the 1980s). Iraqi life under Saddam Hussein is represented, in a sequence that seems almost a parody of the generic propaganda film, by a montage of happy wedding parties, bustling restaurants, a little boy flying a kite, a little girl going down a slide: all of it brutally interrupted by the American bombs. Moore seems reluctant to allow the opposition to express any coherent argument, even if only to knock it down, just as in *Bowling for Columbine* the arguments for gun ownership rights were entrusted to an unprepared and visibly frail Charlton Heston and to the wild-eyed brother of Oklahoma City bomber Terry Nichols.

*FAHRENHEIT 9/11* IS not, finally, a movie about Iraq or Afghanistan, and evidently is not intended to be. It's a movie about America and Americans. The bloody scenes of the Iraq war that follow the dubious montage mentioned above have a frightening effectiveness not because they illuminate in any way the conflicts within Iraqi society but because they demonstrate the unbridgeable gap between the American soldiers and the place where they find themselves. It's as if Moore identified so much with the bewilderment of those soldiers that he can only give us their point of view. The Iraqis themselves are an indistinguishable mass of suffering and resentment, with no distinctions made among different allegiances within the culture. The result, at worst, is another dubious moment when the soundtrack gives us party music—"Come on, party people, throw your hands in the air"—in synch with a crowd of insurgents raising their rifles, who are thereby made to look like a parody of the Arab raiders in some desert adventure movie.

Here as elsewhere in the film Moore has a tendency to make easy caricatural use of any footage involving exotics, whether from Saudi Arabia or Costa Rica. The American soldiers on the other hand are made to seem thoroughly familiar even when they are talking about getting pumped up on a record by the Bloodhound Gang when riding into battle ("The roof is on fire . . . Burn, motherfucker, burn!") or abusing a bound prisoner in Abu Ghraib fashion (a voice redolent of ancient summer camp hazing rituals howls, "You touched his dick!").

It is to America—to Flint—that the film inevitably returns, and it is here that Moore finally clarifies where he has been heading all along.

We get to know a woman named Lila Lipscomb who works at the local employment service; she talks about encouraging her children to join the military because of the educational and travel benefits it offers; and we watch as she tells of learning about her son's death in a helicopter crash in Iraq. In her sincere patriotism, her sorrow, and her rage against a war that her son denounced in his last letter home, she becomes the foil to Bush, an embodiment of everything he is not. (Her presence, and her own articulation of her feelings, is so directly moving that it seems a lapse on Moore's part to intercut a shot of Bush speaking—in a way that in this context can only seem inadequate if not perfunctory—about the grief of those who have lost loved ones in the war.) It is to acknowledge the simple and irrefutable point that the war is happening not just in Iraq and not just on TV but in America that we have been guided through a hall of mirrors to wind up in something like our own backyard.

We are taken, for example, to a shopping mall in Flint to watch two Marine recruiters ply their trade among the mostly African American youths hanging out there. It's a memorable scene—funny, informative about the aggressive yet seductive way in which Marine recruiters do what they do, and quietly devastating in the line it draws between what is said here and what happens in Iraq. This is a moment where Moore folds the movie back into his own life. For me it also triggered the kind of spontaneous reaction that *Fahrenheit 9/11* is expertly designed to elicit. I found myself recollecting an afternoon in late August 2001, in a laundromat at another shopping mall, in upstate New York. The wall-mounted TV tilting down over the dryers was tuned to a seemingly interminable documentary about the arduous training of Army Special Forces, a cinematic recruiting poster that evoked simultaneously the action aesthetic of the *Die Hard* movies and the ferocious camaraderie associated with the warrior cults of 1930s Germany or Japan. After the movie ended it was followed by another in identical style, devoted to the training of Navy SEALs. The afternoon began to take on a disorienting and disturbing quality. Between the poverty of the people in the laundromat—a substantial portion of the town's population was out of work and on welfare—and the unrelieved stridency of the military infomercials, I'd had a sense of glimpsing a possible American future I hadn't quite dared to imagine, of increasingly limited economic prospects and a culture increasingly devoted to the worship of armed force.

A few weeks later—displaced from my lower Manhattan home by the events of September 11—I had occasion to remember that afternoon in the laundromat. By then, however, my concern was not so much with the overbearing aggressiveness of the recruiting films as with the question of whether those elite forces were really as good as they were cracked up to be. In short order so many signs were reversed, so many recent events either buried or reconceived. Days lasted years and opinions and moods took drastic and unexpected turns, as the news bulletins of the morning—the alarms over impending attacks, the freshly revealed evidence of some other hidden band of fanatical conspirators, the latest incident of anthrax contamination, the siege of Tora Bora that for a giddy moment promised to restore order with a decisive victory in the old style—often gave way by nightfall to some fresh and contradictory line of rumor or suspicion. Little could be relied on. A kind of walking amnesia set in, in which events moved too fast to allow people fully to remember what had happened just before. In the grip of an inexorable forward lurch into the next war, the blame for which could be debated and fine-tuned ad infinitum, we stumbled into a future there had not been time even to imagine.

Moving so quickly into the future, even the very recent past seemed to evaporate with no trace. "Was it all just a dream?" asks Michael Moore in voice-over at the beginning of *Fahrenheit 9/11*. "Did the last four years not really happen?" The image on the screen is of fireworks going off as Al Gore—in the company of Robert De Niro and Stevie Wonder—prepares to celebrate his election to the presidency in November 2000. The music has a Bernard Herrmannish tone of lyrical anxiety. The moment is unexpectedly magical and, like much of what follows, functions in a way that goes beyond polemic. Simply by making the recent past visible, by bringing these little pieces of reality into the movie theater, Moore unleashes a reservoir of feeling. It's like the symbolic breaking of a spell. We can begin to remember everything that we had almost started to forget.

*Fahrenheit 9/11* serves as a necessary reminder that, to put it in the simplest terms, we need to see and hear more than the government and the various news channels allow us to see and hear. We need to play back the tapes to refresh our memory of what seems consigned to instant oblivion even as it unfolds. We need to see those images— of Americans and Iraqis alike wounded and dying, for example—that American television tends to withhold, as if the reality of the war could thereby be kept at bay. Michael Moore's version of what has been happening lately is only one possible narrative; but by its very existence it encourages a more active and confrontational approach to the images that surround us, anything to break through the numbing flow of TV news broadcasts and official bulletins that has become something like the wallpaper of a distorted public reality, a stream of images that moves forward without ever looking back.

The opening of *Fahrenheit 9/11* (which has set attendance records for a documentary) generated some responses that might have been extensions of the movie itself. The clumsy attempt by a group calling itself Move America Forward to pressure theaters into not showing the film; the possibly more effective attempt by Citizens United to block the film's television ads; the comparison by Bill O'Reilly on the Fox News Channel of those who applauded the film at its premiere to "people who would turn out to see Josef Goebbels convince you that Poland invaded the Third Reich," or the feverish musings of Kathleen Antrim in the *San Francisco Examiner* ("Will his warped film ignite more violence and provide further provocation for terrorists? Could they be showing this film in al-Qaeda camps to fire up the terrorists?"): Michael Moore couldn't have scripted it better if he had wanted to underscore his warnings about the toll that the War on Terror is taking on public discourse.

*The New York Review of Books*, 2004

# the return of the shaw brothers

AT THE DAWN OF THE 1960s, on the shore of Hong Kong's Clearwater Bay, a world capital of sorts came into being: Movietown, the production center of the seemingly unbeatable Shaw Brothers Ltd., a company that had parlayed a movie theater business in prerevolutionary Shanghai into a global concern dominating both production and exhibition in Chinese-language markets. Looking in aerial photographs like a cross between a low-income housing project and a theme park crammed with ancient Chinese motifs, Movietown was in its heyday a self-contained filmmaking universe open around the clock and churning out as many as seven features at a time—some three hundred were made in the studio's first twelve years—to fill the screens of Hong Kong and Taiwan and Southeast Asia, and beyond that all the screens of the diaspora of London and New York and San Francisco and every other city with a Chinatown.

Movietown's standing sets, employed in movie after movie, would become a familiar alternate world: a phantom China whose temples and palaces, taverns and brothels, labyrinthine fortresses, picturesque rock formations, and subterranean canals provided the setting for a succession of combats, conspiracies, rigorous apprenticeships, bloody sacrifices, and displays of extravagant skill both martial and supernatural. Even though geographically and temporally inaccessible, this lost China—destroyed by history and thereby permitted to flourish as myth—asserted its undying presence through vibrant color schemes and rousingly noisy music and sound effects. The movie offered not just a story but an extension of place to alleviate the claustrophobia of exile. The screen was like a window or a harbor front opening onto a past that signaled its defiant robustness with overpowering displays of physical energy, leaps above treetops, high-speed attacks and evasions, fight scenes in which (as in the incredibly protracted finale of 1972's *The Boxer from Shantung*) a wounded warrior could keep knocking down dozens of opponents for ten minutes with a hatchet embedded in his stomach.

The *wuxia pian* ("films of chivalric combat") that in the early years dominated the Shaw Brothers' releases embodied the oldest of traditions, extending from classic novels like the seventeenth-century *Water Margin* (to which Shaw Brothers paid tribute with a 1972 film version followed by a sequel, *All Men Are Brothers*) and the melodrama and acrobatics of Chinese opera to the swordplay and displays of magic that became a staple of Chinese movies from the silent era on. From those early sources the movies preserved not only a repertoire of devices and situations, but, beneath all the heroic fantasy, an ancient harshness grounded in political realism. In the absence of reliable, uncorrupted law enforcement or any notion of popular sovereignty, heroic action was an improvisational kind of justice, created ad hoc in the midst of emerging confrontations, and shored up by whatever loyalties were available to be called upon.

But Shaw Brothers movies were also harbingers of the modern. Their dazzlingly bright colors and expansive Shawscope compositions revamped the inherited repertoire of adventure stories into artifacts that seemed futuristic: the products of a China yet to be, streamlined and globally competitive, not a version of Hollywood but an alternative to Hollywood. Soon enough, with the advent of Bruce Lee and the triumph of kung fu, Hong Kong filmmakers would look beyond Chinese-language audiences, leading the way to the gaudy era when Tsui Hark, John Woo, and their colleagues briefly made Hong Kong movies into a world model for genre filmmaking—faster, wilder, and more flamboyantly stylized than the American competition.

By then, the splendor of the earlier films was just a memory. In Chinatowns all over the world, the movie theaters were shutting down one by one, Movietown had begun its long decline, and the widescreen epics of great directors like King Hu, Chang Cheh, and Chu Yuan survived, if at all, as truncated, faded, panned-and-scanned, horribly dubbed videos, interspersed indistinguishably with far cruder and cheaper martial arts fodder and valued chiefly as a source of motifs and samples for hip-hop records. The movies of a lost world were themselves consigned to a lost world.

But now, in an unanticipated bonanza, we have been witnessing through the good offices of Celestial Pictures in Hong Kong a flood of digitally restored items from the Shaw Brothers catalogue, with the promise of many more to come. The library amounts to some eight hundred movies. The process of excavation is only beginning, yielding for instance newly revealed splendors of the late 1950s and early 1960s, a period dominated by sumptuously artificial opera films like Li Han-hsiang's *The Kingdom and the Beauty* (1959) and *Beyond the Great Wall* (1964) and heart-wrenching romantic dramas like Chin Tao's *Endless Love* (1961). (All three of those films are marked by the indelible presence of Lin Dai, an actress whose tragic roles were echoed by her own suicide at thirty.)

WITH MANY OTHERS, I feel an almost irrational gratitude for the return of those Shaw Brothers films of the 1970s that had become an increasingly remote memory. It's like being allowed to return to a place where you were happy and that you had begun to assume you would never see again. Just a glimpse of the immense blue skies that often fill that ultrawide Shawscope frame—a shade of blue that seems to exist only in Hong Kong movies of a certain vintage—promises, if not earthly contentment, then whatever it is that movies offer as a nearly indistinguishable substitute.

No DVD can restore the atmosphere of a Chinatown movie theater in the Sixties and Seventies, that sense that the theater was a kind
of town square where all generations were represented, some intently
focused on what was occurring onscreen in whatever violent costume
melodrama or kinky sex farce was unreeling, while others were perhaps more preoccupied with eating lunch, looking after babies, or
keeping an eye on the somewhat older kids roaming in the aisles. No
single movie was more important than the continuity provided by a
steady stream of product, with its implication that there would always
be one more cunningly devised stratagem, one more annihilating collision of a lone swordsman with an army of masked attackers, one
more heartbreaking ballad to embody the force of a frustrated passion
otherwise left chastely to the imagination (at least before the floodgates
of eroticism began to open with the 1972 hit *Intimate Confessions of a
Chinese Courtesan*).

The classic Shaw Brothers movies set about their business from the
first frames and allow for very little downtime as they progress. In the
manner of the storytelling tradition in which they are rooted, attention
is sustained stringently from instant to instant, with overall structure
less important than making sure that something compelling is happening at any given moment. Typically a movie starts with a scene of
vigorous combat that will be explained more or less on the run, the
characters dropping in bits of backstory in between spear thrusts or
feats of levitation. A good deal of the backstory may never be explained
to the satisfaction of a viewer unfamiliar with the legacy of well-known
plotlines on which the films draw freely, and in the last reel the movie
may seem not so much to end as to stop, suspended at a convenient
moment to be resumed at some future time.

The point is not what's going to happen; such resolutions as occur
are more or less inevitable. What counts is to maintain an unbroken
intensity of spectacle, in which every movement and image—every
glance and gesture, every boastful challenge and malevolent chuckle—
is calculated for unimpeded impact. The energy of these movies evokes
to a remarkable degree that of the oldest storytelling or street theater,

a quality owing much to the speed with which they were made by a stock company of actors and technicians kept on their mettle by near-constant employment. (Production conditions were far from utopian, and the restrictive contracts and drastically low salaries offered by Shaw Brothers would finally lead to the defection of some of their best talent.) When Yueh Hua, as an avenging warrior disguised as a scruffy mendicant entertainer, launches into his comical patter-song in a tavern packed with bandits in King Hu's magnificent *Come Drink with Me* (1966), the street theater aspect comes into full play. Juggling, acrobatics, rhymed riddles and stylized insults, magic tricks and tests of strength: nothing that will keep the audience attentive for one moment longer is out of place.

These were movies in which skill was central, a skill not merely alluded to but constantly demonstrated. To see them when they came out was to encounter not only a foreign language but a foreign body language, shaped by skills that were made constantly explicit, with no latent capability left to surmise. Those Shaw Brothers stars who were not themselves martial arts adepts made up for it with a choreographic grace—augmented by wires, trampolines, and intricately deceptive editing—that made Hollywood action scenes seem curtailed and mechanical. "I'm impressed with your whip technique," an admiring warrior tells the imperiously beautiful Cheng Pei-pei in *The Shadow Whip* (1971), in what amounts to a refinement of lovemaking. No combat is too closely fought not to allow time for those interjected bits of analysis—"Someone having such guts must be skilled" or "If you were kidding you wouldn't punch so hard"—that establish a backbeat for the blows and parries. Whatever takes place onscreen is informed and enlarged by language; every duel is partly verbal. The wily magistrates, unctuous monks, and rapacious bandits are all masters both of hypocritical courtesies and baroque vituperation, and there is always an ample supply of comically fearful, vainglorious, or simply dim-witted henchmen for additional theatrical flavor.

To see the Shaw Brothers stock company demonstrate how an acting technique of nearly total artificiality, a technique based on rigidly defined character types and a repertoire of fixed gestures, can create as convincing an illusion as supposedly more naturalistic styles would be enough to keep these movies watchable. These are ensemble works in which no player, however minor, ever relents for a second. All villains are transparently villainous, all heroes self-evidently sincere. Lechery, cowardice, senile weakness, low cunning, and wounded pride are displayed in the manner of puppet theater, with decisive figuration and vigorous grace seemingly more valued than nuance or ambiguity. Only seemingly, because nuance and ambiguity creep in anyway, as the avenging loyalists incarnated by Jimmy Wang Yu (*The One-Armed Swordsman*, 1967) or Ti Lung (*Blood Brothers*, 1973) become increasingly nihilistic and conflicted, and even David Chiang, the impishly smiling, sometimes lute-strumming hero of so many films, acquires intimations of a psychopathic edge.

THE EARLIER RELEASES have a particular charm; they are stylized in ways that would be phased out as Hong Kong movies reached wider markets, and their combat scenes are leavened by romance, domestic comedy, and musical diversion. These are wonder tales, in which a mysterious stranger can walk without leaving footprints in the snow (*The Shadow Whip*), or in which a slain warrior may rise out of his body, ascending heavenward in astral form (*The Trail of the Broken Blade*, 1967). *The Temple of the Red Lotus* (1965), a huge hit that sealed the popularity of *wuxia pian*, culminates in a long sequence in which the hero—owing to the arcane rules of the clan he has married into— must confront in combat his wife's sister, mother, and grandmother.

*The Knight of Knights* (1966), a particularly rich mix, pits a masked hero against a conclave of corrupt and lecherous monks (the sustained leering grin of the foremost lecher is something to see) who keep abducted women prisoner in their monastery while plotting to assassinate a magistrate by toppling his pagoda into the sea. (The toppling is initially demonstrated with the use of a builder's model, a striking instance of these movies' concern with architectural technique, whether in the form of traps, hiding places, or ingenious means of invasion and infiltration.) It also finds rooms for a poignant, musically narrated interlude in which the chaste hero and heroine must dry off their clothes by the fire, separated only by a screen: it's like a demonstration that virtue is finally the ultimate aphrodisiac.

Women had a much greater role to play in the early swordplay era, with woman warriors like Cheng Pei-pei, Xu Feng, and Angela Mao taking charge in a fashion that remains exhilarating. Later films, by contrast, particularly under the guidance of the extraordinarily prolific Chang Cheh (he directed nearly one hundred movies), would concern themselves ever more relentlessly with the fate of the male body, as blood-soaked heroes took longer and longer to die, gathering their energy for one more leap to take out one more assailant. The lighter elements that had been part of the genre tended increasingly to give way to a more doom-laden atmosphere. The question was no longer whether the hero would survive but whether he would succeed in killing all his opponents before finally collapsing. The blood leaking from the corner of his mouth was the inevitable signal that his time was up.

Pure fantasy found a home, however, in a cycle of films adapted by Chu Yuan from a series of twentieth-century novels by Gu Long, including *The Magic Blade* (1976), *Killer Clans* (1976), and *Clans of Intrigue* (1977). Here we are plunged into a dreamlike universe inhabited solely by martial arts masters who operate through arts of magic, disguise, and secret weaponry like the mystical Peacock Dart. The director had already made the notorious *Intimate Confessions of a Chinese Courtesan*, a film that manages to blend brutal realism, a sexual explicitness that broke decisively with convention, and rough-hewn comedy (on the favorite Chinese theme of senile lechery) before culminating in a scene of mutual annihilation as the courtesan and her madam more or less slice each other to pieces. In his Gu Long adaptations, Chu Yuan revealed himself as a master of luxurious reverie. The films are exquisitely aestheticized fever-dreams that dissolve as you watch them, leaving only brightly colored fragments behind.

It is fitting that these should reemerge at a moment when their ghostly presence has been making itself felt in contexts ranging from Tsai Ming-liang's minimalist *Goodbye, Dragon Inn* (2003), with its nearly empty movie theater showing the King Hu classic *Dragon Inn* to spectators seemingly stranded in time, to Tarantino's appropriation of the Shaw Brothers logo for the opening of *Kill Bill*. With all respect to Tarantino, there is indeed nothing like the real thing, and even those who don't find it necessary to track down all eight hundred Shaw Brothers releases may find that these apparently escapist fantasies evoke, finally, something uncannily solid: indeed, nothing less than a world.

*Artforum*, 2004

# the man in the smoking jacket

## 1.

IN 1920 CARY GRANT—or properly speaking, Archie Leach—was a sixteen-year-old Bristol-born music hall acrobat, specialized in stilt-walking and pratfalls, who was on his way to America for the first time as a member of the Bob Pender troupe. In 1927, after various show-business ups and downs, he was a largely out-of-work actor living in a single-room-occupancy hotel in New York, working sometimes as a male escort, sometimes as a tie salesman, sometimes as a sandwich board man for a Chinese restaurant. In 1935 he was a movie actor who, despite having appeared (over a period of only three years) in twenty films opposite such costars as Marlene Dietrich, Mae West, Carole Lombard, Loretta Young, and Myrna Loy, had failed to live up to the high expectations of his bosses at Paramount, who had signed him in the hope that he would prove a star of the magnitude of Rudolph Valentino or Gary Cooper.

It is astonishing in retrospect to see him in a movie like *Born To Be Bad* (1934), getting effortlessly upstaged by a cigarette-smoking Loretta Young in deliriously campy "bad girl" mode. Grant, in the thankless part of a dairy company executive who falls for Young's sleazy charms, looks like a radiantly handsome but inert male model who has rented out his face and physique to Paramount while his thoughts wander elsewhere.

Then, with mysterious suddenness, he clicked on. He imposed his presence in a striking character role, as a roguish Cockney vagabond, a high spot of George Cukor's commercially disastrous *Sylvia Scarlett* (1935), and then came unmistakably into his own as half of the divorcing couple in Leo McCarey's screwball masterpiece *The Awful Truth* (1937). From that point on he enjoyed—in both the audience's pleasure and his own creative control and financial well-being—something like a perfect career as a movie star. In a move that was then radical, he cut himself loose from long-term studio contracts, and through a shrewd choice of assignments was able, with remarkable consistency, to work with exceptional scripts and superior directors: Cukor, McCarey, George Stevens, Joseph Mankiewicz, Stanley Donen, and above all Howard Hawks and Alfred Hitchcock. A movie career that started in 1932 was still peaking in the late Fifties and early Sixties with tremendous box office hits like *Operation Petticoat* (1959) and *That Touch of Mink* (1962). Then, with the elegant discretion of which he had made himself the embodiment, Grant withdrew from the scene just before signs of old age could dent the screen image he had elaborated with such perfectionist devotion.

When I first encountered Cary Grant in childhood in regularly repeated television reruns of such films as *Gunga Din* (1939), *Mr. Lucky* (1943), and *The Bachelor and the Bobby-Soxer* (1947), he seemed both amusingly peculiar—those singular vocal inflections, especially, set him apart from any other actor—and enviably high-spirited. It became evident as well that for the female relatives and caretakers with whom I watched these movies Cary Grant was something quite special, an image of the dream date, the perfect man. His name was spoken with an affectionate sigh, as if he symbolized a better world somewhere on the other side of the screen. Yet on a closer look there was something isolated about him. With each of his movements and line readings he drew a boundary line between himself and everything else in the frame. Anyone that perfect would have to be something of a closed system. He suggested, however, that such a fate might be quite desirable.

There is an emblematic scene in the otherwise mild comedy *The Bachelor and the Bobby-Soxer* in which Grant, playing a successful painter of supposedly scandalous habits, returns alone to his luxurious apartment in a sleekly tailored double-breasted suit. What follows is a systematic cataloguing of the joys of bachelor life: Grant ascends to the second floor of his duplex to change into a smoking jacket, then reemerges and walks over to his top-drawer postwar sound system to play some music on the radio. He switches the radio dial away from a discussion of "currency fluctuations" until he finds an orchestral arrangement of "My Shining Hour." A small smile registers his satisfaction with the music, the smile sustained as he goes over to mix himself a highball and then—to complete the picture of this solitary paradise—settles in an easy chair with a serious-looking book that he begins to read with what looks like voluptuous contentment. Every move in the sequence might have been choreographed, to illustrate that ordinary life could be a suite of smoothly executed, intensely pleasurable actions, the intense pleasure derived merely from contemplating the smooth execution.

Apparently it wouldn't be bad at all to be utterly alone, as long as one was Cary Grant. He suggested the possibility of a narcissistic self-sufficiency grounded in the consciousness of one's own physical and behavioral perfection. There are other scenes, and films, that have a great deal more to do with Grant's singular excellence as a screen actor; but this little episode encapsulates Grant's supremacy as a screen idol. He was simply the man who lacks for nothing and who does everything the way it should be done. Even if comic situations stripped him of his dignity and elicited from him exquisitely timed displays of petulance and near panic, none of that diminished the underlying sense that here was someone miraculously exempt from flaws, an impeccable specimen—"the world's most perfect male animal," in *Time*-speak—and thus a designated surrogate lover, companion, or self.

Marc Eliot begins his biography (published, along with Gary

Morecambe and Martin Sterling's *Cary Grant: In Name Only*, to coincide with the centenary of Grant's birth) with the actor's own aphoristic summing-up: "Everybody wants to be Cary Grant. Even I want to be Cary Grant." A few lines down Eliot quotes Grant again, responding to a reporter's question about his goal when he started out: "I pretended to be somebody I wanted to be until finally I became that person. Or he became me." It's in keeping with Grant's onscreen persona that he should be his own wittiest and most succinct commentator. Between them these two remarks almost obviate the need for a biography. He has already told us his story, with the same concision and exact definition he gave to his acting; or he has at least warned us that whatever story we hear, it isn't ever going to be the story of that man up on the screen.

If Grant always seemed the movie star's movie star, it was perhaps because he conveyed such lucid consciousness of what was involved in the exchange between star and spectator. It was as if he was giving the high sign to anyone in the audience smart enough to pick up on his signals. Everybody wanted to be Cary Grant in order to partake of that effortless self-awareness, that remarkable capacity to be in on every joke, even the ones of which he allowed himself to be made the butt. What makes Cary Grant different from other actors is the way he suggests—by rapid and barely discernible means, a glance, a wink, a shrug, a turning aside—a constant awareness of that gap between the surface that is all we can know of him and what actually is. He plays intelligence so persuasively that we feel a kind of privileged complicity merely by appreciating the performance.

No movie actor ever achieved quite so total a mastery of surface. Watch him in his first scene in *His Girl Friday* (1940), as—with every vocal inflection and physical gesture, with flexing fingers and lifted eyebrows, with tiny shifting movements, sideways, up and down, leaning forward or back, that constantly reposition him in relation to others—he keeps the spectator absorbed in the spectacle of his self-presentation: and in the midst of all that there is the smile that floats elsewhere, as if he were actually perched a long way off admiring the formal perfection of his own performance. He is both funny and beautiful, all the while portraying a character—the newspaper editor Walter Burns—ruthlessly self-absorbed and indifferent to others, a tyrannical child with real-world authority, capable of savoring his own self-pity even as he sets up his next con.

We learn from his biographers that Grant's concern for surface went well beyond his own performance, extending to the minutiae of set decoration and lighting, so that he might delay the day's shoot by insisting on "doorknobs painted different colors, windows changed, camera angles altered, lenses switched." By the same token he seems to have taken great care to conceal whatever lay beneath the surface, at least until the LSD therapy that he began in the late 1950s (when the drug was legal) prompted some unanticipated soul baring: but even then his revelations were more about his inner life than about how he actually spent his time when the cameras weren't running.

As a result neither of these new biographies, for all the details that they amass, persuades us that we are getting more than furtive and incomplete glimpses of a life designed to be hidden. Marc Eliot's *Cary Grant* is much the more elaborately researched and turns up a fair share of surprising revelations along with much innuendo and surmise, while the Morecambe and Sterling book, on the whole far more respectful of Grant's public image, fills in usefully with some diverting quotes and anecdotes. Finally, though, we are left with a fascinating incoherence, not so much a life as a jumble of possible lives. We are led to suspect that the pains Grant took over his professional life—aside from the care lavished on performances, scripts, and production details, he also served virtually as his own agent and was closely involved in the fine points of every contract he ever signed, right down to which of his tailored costumes he got to keep (ultimately, all)—left him little time to impart much order or direction to what happened offscreen. What he could not control he did his best to hide, and in the process he turned his life into a maze of false mirrors and beguiling misdirections. This was a matter not just of self-protection but of aesthetics. He believed that movie stars should be mysterious, and that to show the public too much was to destroy the source of their power.

## 2.

WHAT FEELS MOST solid in Grant's story is its point of origin in a world as far removed as possible from the ambience of a Cary Grant movie. Archie Leach was born in Bristol to Elsie Kingdon, a shipwright's daughter, and Elias Leach, a tailor's presser at a clothing factory, and grew up in an atmosphere of domestic misery that he later acknowledged, with a mother obsessed with orderliness—"I was fined for spilling things on the tablecloth"—and in perpetual mourning for her first child, who had died in infancy, and a wayward father who would ultimately set up house elsewhere with another woman. When he was ten he came home from school to find his mother absent. He was told at first that she had "gone away," and later at least one relative suggested that she had died. Cast adrift when his father refused to take him into his new home, he spent a summer sleeping in flophouses and working on the docks of Southampton running errands for the troops shipping out for the war. A classmate from Bristol would later say of him: "He was very scruffy. An ugly duckling. Always poorly dressed. And we tended to ostracize him because of that."

He was drawn to music halls and cinemas from an early age, by thirteen was working as a lighting assistant at the Bristol Hippodrome, and not long after teamed up with the vaudeville troupe of Bob Pender. Pender taught him acrobatics and encouraged him to work on losing his brogue, an effort at self-transformation that led to his developing his own personal dialect: a flawed imitation of sophisticated speech that became a model of it. When he was expelled from school a year later—supposedly for stealing from a church, though it may have been more prank than serious delinquency—he became a full-time member of the troupe, touring extensively in England, Europe, and even, Eliot suggests, "the larger theatrical outposts of the Middle East." In 1920 they sailed for New York. On board the *Olympic*, we are told, he befriended fellow passengers Mary Pickford and Douglas Fairbanks, thus initiating the transformation of Archie Leach's fairly bleak reality into the luminous dream-life of Cary Grant.

It is here, on the threshold of this new world, that Grant already begins to elude detection. Eliot's account of his life between 1920, when he opened at New York's Hippodrome in *Good Times*, "a world-class extravaganza, complete with elephants, zebras, monkeys, horses, acrobats, fireworks, dazzling light shows, solo singers, cyclists, dancers, chorales, musicians, magicians, and a self-contained water show," to 1932, when he shot his first picture for Paramount, *This Is the Night*, is a compound of rumor and hypothesis intercut with show-biz statistics and Grant's own very selective recollections. He stayed on in America, touring the vaudeville circuit with Pender's troupe and then on his own, encountering James Cagney and the Marx Brothers; he worked as a black-tie escort and made the rounds of Park Avenue parties passing for the kind of sophisticate he would play in the movies, "gaining a name as the number one gigolo in town"; he perfected his look by pomading his hair and laboriously polishing his teeth.

> He was especially proud of his great teeth and practiced fixing his smile in such a way as to show them off to their fullest advantage. He brushed them compulsively, several times a day, often until his gums bled. . . . He carried a brush with him at all times and in company would excuse himself after smoking a cigarette to get to a men's room, where he would scrub any dulling residue, real or imagined, from his three-packs-a-day habit.

When other employment failed, he reverted to stilt-walking at Coney Island.

He roomed on Barrow Street with an older Welsh set designer who was "extremely effeminate and openly and unashamedly gay," and who Eliot presumes was not only Grant's lover but his instructor in matters of social style. The Morecambe and Sterling book, by contrast, remarks with tortuous discretion:

> Archie's sex life at this point remains shrouded in some mystery, but there's no doubt that this superbly handsome,

charming young Englishman was compellingly attractive to
New York women of varying ages. . . . Though nothing has
ever been proved, it is possible he was assumed to be gay by
those directors and producers of a similar nature.

After several years the relationship ended badly and Grant began
living alone, clinging to the fringes of show business, evidently at a
very low ebb.

The late 1920s found him, in Eliot's account, a familiar of the "elite
gay Broadway social scene," where he made useful connections and
began to clamber out of a long period of depression and isolation.
He frequented a show-business set that included Moss Hart, Preston
Sturges, Humphrey Bogart, and the playwright Edward Chodorov,
who later remarked that "he was never a very open fellow, but he was
earnest and we liked him." That remark is about the most incisive
description of Grant to emerge from this entire period: his movements
can be tracked, at least in part, but there is scarcely a hint of what went
on within him. He worked on polishing his image as assiduously as
he polished his teeth, perfecting his manners, his accent, and the flair
for clothes he had picked up under his father's tutelage ("Shoes are
important" was one major life lesson). When, after a string of increasingly successful Broadway appearances, he made it to Hollywood and,
at Paramount's strong urging, changed his name to Cary Grant, Josef
von Sternberg completed the metamorphosis by demonstrating that
he should part his hair on the right side instead of the left.

WHAT IS ODD about the bare account of Grant's early career is its
tempo. Show-biz biographies tend to be imbued, especially in their
early stages, with the élan of the striver; Grant moves at a more erratic
pace, and it is hard to tell when he is pushing himself forward and when
he is drifting on a tide of circumstance. His compulsive self-discipline
in matters of self-presentation—the powerful impulse to ensure that
every aspect of what the world sees is not merely beyond criticism, but

also apparently effortless—is shadowed by a tendency to hide out or go against the current. Once he becomes established as a movie star, his patterns become even harder to read: not least, perhaps, for himself.

He was anchored by unwavering professionalism as an actor and filmmaker, and an equally unwavering regard for money. He had as much genius for business as for acting, and parlayed the freelance status on which he insisted after 1936 into a large fortune, infuriating the studio heads who, in Eliot's interpretation, saw to it that he never got an Oscar until his honorary award in 1970. His penny-pinching (he was a notoriously bad tipper and would present a bill for laundry and phone calls to houseguests who overstayed their welcome) became legendary. Beyond the stinginess lay something like austerity; the mansions in which he lived were often barely furnished. His stated ambition for his later years was to lie in bed reading.

Ordinarily we read biographies to get an idea of what it would have been like to know the subject. In the case of a movie star like Grant, however, we feel we already know him and have an intimate sense of his gait and tone of voice and facial reactions, so that we picture him in the scenes described by the biographer as if they were episodes from lost movies, movies that often seem oddly refracted versions of the ones we know. When we read of his long, on-again, off-again cohabitation with Randolph Scott in the 1930s—an open secret that Eliot describes as "one of the longest, deepest, and most unusual love relationships in the history of Hollywood"—we conjure up Grant and Scott's poolside scene in *My Favorite Wife* (1940), with Irene Dunne suddenly a bit superfluous.

The account of Grant and Scott breaking up and each getting promptly engaged, then traveling together in November 1933 on an ocean liner to London where Grant was to meet up with his fiancée, Virginia Cherrill—a crossing on which Grant supposedly devoted himself to lounging in silk pajamas, drinking excessively, and playing dismal music on the piano—might have come from some slightly more subterranean screwball comedy of the era. Or, indeed, from the moment in *Bringing Up Baby* (1938) when Grant, in Katharine Hepburn's bathrobe, announces to her astonished aunt: "I've suddenly gone gay!" Even Eliot's theory that Grant may have been recruited by the FBI in 1942 to spy on his second wife, the Woolworth heiress Barbara Hutton, who was suspected of funneling money to the Nazis to protect her Danish ex-husband, resonates with plot elements of two of his films from the same period, *Once Upon a Honeymoon* (1942) and *Notorious* (1946).

Some of the speeded-up splits and reconciliations, lockouts and pursuits of Grant's various marriages and love affairs (after the final parting from Scott, men disappear from the story) sound like nothing so much as the prom-night imbroglios of a bunch of adolescents just in the process of finding themselves, or more exactly of not finding themselves. Grant often comes across as someone who never quite had time to grow up and tried to make up for it hurriedly, between pictures. There is an air of barely contained chaos and emotional catastrophe that explodes in episodes of extreme possessiveness and violent jealousy (at one point he rammed the car of Oscar Levant, his rival for Virginia Cherrill's affections), heavy solitary drinking, prolonged depressions, and what may have been a botched suicide attempt.

He had at least one major legitimate motive for confusion. On returning to Bristol in 1934 as the triumphant movie star, he was informed, in a plot twist worthy of an early thirties melodrama, that his mother had not in fact died, but had been confined (due to a "nervous breakdown") to the Fishponds mental hospital ("one of the worst medical facilities in all of Great Britain," according to Eliot) for the past eighteen years. This was evidently a matter of convenience for Grant's father, freeing him from his wife so that he could devote himself to his new family. Grant obtained her release and saw her at regular intervals for the rest of her life, but this shock must have made his previous adult life appear abruptly unreal, or perhaps compounded a sense of unreality already present.

The contrast between Bristol and Hollywood—between the world from which he had escaped as quickly as he could, but whose claim on him came back in the grotesque form of his mother's fate, and the alternate world created by the studio system, that industrial farm where marketable talents were bred and luxuriously stabled but never

allowed too much freedom—must have exacerbated his feeling of having nowhere really to call his own. He rebelled against both spheres,
clearing out of Bristol and then slipping from the trammels of the
studios by making himself a free bargaining agent. But his biography
gives the impression of a fundamental unease only alleviated, and then
only temporarily, by making one picture after another.

At his worst moments the biographical Grant—as opposed to his
eternally young and pleasure-giving cinematic double—begins to look
like a classic twentieth-century neurotic, Western World division, sex-
ually and emotionally confused, grumpy, peevish, self-pitying, com-
plaining, a discreetly alcoholic chain-smoker, obsessed with personal
appearance and social decorum, counting every penny while seeking
wisdom in spiritual tracts and self-help manuals. Or he begins to disappear altogether, a cipher cunningly miming all the shades of emotional
response while nursing a morbid shyness. The line between feeling
and acting is never clearly defined: he never studied acting, and always
acknowledged that to some extent he was playing himself. (One thinks
of James Mason murmuring—after Grant has protested his utter innocence—in *North by Northwest*: "With such exquisite play-acting, you
make this very room a theater.")

In his later years, particularly after his marriage (the third) to the
young actress Betsy Drake in 1949, Grant actively sought mystical
enlightenment and psychological release. He went to live in the desert with Drake to try to radically simplify his life; he cured himself of
chain-smoking through hypnosis; they traveled through Asia seeking
out "various religious, mystical, and psychological figures" (unfortunately left unidentified by Eliot). In 1957 he began to take LSD under
medical supervision, and ultimately became an enthusiastic spokesman for the drug, telling the reporter Joe Hyams (in an interview he
came to regret):

> I have been born again. I have been through a psychiatric
> experience which has completely changed me. . . . Now I
> know that I hurt every woman I ever loved. I was an utter

fake, a self-opinionated bore, a know-all who knew very
little. . . . The moment when your conscious meets your
subconscious is a hell of a wrench.

Grant wrote extensively about his LSD experiences, speaking
of passing "through changing seas of horrifying and happy sights,
through a montage of intense hate and love, a mosaic of past impressions assembling and reassembling." It is startling to realize that Grant
was undergoing these visionary revelations just around the time he
was starring as the self-centered, martini-drinking, decidedly unen-
lightened adman Roger Thornhill in *North by Northwest*: another
instance of the ultimate inscrutability of Cary Grant.

The debonair wit and man about town, rakish and nonchalant in
tuxedo or smoking jacket—Wilde's Algie in *The Importance of Being
Earnest* provides the classic instance—flitted through drawing-room
comedies of the late nineteenth and early twentieth centuries as an
emblem of unfettered pleasure-seeking and sophisticated detachment.
How odd that a muscular, thick-necked youth sprung from a gloomy
lower-middle-class Bristol household should transform himself into
the apotheosis of that type. The Cary Grant that Archie Leach invented
was the imitation of an imitation—specifically, by his account, a compound of Noël Coward, Jack Buchanan, Rex Harrison, Fred Astaire,
and Hoagy Carmichael: "When I was a young actor, I'd put my hand
in my pocket trying to look relaxed. . . . I was trying to imitate what
I thought a relaxed man looked like." In the end, of course—as he
romances Deborah Kerr on shipboard in *An Affair to Remember* or
strides into the Oak Room of the Plaza as if it were his natural habitat
in *North by Northwest*—he becomes the "real thing" that latecomers
can only imitate.

Except to the dwindling band of those who actually knew him, any
"real" life led by Cary Grant is wraithlike compared to his alternate,
realer-than-real cinematic life. This could be true of any actor, but
if Grant still strikes us as supreme in his domain it's because all the
contradictions of his being are present on the screen. The masks and

the elusiveness are there, but so is a disarming sincerity: the sincerity of someone who has scarcely had time or opportunity to develop an inner life. For all his masterful control of surface, there is something unguarded about the way he lets us watch him in the very act of thinking.

In a sense he is always being himself, but because he has so many selves to choose from, he is never the same person twice. Recall Grant in his best performances—among them *The Awful Truth*, *Only Angels Have Wings*, *His Girl Friday*, *The Philadelphia Story*, *Suspicion*, *Notorious*, *Monkey Business*, *An Affair to Remember*, *Kiss Them for Me*, *North by Northwest*—and it becomes apparent that he embodies a distinctly different personality in each, even if they might use the same gestures and flash the same smile. Small wonder that the directors who elicited his best work from him, Hawks and Hitchcock, thought of casting him respectively as Don Quixote and as Hamlet: having seen what he could do, they suspected that he could probably do anything.

*The New York Review of Books*, 2004

# gangsters with toothbrushes

ALBERT SIMONIN'S NOVEL *TOUCHEZ PAS au grisbi* is said to
have had a revolutionary impact on French crime writing, and Jacques
Becker's film version had a similarly transformative effect on French
crime films, yet film and novel bear little resemblance to each other.
In fact Becker, with the help of Simonin, pretty much threw the book
out the window. Told in the first person by the aging career criminal
Max le Menteur (played in the film by Jean Gabin), Simonin's novel is
an exuberant exercise in argot for its own sake, and even comes with a
glossary to help the reader wade through its impasto of criminal discourse. Crowded with incident, casually violent, narrated with a sort of
comic grandiosity, it works its effects entirely through the power of an
unleashed dialect, and the effect is something like a Gallic marriage of
Damon Runyon and Mickey Spillane.

Becker keeps the milieu and a good number of characters, and
changes everything else. The wise-guy, almost vaudevillian tone of the
book gives way in the film to a clipped melancholy, unblinking and
loaded with gravity. Exaggerated speech becomes a series of laconic
exchanges, with the previously garrulous Max—Simonin's endlessly
talkative narrator—the tersest of all; carefree promiscuity gives way to a
mood of aging desire; and violence is kept to a minimum, even though
the threat of violence is everywhere. As for humor, it is everywhere
and nowhere, a hard-bitten humor that seasons every conversation

without ever suggesting anything like relaxed enjoyment. Plot, finally, which abounds in Simonin's novel, here becomes—at least until the final violent explosion—a chain of suggestive pauses. Becker's genius in *Touchez pas au grisbi* is to focus resolutely on what comes before or after or falls in between the decisive actions. It's a film where we learn how gangsters brush their teeth.

The heist on which the plot depends isn't shown or even explained. The scenes of confrontation are treated as tedious interruptions—a matter of going to work—in what would otherwise be a comfortable life of leisure, whether passed in Madame Bouche's restaurant (where the only problem is shooing away the squares who sometimes wander in) or in the bedroom of a bejeweled American who "really doesn't know" who and what Max is. *Grisbi* unfolds as a series of tableaus so vivid that we scarcely notice how insignificant the story is: each scene has its own reality, its own fascination. New characters emerge with no explanation, and past entanglements are never clarified. When *Variety* reviewed the movie after its Paris opening, it had high praise for Becker's "fine job" but was careful to note that the movie was "not of sufficient suspense and entertainment value for more general situations . . . It lacks the U.S. counterpart of pacing, action and movement." They had it right: on repeated viewing *Touchez pas au grisbi* looks ever more radical in its narrative fragmentation.

As in Becker's final masterpiece *Le Trou*, with its meticulous played-out drama of imprisonment, escape, and betrayal, everything here is about time. In the world of *Le Trou*, time is dictated by prison sentences and prison routine; here it's ordered by the less obvious but equally inexorable pressures of another kind of prison, in which the inmates police each other even as they keep tabs on their own aging bodies. The actual police have virtually no role to play in *Grisbi's* parallel order of reality. It's the gangsters who inhabit a realm of constant mutual surveillance, the domain of permanent mistrust of which Max is master only because he's two degrees smarter than anyone around him. The speed with which he has to act is weirdly accentuated by the deliberate slowness of Gabin's movements, the almost tidal fashion in which he navigates his way through the spaces—streets and nightclubs and back rooms and cellars—to all of which he seems massively indifferent. He'd always rather be somewhere else. His expression returns again and again to the scowl of someone who is being disturbed yet again by the need to correct someone else's mistake or get the jump on someone else's duplicity.

In traditional gangster movies, the hero seeks power, attains power, overreaches, and goes down in flames. Gabin's Max, by contrast, has already attained a power that he doesn't really want or need anymore, and wishes only to get away—get out of the movie we're watching—so he can drink his champagne, make love to his gorgeous American girlfriend, and listen to that harmonica tune that he likes so much. In one of *Grisbi*'s boldest moves, Becker gives us one brief scene of Max alone, uttering his regrets in voice-over; he takes us inside Max's head for a moment of totally unexpected interiority. A moment is all that is needed to make us feel that we've taken the measure of his life as he experiences it, and can now see the surrounding play of masks and shadows from his point of view as a nuisance, an intrusion, something to be cleared away while there's still time.

Max has only one strong human tie that we're privy to, his friendship with Riton—the hapless fellow operator whose stupidity in allowing himself to be deceived by Jeanne Moreau's Josy will cost him all the grisbi. It isn't the most demonstrative of friendships; it has more the feel of a long marriage that can't be renounced for all its grating regrets. Gabin looks at René Dary as if constantly and silently raging at the fate that has linked him to this doomed character. ("Poor Riton," he tells him uselessly, rhyming in anticipation with the "Poor Gaspard" that ends *Le Trou*.) The bond between them is displayed only through a series of gestures in *Grisbi*'s most memorable scene, the long sequence in Max's hideaway apartment where the pouring of wine, the spreading of pâté, the laying out of pajamas for his friend are performed with the solemnity of ancient rituals, all the while Gabin's face retains its stone-graven impassiveness.

It is a face that has already resigned itself to the almost inevitable failure of all projects of escape or evasion. Everything that happens around him is like a movie or a cabaret performance that Max is watching, a show he's seen too many times. In *Grisbi* gangsters play at being gangsters, showgirls play at being showgirls. Even the anni-hilating violence of the last reel has a theatrical feel, as the opposing gang members stride toward each other with their machine guns as if going through the paces of a well-rehearsed musical number. All of them know the lines and the moves required of them; only Max possesses the extra dimension of self-knowledge that enables him to take an ironic distance from the spectacle, for all the good it does him. He too finally is only another player, accepting defeat with practiced grace. The magnificent jukebox playing his favorite tune—the image with which the film ends—is like a mute godlike presence presiding over that defeat with a mechanical semblance of joy.

The Criterion Collection, 2005

# calligraphy in blood

KIHACHI OKAMOTO'S *THE SWORD OF DOOM* (1966) is likely to strike the unalerted viewer as an exercise in absurdist violence, tracking the career of a nihilistic swordsman from his gratuitous murder of an unoffending old man to his final descent into what looks like a rehearsal for global annihilation, as, in a kind of ecstasy, he slaughters a seemingly endless army of attackers both real and phantasmal. The extreme but stylized violence of Okamoto's film epitomizes a style of Japanese filmmaking that profoundly influenced such directors as Sam Peckinpah and Sergio Leone, and it would be easy—and not entirely inaccurate—to read the film in the light of the cynical antiheroic trends that surfaced in genre films all over the world in the 1960s, and surmise that it represented the same kind of break with heroic tradition as, say, spaghetti Westerns. It should be kept in mind, however, that *The Sword of Doom* is only the most recent in a long line of stage and film versions of an extraordinarily long, structurally meandering novel that has remained popular ever since the appearance of its first installments a year after the death of the Meiji emperor (the ruler who oversaw Japan's transition from hermetically sealed feudal state to modern industrialized nation), and whose ostensible theme is religious.

The novel *Daibosatsu Tōge* (*The Pass of the Great Buddha*, *The Sword of Doom*'s Japanese title) originated as a newspaper serial in 1913 and continued to appear for three more decades; forty-one volumes were published before it was left uncompleted at the death of its author, Kaizan Nakazato (1885–1944). Nakazato, a sometime telephone operator and assistant teacher, avowed himself a literary disciple of Dostoevsky and Victor Hugo, and was deeply influenced by Christianity and Socialism; he was a pacifist during the Russo-Japanese war, and kept himself aloof from cultural entities associated with the military government in the 1930s and 1940s. His novel was intended as an expression of Mahayana Buddhism, with the earthly actions of its characters, and most especially of the demonic swordsman Ryûnosuke Tsukue, nothing more than the working out of karmic law.

The political background—the struggle of various shadowy groups either to uphold the power of the Shogunate or to bring about the restoration of direct imperial rule—is itself only one layer in Nakazato's cosmic vision, in which the hero's seemingly evil path is dictated by forces beyond his control. However, Ryûnosuke is a character who seems to have escaped from his author's control, taking on independent life as an icon of popular culture, an embodiment (in the words of the scholar Cécile Sakai) of "the fascination of Evil . . . which gives him his seemingly paradoxical charisma." He is the archetypal fallen angel of early modern Japan, a figure who elicits sympathetic identification by the uncompromising intensity with which he follows his path, even if the path seems to lead into darkness.

Even while the novel was still appearing in installments, stage adaptations were made of its early episodes, and these were followed by a two-part 1935 film version (now presumed lost) whose directors included Hiroshi Inagaki, known for his later *Samurai* trilogy and his 1962 version of *Chûshingura*. After the war, the novel was remade repeatedly, in three parts (1953) by Kunio Watanabe, in three parts (1957–1959) by Tomu Uchida, and in three parts (1960–1961) by Kenji Misumi and Issei Mori. The freeze frame that concludes Okamoto's film is not an ending but a pause while awaiting the later installments that were never made (installments in which, among other things, the hero goes blind and changes sides to support the imperial faction). The gaps and unresolved story lines that are apt to bewilder a viewer coming to the film cold would not pose a problem for an audience thoroughly familiar with the source material. Okamoto's film might almost be called *Famous Scenes from "Daibosatsu Tôge,"* a series of set pieces content to skip over much connecting matter.

This is not to say that the film's enigmatic qualities are due solely to the misunderstandings of Western audiences. A sense of the mysteriousness of violence is essential to Nakazato's novel and Okamoto's film alike. Ryûnosuke is at once hero and villain, demon and potential bodhisattva, and Tatsuya Nakadai's stunning performance incarnates perfectly the paradox at the heart of the character: Does he act or is he acted upon? In what sense does he choose his destiny? He seems at times the spectator of his own destructive course, alternately anguished or blackly amused, but essentially powerless to change what happens. His unique style of swordsmanship—*mumyô otonashi no kamae* (form without sound or light)—as enacted by Nakadai has a weirdly passive quality. He seems to go limp, to withdraw into himself, as if the invariably lethal blow was directed not by the exercise but by the abandonment of will. In terms of the body language of sixties cinema, his posture symbolizes as well a kind of sullen hipsterism, a serpentine deviousness, in the face of the forthright heroic stance of Toshiro Mifune as the noble instructor Shimada.

It's fitting that a film whose characters are so intensely preoccupied with form—who pay such unremitting attention to angles of thrust, movements of feet, pauses and sight lines—should itself be so stunning on a formal level. In an era of Japanese filmmaking marked by such masterpieces as Kurosawa's *Throne of Blood* and Kobayashi's *Harakiri,* and when even the most routine samurai pictures tended to look very good indeed, *The Sword of Doom* stands out for the rigor and calligraphic pictorialism of its widescreen compositions. It's as if the formal qualities of the swordsmanship so amply displayed in the film's major set pieces—the duel with Bunnojo at the temple and its aftermath, Ryûnosuke's visit to Shimada's *kendô* school, the confrontation in the snow in which Shimada wipes out Ryûnosuke's associates, and the apocalyptic finale—were mirrored by the slashing precision and constantly shifting perspectives of the staging and camera work.

Okamoto, who trained as an assistant to the great Mikio Naruse, was only one of many highly competent genre directors of the time. Known as much for his war films (*Japan's Longest Day*, 1967; *The Human Bullet*, 1968; *Battle of Okinawa*, 1971) as for such period films as *Samurai Assassin* (1965), *Kill!* (1968), and *Red Lion* (1969), he often cultivated a satirically humorous tone. In fact, *The Sword of Doom* was a project imposed on him by the Toho Company after their dissatisfaction with his more personal *The Age of Assassins*. Neither as intensely personal a filmmaker as Kurosawa nor as subversive an experimentalist as Seijun Suzuki, Okamoto in *The Sword of Doom* nevertheless demonstrates—with the help of Hiroshi Murai's magnificent cinematography—a mastery of surface that makes the film hypnotically pleasurable to watch. (Thanks to Masaru Sato's slashing score, it is also intensely pleasurable to listen to.)

Its surface, one might say, *is* its depth. If indeed "an evil soul is an evil sword," then form and gesture are a graph of profound undercurrents. The unrelenting visual inventiveness of *Sword of Doom*, culminating in the final massacre with its thousand and one variations on the theme of killing with a sword, is not a matter of flashy illustration but the essence of what the film is about. Gesture here takes on a life of its own. The human killing machine, blinded and stumbling in his own blood, has become something like a force of nature, a destructive essence. The undeniable visual beauty of the scene is inseparable from its horror. The perversity of the central character takes over the film itself, and perhaps we did not need the sequel that Okamoto never made. What really could surpass that freeze-frame of the swordsman caught in mid-rampage, bent on continuing to kill as if it were a way for him finally to extinguish himself?

The Criterion Collection, 2005

# the comfort of martians

1 .

STEVEN SPIELBERG'S *WAR of the Worlds* is a movie at once authentically uneasy and deeply nostalgic. The nostalgia is for long-cherished cozily scary fantasias concerning alien invasions and men from Mars as filtered through boyhood comic books and drive-in movies and tattered paperbacks, a whole century of cheap thrills summed up and transfigured in a return to their primal source, H.G. Wells's 1898 novel. But Spielberg doesn't try to reproduce the camp goofiness of *Mars Attacks!* or the video game hijinks of *Independence Day*: he wants us to care about what is happening in front of us, as if we were contemplating this scenario for the first time.

That would require a return to childhood, a return to the childhood of the genre to which he has devoted so much of his energy and to whose historical permutations he can (and in this movie does) allude almost reflexively. (In passing I registered fleeting, virtually subliminal hints of *The Birds*, *Alien*, *Night of the Living Dead*, *The Day of the Triffids*, *Panic in Year Zero*, *Quatermass and the Pit*, and *The Poseidon Adventure*, not to mention Spielberg's own *Jurassic Park*, whose raptor in the kitchen is paralleled here by aliens in the basement.) We would need to feel again how much our nostalgia is imbued with real terror, even if it was a terror at one remove, just distant enough to let us play inside it. *War of the Worlds* aspires to be a compendium of Wells and all that sprang from Wells, an all-in-one package that might serve as something like a child's introduction to cosmic fear. It feels inevitable that the movie should come to revolve around the haunted face of a child, the inscrutably traumatized ten-year-old played (with an intensity in itself rather disturbing) by Dakota Fanning.

The world seems particularly expendable in Spielberg's opening scenes when we see it from the vantage point of Tom Cruise's Ray Ferrier, a New Jersey dockworker living in disordered solitude since his wife left him, and brimming with hostility at the prospect of being dumped with the kids while his ex goes off for the weekend with her new partner. (Cruise, in a performance more restrained than he has been giving on television lately, manages capably his character's journey out of sullenness into the sustained urgency that the rest of the picture requires of him, but it is not a role that calls on much range.) Spielberg's foray into kitchen-sink realism conjures up a mood of dead ends, of life as a continual round of taunting and bickering in prefab houses. Imagine the movie continuing in this vein without the arrival of the aliens. In the event—no surprise—the extraterrestrial invasion will provide a chance for some real quality time enabling Ray to discover that he does actually care whether his children live or die.

This family drama seems too calculated an interpolation, fulfilling too neatly the Hollywood requirement that all movies must involve the "redemption" of at least one central character. The H.G. Wells novel followed a more austere and solitary course, as its anonymous hero mostly hid out and watched from the sidelines while the disaster unfolded. He was there as an observer; it was the fate of the race that was in question. Here we are often distracted from the magnitude of the catastrophe by worrying about what will happen to Ray, his teenage son, and his ten-year-old daughter, as if—with inescapable movie logic—the fate of the rest of humanity took second place to Ray's need to establish a good relationship with his kids and get them safely back to their mother in Boston.

It is hard to work up much interest in a redemption that is a foregone conclusion, but it doesn't matter much since the overwhelming speed and scale of the events that overtake this family unit leave them blessedly little time for extended conversation. After the son runs off to join up with the soldiers who are counterattacking the aliens—the dialogue suggests a floating analogy with the Iraq war—we are down to father and daughter, with Cruise hoarsely singing the Beach Boys' "Little Deuce Coupe" as a consoling lullaby in the face of ultimate horror, and Fanning beginning to take on the stature of a designated martyr for humanity in general in a world where the worst suffering is to survive.

The personal drama, such as it is, reaches its peak with a very effective scene that works a variation on Wells. In the novel, the hero is finally forced to knock senseless the curate with whom he has taken shelter, and whose gathering hysteria endangers both of them. It is left ambiguous whether he has killed him or knocked him out, but the narrator notes by way of apologia:

Those who have escaped the dark and terrible aspects of life will find my brutality, my flash of rage in our final tragedy, easy enough to blame. . . . But those who have been under the shadow, who have gone down at last to elemental things, will have a wider charity.

Spielberg enacts a comparable scene in which Ray is forced to kill the raving survivalist (played rather hammily by Tim Robbins) who has offered them refuge, and must blindfold his daughter so that she catches no glimpse of the act. The blindfolded eyes serve to underscore the recurring image of Dakota Fanning's wide-open eyes elsewhere in the film, while the matter-of-fact bluntness of the offscreen killing weighs more heavily than the explosions, fireballs, and flying debris that accompany the advancing aliens. It's a bleak moment that offsets the impulse, here and there indulged, to unleash the special effects for the full summer blockbuster joyride.

*War of the Worlds* is chilling in all the places where it's supposed to be: in the splitting apart of the pavement as the aliens—planted underground long ago—first emerge; in their attack in their giant tripods on the ferry boat trying to cross the Hudson to evade them; in the exploratory twisting of the aliens' extensible observation arm through the basement where the humans cower silently. Spielberg does this sort of thing as well as any director ever has, and still seems to enjoy it. The catastrophe is delivered as promised: as it must be, to fulfill the promise of an adrenaline-fueled theme park ride to keep the American summer—not to mention the American movie business—alive. Some of the most efficiently frightening scenes—that arm in the basement, for instance, which is milked for all it's worth—serve as something like comfort food, reassuring us that we've seen this sort of thing before but that this time it's going to be better than ever.

Yet the movie is full of indications that Spielberg wants if not to spoil the fun then at least to complicate it, to lace it with a dash of what might even be anguish. He wants to let something of the real world in, most markedly through visual echoes of September 11 and its aftermath. On the one hand the movie is a game, a conscious display (if we needed it at this stage) of Spielberg's technical mastery; on the other it reaches toward what might be prophecy, or passionate allegory, or exhortation to mindfulness of real human suffering. This is where the unsettling part comes in, because for all his deliberateness as a filmmaker Spielberg cannot altogether control the undertones of despair and gnawing anxiety that his images elicit.

The reminders of September 11 interwoven here—panicked dust-covered people running through the streets, handmade wall posters for missing loved ones, stunned bystanders wandering through airplane wreckage—summon up a dread that spills over into everything else, until the movie itself begins to seem an entertainment played out on the site of a disaster, like the street performances that sprang up in the ruins of bombed Japanese cities. Contemplating the face of the little girl who appears genuinely traumatized by all those corpses floating down the river, some lines of Emily Dickinson drift into mind:

Would not the fun
Look too expensive!
Would not the jest—
Have crawled too far!

The war going on here seems to be a war over where exactly the fun starts or stops.

That conflict between uncomplicated fun and real-world grief can hardly be resolved in Spielberg's movie, but the pressure it creates finds its outlet in certain images of exceptional beauty. It's in the scenes of the Martians themselves, and the havoc they wreak, that Spielberg finds a way out of his dilemma in vistas that have the solemnity of one of John Martin's Victorian tableaux of the Day of Judgment. He plants the alien tripod machines, with their annihilating heat rays and their spindly legs that flex like tendrils—with a dedicated fidelity to the descriptions of H.G. Wells that make them look positively antique—into a world just drab and wounded enough to pass for real.

The aura of virtual historical reality that Spielberg labored to create for the ghetto takeover in *Schindler's List* or the Omaha Beach landing in *Saving Private Ryan* or the slave ship scenes in *Amistad* is here imparted to an invasion that might as well be historical: the devastation of twenty-first-century New Jersey by illustrations from a Victorian scientific romance. These almost fussily perfect vistas, like the moment when the alien machines are seen from a distance standing knee-deep in the Hudson to feed on their human prey, bring to mind a peculiar kind of history painting: Landscape with Tripods, perhaps, an exercise in the Spielbergian sublime, where what devastates us does, from a certain angle, possess an undeniable abstract beauty. These spacious setups have a gaudy splendor far removed from the cramped dullness of the ordinary world on which the aliens intruded, a world in which the sole note of aesthetic liveliness was provided by a children's cartoon show.

The effect is of reliving scenes we experienced in the novel, in Orson Welles's notorious radio play, in the comic book, and in the 1953 movie version, but with the suggestion that this time they're really at hand.

We have arrived at that apocalypse so assiduously imagined in all its variations for the last hundred years: the foundering of the everyday and its shockingly abrupt replacement by a different order of things, an order from which there can apparently be no more than a temporary escape. Earth is overgrown with red alien weeds.

The movie fulfills itself in such images, even if it cannot sustain their mood into the final scenes. Spielberg is faithful to the rough outline of the novel—the sudden collapse of the aliens and the revelation that they have died from exposure to Earth's bacteria—but he cannot give it the solemnity of Wells's last pages. Here the wrap-up seems almost as perfunctory as one of those fifties sci-fi movies where the air force discovers, say, that the flying saucers are susceptible to high-frequency noises and saves the planet in the last five minutes. The difference is that in Wells the protagonist walks through a dead and emptied London—"The windows in the white houses were like the eye sockets of skulls"—and is utterly alone when he hears the wailing of the dying Martians: "Ulla, ulla, ulla, ulla." The scene, like many in the novel, has an uncanny poetry that in Spielberg's version is crowded out by the mob of onlookers and soldiers who make nonsense of the idea that the human race has come close to extinction.

At this last juncture Spielberg pulls his punches, refraining from giving us the full taste of human defeat on the scale that Wells proposes. In the novel, after all, it is clear that humanity has been defeated. The movie ends with Morgan Freeman reading an adaptation of the passage where Wells exults briefly in the defeat of the invaders by bacteria to which humans themselves have become immune:

> By the toll of a billion deaths man has bought his birthright of the earth, and it is his against all comers; it would still be his were the Martians ten times as mighty as they are. For neither do men live nor die in vain.

But this is a passive victory, a triumph of evolutionary biology. And further on, characteristically, Wells's narrator changes course again.

After indulging a reverie about human life "spreading slowly from this little seed bed of the solar system throughout the inanimate vastness of sidereal space," he brings himself up short: "It may be, on the other hand, that the destruction of the Martians is only a reprieve. To them, and not to us, perhaps, is the future ordained."

Wells's narrator follows this with an observation that might be the unspoken epigram of Spielberg's movie: "I must confess the stress and danger of the time have left an abiding sense of doubt and insecurity in my mind." The doubt and insecurity permeate the film, even if the director acknowledges, with a final scene of the family all safely reunited, that there might be a limit to how much insecurity his audience will tolerate.

2.

IN H.G. WELLS'S novel the narrator who tells us of the Martian invasion refers to his subject as "the great disillusionment." Spielberg's theme will, I suppose, be described by some as the loss of innocence, the American innocence that has been lost so many times only, apparently, to regenerate so that it may be lost yet again. The innocence lost in his film would be a lack of awareness of just how vulnerable we are to destruction by unknown forces. Wells's "disillusionment" is much broader in its scope, just as his novel contains within it the seeds of a thousand variations, including the 1953 film produced by George Pal with its ambience of nuclear terror, graphic interpretations by artists ranging from Edward Gorey to Lou Cameron (whose 1955 comic book version for *Classics Illustrated* is a model of spareness and restraint), a rock opera in the 1970s, and the 1938 radio production by Orson Welles, which persuaded a good many unwary listeners that they were hearing live breaking news reports of Martian invasion.

The novel has not been exhausted, being one of those open-ended works that combine infinite suggestiveness with the most rudimentary of narratives. The Martians are more intelligent than we are; they arrive and devastate us as men would tread on an anthill; we would without question be destroyed except for that lucky business of the bacteria the Martians somehow failed to anticipate. Everyone remembers certain instants in Wells's book—the first sighting of what appears to be a falling star, the discovery of the cylinder, the first encounter with the power of the Martian heat ray—but as far as plot goes the novel is monotonous in the extreme. The monotony comes from the scenes of wartime suffering that from his vantage point Wells could only imagine. Essentially the Martians go from place to place and destroy everything they find. The humans flee or resist in vain, despair, loot, get drunk, die miserably, hide out in coal cellars. One day it ends.

Because the story is so simple that it can be told in a single sentence, Wells tells it again and again, each time from a different angle. His anonymous narrator—a writer with scientific interests, apparently, comfortably settled in suburban Woking, Surrey, with a wife from whom he is separated for most of the book and an equally sketchy brother, inserted none too artfully, whose sole function is to provide eyewitness testimony of events taking place in London—is not so much a character as a mind set adrift by circumstance. What is most striking in rereading *The War of the Worlds* is how swiftly its moods and angles of vision can lurch from point to point. Adaptations inevitably smooth over the book's texture, which is the result of thought revising itself, of emotions mutating unpredictably, of viewpoints turned on themselves.

Likewise Wells's prose can dart from sermonic eloquence to notation as dry as a railroad timetable. The confident assertions of nineteenth-century thought give way to a stammering bluntness as the narrator finds himself unable to tell others what has happened: "I felt foolish and angry. I tried and found I could not tell them what I had seen. They laughed again at my broken sentences." The book has so often been turned to graphic and cinematic uses that it is easy to forget the changes it works in language alone.

What Wells's narrator meditates on is a game devised by Wells himself, with a measure of detachment verging on the misanthropic. In his *Experiment in Autobiography* he described how he "wheeled about the district marking down suitable places and people for destruction by my Martians." The book might then be imagined as the soliloquy of a man who bicycles through the suburbs of 1890s London imagining their destruction, along with the devouring of their inhabitants by blood-drinking aliens. A secret antisocial fantasy is played out with the enthusiasm of a schoolboy moving pins around on a war map. In his private game he becomes complicit with the super-intelligent, all-powerful, casually murderous Martians; he allows some part of himself to go off on a vicarious rampage overseen by "intellects vast and cool and unsympathetic," a company he might well have preferred to the scared scurrying earthlings of the suburbs who play for the most part such an inglorious role in his novel.

All the same, another part of him contemplates the resulting carnage with horrified awe. A mood of trauma sets in, amplified in various registers by every person he happens to meet, like the "timorous, anemic" curate who complains: "Why are these things permitted? . . . What are these Martians?" There is no right response because what the Martians perceive is by definition beyond us. They are the devouring Other, superior, pitiless, and unknowable. Malevolence has nothing to do with it. All they can do for human beings, besides annihilating them, is to provide a momentary occasion to look at the human situation in a different light, to reconfigure existing definitions of what humans are.

At the same time, the protagonist's disordered wanderings take on a visionary flavor. The narrator turns the events over and over, finding upsetting metaphors for the events that have occurred and equally upsetting contradictions in the way he reacts to them, reliving random encounters and insights in the midst of chaos as if they were episodes in some future scripture: "It came to me that I was upon this dark common, helpless, unprotected, and alone. Suddenly, like a thing falling upon me from without, came fear." Biblical echoes proliferate even as the hero lashes out, for instance, at the curate's evocation of "the great and terrible day of the Lord": "What good is religion if it collapses under calamity? . . . Did you think God had exempted Weybridge?

He is not an insurance agent, man." In its way the book belongs to a characteristic English mode of allegorical, more or less insular peregrination that can be discerned in works as disparate as *Piers Plowman*, *The Pilgrim's Progress*, Daniel Defoe's *A Journal of the Plague Year*, John Clare's hallucinatory account of his journey on foot out of Essex, and *The Wind in the Willows*. (W.G. Sebald's *The Rings of Saturn* is a recent addition to that canon.)

All assertions in Wells's novel are tentative; after the great disillusionment comes the age of permanent doubt. What appears true at a given moment—such as the ability of the human beings to outwit the Martians or defeat them with firepower—is bound to be demolished at some further point in the journey. Any hint of the heroic is invariably darkened, inverted, questioned, notably when the narrator is caught up in the early, optimistic expectation that the Martians, still just crawling out of their cylinders, will be quickly exterminated:

> Something very like the war-fever that occasionally runs through a civilized community had got into my blood. . . . I can best express my state of mind by saying that I wanted to be in at the death.

As a narrative about Alienated Man picking away at his own motives, the novel might be an ancestor of *Nausea* or *The Stranger*:

> Perhaps I am a man of exceptional moods. . . . At times I suffer from the strangest sense of detachment from myself and the world about me; I seem to watch it all from the outside, from somewhere inconceivably remote, out of time, out of space, out of the stress and tragedy of it all.

*The War of the Worlds* is not so much an adventure story or a work of prediction as it is an extended contemplation of human limits and the overall tenuousness of human survival. The conformist life of the lower-middle-class Victorians savagely derided by Wells's Artilleryman (a character who erupts into the book near the end and is allowed a long and unforgettable rant), the sort of people among whom Wells grew up—

> working at businesses they were afraid to take the trouble to understand; skedaddling back for fear they wouldn't be in time for dinner . . . and sleeping with the wives they married, not because they wanted them, but because they had a bit of money that would make for safety in their one little miserable skedaddle through the world . . .

—is a thin layer bounded on one side by the uncontrollable world of microbiology and cellular evolution, on the other by the infinite coldness of an outer space that might well spawn an advanced intellect divorced from empathy. It is an impersonal and uncontrollable Darwinian process that sets up the inhabitants of Woking and Weybridge to be the victims of a mechanized warfare waged by beings incapable of pity for them, and leads to a Victorian gentleman being reduced (as we do not quite see Tom Cruise reduced) to gnawing the bones of cats and rabbits for sustenance.

Although Wells's novel is shot through with satiric humor, the profound anxiety at its center remains palpable. It is the trauma of anticipation, foreseeing already the moment when someone will be forced to admit: "Cities, nations, civilization, progress—it's all over. That game's up. We're beat." What emerges in response to that fear is a reluctant identification with animals. The hero acquires

> a persuasion that I was no longer a master, but an animal among the animals, under the Martian heel. With us it would be as with them, to lurk and watch, to run and hide; the fear and empire of man had passed away.

He imagines himself a rabbit returning to his burrow, to find that men have dug it up to lay the foundations of a house. Such images proliferate like hiding places—comfortless hiding places—within the monotonous accounts of human civilization burned and laid waste.

Wells's novel remains a much tougher work than any of its offspring, and a richer one. Orson Welles and his scriptwriter Howard Koch took one aspect of the story—the breakdown of modern communications under the stress of the invasion—and translated it into a still exhilarating game in which radio's means were turned against itself and drama culminated in dead air giving the answer to the question: "Isn't anyone there?" George Pal's 1953 film turned the book into an efficiently paranoid Cold War entertainment, with tactical nukes failing to stop the invader, civil defense officials politely overseeing mass evacuations, and those left behind piling into churches as a last resort.

With Spielberg, the trauma of anticipation that animated Wells gives way to something like nostalgia for that trauma. Its legacy of perverse beauties—the by-now-antique images he lovingly refurbishes—is after all so much more bearable than the actual disasters that have followed. It is as if, in the face of more pressing terrors, Spielberg sought the comfort of Martians. For all its faithfulness to the demands of blockbuster filmmaking—with all that implies of playing to emotion and steering away, as Wells never does, from the convolutions of thought—his movie is also just faithful enough to Wells to convey what cold comfort that can be.

*The New York Review of Books*, 2005

# a memory of *columbo*

WATCHING TV IN THE EARLY seventies—watching in the company of others, not that solitary viewing that back then we still viewed as a final humiliation of the damned—was an experience always incomplete. The reception was never good; and you were stoned, or you were with people who were stoned; there was music playing loud in the next room, whose hilarity spilled over into any attempt to follow the plot of an episode whose beginning you had almost certainly missed; and the programs, even when not interrupted by others, interrupted themselves with commercials and station breaks whose recurrence provoked a small spasm of resentment.

Watching television was supposed to be something easy. Its emblematic purpose was to be the easiest thing in the world, the pleasure of last surrender, requiring zero emotional or intellectual investment; but it was all too easy to be distracted from that very distraction, so that it became unaccountably disorienting. You forgot what you were watching even while you watched. What was most difficult perhaps was to maintain the belief that you cared at all about what was supposed to be happening in the story. This "caring" had no emotional substance—you were not yet that far gone—but it was at least structurally analogous to actual feeling, a kind of mimic empathy. The experience was like a lesson in how deeply you could withdraw from human contact and still maintain a simulation of social communion. Somehow it was important that the television be on, as a stay against drift, even if finally it was an anchor made of blur.

In the midst of all that, *Columbo* emerged with its unshakable clarity. No blur there. No matter where you came in, you could gauge precisely where you were in the unfolding of the narrative, and you even knew why you cared. In the extreme repetitiveness of its elements, the show went beyond formula into the realm of ritual, a realm to which it laid claim from the outset with its eternal repetition of the primal fantasy of the child who secretly nurses malice: the planning and execution of the perfect crime.

This crime occurred somewhere in a deliciously fake version of a Southern California inhabited almost exclusively by wealthy white people and their variously harassed or obsequious hangers-on. Their world had a voluptuous tackiness, with its sickly pastels given further emphasis by the garish tones of seventies fashions, those pinks and yellows and oranges that turned the television screen into a kind of damaged bouquet. Everything spoke outwardly of pleasure, a pleasure reinforced in the show's early episodes by the exquisite surfaces of Russell Metty's cinematography, the hip fluency of Gil Mellé's or Oliver Nelson's scoring, and (in the series opener "Murder by the Book") the energetic mise-en-scène of Steven Spielberg. This was a pastoral paradise of wealth masquerading as happiness, against a background of the mansions and marinas, art galleries and ski resorts and upscale boutiques that alleviated the hard lines of the machinery designed to protect this life, this network of enclaves, against unpleasant or unscheduled intrusions.

In this paradise there lurked always a devilish malcontent, whether art critic or crime writer or much-decorated general or imperious industrialist. As if his deceptiveness—the oily good manners, the self-satisfied smirks, the undisguised contempt for his perceived inferiors, the general tone of narcissistic grandiosity—were not sufficiently brazen, we were permitted to watch him plan and execute his crimes with the aid of the fudged timetables and rigged-up alibis indispensable to that cherished art. These devils did not operate in isolation. Sometimes they existed within the heart of a den of fawning vipers, sometimes they surrounded themselves merely with haplessly deceived victims and unconscious abettors, but whatever was false in them tainted their whole world.

They knew this and exulted in it, and we were invited to share their sense of triumph. *Columbo's* guiltiest pleasure was the way it encouraged us, through these surrogates, to revel in self-serving vanity, indifference to the needs of others and exploitation of their weaknesses, enamored contemplation of our own Machiavellian brilliance. Within the samsara of bourgeois appetite—among all those cars and yachts and other petty toys—the sin of pride was nurtured as a kind of spiritual or aesthetic pursuit.

It was a land of fable. The first shall be the last, the overweening shall be brought low. The intrusion in this bubble world of the man in the wrinkled white raincoat was the only event, in a schema as hieratic as any Noh play or medieval morality. In the profound pleasure of not having to follow a story, because the story was already known, there was nothing to do but admire grace notes and variations while appreciating the changelessness of fundamental elements. It was not only delightful but strangely moving to find in the heart of tackiness the reenacting of an ancient agon, devil-mask facing god-mask in extremis.

On the one hand there was that seductive hotel-suite world of luxurious fakery, with a preening egotist at its core; and on the other there was Peter Falk, dropped as if from another planet, or at least from New York, into this beachfront waxworks. It was always a little puzzling how he ended up in the LAPD, since he seemed utterly isolated from his colorless colleagues. This was the last man on earth, the last authentic human, a note of dissonance destroying by his mere presence the triumph of harmonious illusion. From episode to episode the same necessary act of demolition was to be enacted, in exactly the same way, the demolition of an alluring surface.

How profound was this Columbo! We couldn't get over it. He had all the earmarks of the hidden teacher, the secret messenger. He was like the Socrates of the *Symposium*, the way Rabelais described him:

"Seeing him from the outside and judging by his external appearance, you wouldn't have given a slice of onion for him, ugly of body as he was and ridiculous in his bearing . . . simple in his manners, rustic in his clothes, poor in fortune, unfortunate with women, inept in public duties . . . always concealing his divine knowledge."

He was the power of passivity exemplified in the Taoist notion about water, the softest and most yielding of elements, wearing away rock. There was decidedly something East Asian about the guy. He was one of those ragged wandering monks who never spoke to the point, conveyed everything by indirection, harmless until you tried to get a hold on him. He made himself available as an object of contempt, and his opponent could never resist the invitation. It was like a nonviolent version of the scene in *Bad Day at Black Rock* where the one-armed Spencer Tracy, finally pushed to the edge by a town inhabited exclusively by racist bullies, knocked down a rampaging Ernest Borgnine with a single well-timed karate chop. Columbo's martial art was a mental judo—a drunken monkey kung fu made of simulated shambling, shuffling, awkward pausing, bashful overpoliteness.

By withdrawing utterly into himself—withholding all anger, all direct attack—he opened an abyss into which his opponent fell. Thus embarrassment triumphed over shamelessness. He made himself a mirror to the falseness of the concealed murderer, letting him see precisely what he projected, offering no outward resistance, relying on ingrained habits of ego-obsession to bring him down. He made no effort to deceive and did so anyway. As a Zen detective he knew intuitively who was guilty from the minute he walked in the room. No need for the elaborate ratiocination of a Sherlock Holmes or Poirot: it was only a question of laying bare a guilt that had been clear from the beginning.

It was another considerable pleasure that he did not philosophize overtly—there was none of the explicit social criticism of, say, J.B. Priestley's *An Inspector Calls,* none of the maudlin moralizing that television loved—because everything he did amounted to a philosophical statement. It was left to the culprit, when finally exposed, to generalize about the significance of what had taken place. Columbo's role was simply to elicit an admission of truth from those who had been most deceptive, and ultimately most self-deceptive (as if there could be a difference between deception and self-deception). Between criminal and detective there was something like a student-teacher relationship, with the roles outwardly reversed until the denouement. Thus, Columbo was ever the pupil, learning about the art of crime fiction from the murderous novelist, playing "Chopsticks" (at the Hollywood Bowl) for the benefit of the master musician.

In the myth of the disguised god mocked by ignorant mortals, the last scene is always the revelation of the god's identity and the violent punishment of those who abused him. Columbo however retained an air of mildness even in the final unmasking, encouraging a similar politesse on the part of those he exposed, never more movingly than in his confrontation with John Cassavetes in the episode "Étude in Black," with Cassavetes's sincere acknowledgment of Columbo's— that is to say, of Falk's—unquestionable genius. What happened in the end was a kind of revenge for all the petty slights and contemptuous dismissals to which the detective had been subjected, but Columbo did not revel in it. He brought to it instead a tone of sadness and long suffering. Whatever anger was in him could only be surmised from the implacability of the pursuit.

I think we did not appreciate Columbo fully until we were exposed to Haldeman, Erlichman, and the rest of the Watergate crew of devious master criminals. How they confirmed the essential realism of those episodes in matters of malevolent deception and overweening pride; and how one longed to see them taken apart, in his gentle relentless fashion, by the lieutenant. Perhaps it is not too late for the man in the wrinkled overcoat to come calling on one or another of their successors, a Cheney or a Rumsfeld, and proceed in the old-fashioned way to the breaking down of alibis.

*Black Clock*, 2005

# hero in waiting

IN *YOUNG MR. LINCOLN* JOHN Ford achieves the perfection of his art. Never were his matter and his method more aptly fitted, and never were his tendencies toward sprawl and overemphasis more rigorously controlled. It is a masterpiece of concision, in which every element in every shot, every ratio, every movement, every shift of viewpoint seems dense with significance, yet it breathes an air of casual improvisation. While its surfaces paint, with relaxed humor and effortless nostalgic charm, an imaginary antebellum America, it sustains an underlying note of somber apprehension all the more powerful for being held in check.

Ford finds a mood that avoids the clutter and ponderousness of most Hollywood history movies, a mood more of parable than of textbook chronicle. That preoccupation with history and its contradictions—the variance between actual human experience and the official version that will be constructed after the fact—that suffuses films as different as *They Were Expendable* (1945), *Fort Apache* (1948), and *The Man Who Shot Liberty Valance* (1962) resonates troublingly at the heart of this film, for all its apparent serenity. Nothing here is as uncomplicated as it seems designed to appear, which may be why the editors of *Cahiers du Cinéma*, in a celebrated, if by now scarcely readable, special issue in 1970, brought the full force of their post-'68 Althusserian-Lacanian rhetoric to bear on the film in a scene-by-scene analysis, as if here the secret mechanisms of the American ideology itself might be decoded and exposed. In trying to pin down the meanings of Ford's art, however, *Cahiers* missed his mercurial—and, admittedly, sometimes infuriating—ability to be in two places at once. If Ford's Lincoln exhibits at once a radiant sincerity and the devious subtlety of a trickster, he is to that extent the director's mirror image.

Bertrand Tavernier described *Young Mr. Lincoln* as "worthy of Plutarch,"[1] and there is indeed something ancient in the bareness with which Ford lays out his episodes, allowing each scene its independent life and leaving much unspoken. As history, it is on many points not much more accurate than Plutarch; like the Greek historian, Ford relies freely on anecdote, rumor, and imaginative reconstruction to fill out his portrait. But, in a way, that is the point: he carves out a space beneath or before history in which past events, not yet ossified into the stuff of monuments, retain the lithe flexibility of what is not yet formed. The myth of the Great Man is subverted by presenting a hero who has not yet become himself, who is all the more admirable for still being in a state of pure potentiality. The film radiates a youthful joy while at the same time insistently implying that the hero's destiny will necessarily mean the loss of all joy.

Henry Fonda's remarkable performance is impossible to consider apart from Ford's framing of it. His location in space, his relative distance from those around him, his physical stance, his degree of comfort or discomfort: these are constant reference points. We can't take our eyes off him, and yet there are moments when he is almost lost in the crowd. His blossoming as a politician, as he confronts the mob seeking to lynch his clients, is balanced by the moments of turning away, of looking into the distance or into himself. Every point of contact or loss of contact is registered with an electric hypersensitivity, not least in scenes that seem bathed in pastoral tranquility.

We are invited to indulge a naive lyricism that always proves deceptive. The linked sequences encompassing Lincoln's muted courtship of

---

[1] Bertrand Tavernier, "La Chevauchée de Sganarelle," *Présence du Cinema*, no. 21, March 1965.

Ann Rutledge and his visit to her grave are as beautiful as anything
in American movies, but it is not a simple beauty. Even the initial
moments, of Lincoln sprawled on the riverbank with a law book, head
on the ground and legs propped up on a tree trunk, the camera revers-
ing to give us the same posture from opposite angles, before Lincoln
himself reverses his position, scratching his leg as deliberately as he
absorbs the moral principles of law, hint at what can't be shown or
said. Ford consistently undermines any overemphatic or oversimpli-
fied explanation of events, or of Lincoln. His consciousness is the center of the movie, and it remains as much a mystery as the river that is
constantly evoked.

Young Mr. Lincoln is the product of an era when, elsewhere in the world,
political mysticism was finding form in movies like Triumph of the Will
and Alexander Nevsky: geometric odes to ritualized collective redemption. Ford seeks a cinematic language fit for democratic myth, and finds
no easy resolution of the paradox that Lincoln, the great democratic hero,
triumphs by a real intellectual and moral superiority (not to mention the
physical superiority of the champion rail-splitter) over his fellows.

The singularity of Lincoln is the most difficult of things to depict
in the vocabulary of American genre tradition, a tradition in which
singularity is more frequently associated with evil or failure, while
heroism, leadership, and success are linked to figures seen to be at
heart one of the guys, one with the people. We are shown Lincoln as
natural-born populist, a canny joke-teller and judger of pie contests,
spirited participant in tug-of-war contests and tar-barrel burnings, a
courtroom lawyer whose self-deprecation is clearly effective strategy, a
budding politician who surely knows the political value of his heartfelt
pleas for the poorest and humblest. Yet who are these people for whom
he speaks? Take away Lincoln, and who is left in the movie to offer
anything like a sense of direction or vision? This America of the 1830s
looks like a squalid class-based society with prating politicians at the
top and resentful bullies at the bottom, while good Christian folk like
Abigail Clay (Alice Brady) suffer in silence, and amiable drunkards loll
on the sidelines as they venture another snort.

Lincoln is of them yet apart from them: a loner of a different sort than John Wayne in *The Searchers* (1956), but no less alone. "People used to say I could sink an ax deeper than anybody they ever saw," he remarks; he might be hinting, for anyone subtle enough to catch the hint, at his own depths, while at the same time maintaining a guileless front that could pass for country boy naïveté. We are led to understand—always obliquely—that the depth of his self-awareness makes everything around him look like an absurd and mindless puppet show. The movie studies Lincoln's shifting relations with the ignorant, fickle, rowdy, self-interested inhabitants of Springfield, demonstrating how profoundly he understands them, how effortlessly he can amuse and manipulate them, and at the same time how utterly alien they must be to him. (When he wins the tug-of-war by tying his end of the rope to a wagon, is he showing a capacity for cheating or merely demonstrating that he has more important struggles to spend his energy on than such mindless contests?)

He has indeed "a certain political talent," as his future rival Stephen Douglas remarks—an ability to calculate others' reactions that could be almost frightening in its implications—yet he is most himself when he withdraws, standing apart, in the background, at Mary Todd's while the high society dancers circle in the foreground; or turning his back on Mary to stare toward the river; or looking away and downward as he says, "Ann died too"; or bending his head raptly as he opens a law book for the first time; or losing himself in music as he plays "Dixie" on the Jew's harp while riding past the river.

In the film-within-a-film that tells the story of Lincoln's defense of two brothers accused of murder, the chaos of the courtroom provides a vision at once comic and horrific of an unidealized democracy. Fordian humor is in full sway, with a bespectacled judge shouting "Put them jugs away!" while attempting to impart some order to the proceedings. The prosecutor—unforgettably embodied by Donald Meek, who seems nearly mummified—supplies volleys of rhetorical hot air that foreshadow, ironically, the kind of all-American rhetoric that would eventually attach itself to Lincoln's legend. At the heart of the courtroom scenes are several close-ups of Lincoln in the full splendor of his solitude, brooding and wrathful as he contemplates the injustice that seems about to triumph.

The trial—based very loosely on Lincoln's successful defense of William Armstrong in 1858, with the aid of an almanac—provides a neatly resolved narrative, complete with happy ending, within a film notably lacking in both plot and resolution. Instead we have scenes from an uncompleted journey—scenes structurally akin to the emblematic episodes in some medieval saint's life—culminating in that walk up the hill, in which the isolated figure of Lincoln is further delineated by a violent thunderstorm that seems to embody a prophetic rage that had lurked all along within the film. The storm's fury, symbolically prefiguring the Civil War, marks the point at which the world of the film—a world essentially comic in its promise of justice and harmonious endings, a world that with a few changes might be that of the comedies Ford made with Will Rogers, *Judge Priest* (1934) and *Steamboat Round the Bend* (1935)—collides with the unforgiving cataclysm that is history.

When Lincoln walks into history, he walks, in a sense, out of the world of John Ford's cinema. Ford was rarely comfortable portraying great historical moments head-on, and on those occasions when he did, as in the assassination of Lincoln in the earlier *Prisoner of Shark Island* (1936), it has something of the quality of a Currier and Ives print: the event is already its own monument. What interests him is the freedom that exists outside history, the freedom symbolized, in its lighter aspect, by the fleeting pleasures of camaraderie and communal merrymaking that he loves to linger on. Heroes are hard to find in his movies—those who seem to be often aren't (Henry Fonda in *Fort Apache*); or represent only half the story, the other half having been buried (James Stewart in *The Man Who Shot Liberty Valance*); or will be shown not victorious but defeated (Robert Montgomery in *They Were Expendable* or John Wayne in *The Wings of Eagles*). Ford accepts triumphalism as a necessary evil—accepts the need for a Great Man and a monument to affirm his greatness—but his movie is not quite that monument. It is more a lament for what the world might almost have been, if there had been no need for a Lincoln to save it.

The Criterion Collection, 2006

# the gleam of luminous water

THE CREATIVE CAREER OF VAL Lewton—the part with a continuing afterlife—lasted just four years, from the spring of 1942, when
pre-production work began on his film *Cat People*, until April 1946,
when *Bedlam*, the last of the eleven films he produced for RKO, was
released. Nine of those films (all but the studio-mangled melodrama
*Youth Runs Wild* and the underrated Maupassant adaptation *Made-
moiselle Fifi*) have been released on DVD as "The Val Lewton Horror
Collection," providing a welcome opportunity for re-immersion in a
body of work whose power to fascinate seems to have grown over time.

Probably unavoidably, the films are being marketed with the same
misleading poster art and the promises of "chillers," "shockers," and
"tales of terror" that inveigled their original audiences into anticipating
something quite different from what they got. What they actually did
get remains mysterious enough to keep these movies from becoming
comfortably campy artifacts of another era. Like flowers preternatu-
rally slow to unfold, they seem to be still in the process of revealing
their final form: odd as it may be that such miraculous freshness
should emanate from movies whose themes are inescapably decay,
morbid regret, the temptation to welcome death.

Even when we know them well they continue to instill, as in John
Ashbery's description of *The Seventh Victim*, "the feeling that the
ground under our feet is unstable." What Lewton's movies are actually

about, in the most literal sense, is always open to question. One can watch *I Walked with a Zombie* or *The Seventh Victim* or *Isle of the Dead* many times without being able to give a coherent summary of their plots. On its release, Bosley Crowther in *The New York Times* thought that *The Seventh Victim* "might make more sense if it was run backward." (Lewton's most narratively coherent picture, *The Body Snatcher*, adapted from Robert Louis Stevenson's story, though admirable in many ways, has less of his distinctive poetry than the others.) In American film, the only predecessors that come to mind for such destabilizing effects are Edgar Ulmer's formally rigorous Gothic delirium *The Black Cat* (1934) and Joseph Cornell's *Rose Hobart* (1936), in which Cornell took the seventy-six-minute jungle picture *East of Borneo* (1931) and condensed and recombined its sequences into nineteen minutes of mesmeric suggestiveness, a dream vision of what remains of movies after their stories have gone.

Alexander Nemerov's critical study of Lewton, *Icons of Grief: Val Lewton's Home Front Pictures*, demonstrates, by its nearly trancelike dedication to defining the elusive essence of these films, the capacity of Lewton's work to draw commentators ever deeper into the mood of dreamy morbidity that infuses *Cat People* and *The Leopard Man* and *Isle of the Dead*. Lewton is the Ancient Mariner of filmmakers. Like the old sailor at the beginning of *The Ghost Ship* or the ominous calypso singer in *I Walked with a Zombie*, he hooks you with the beginning of a tale and leads you on through the bewildering paces of a journey whose significance (could it ever be determined) might hinge on fleeting, apparently random encounters with minor characters or with abrupt and inexplicable deviations from the main trail. His films might be described as mood pieces interrupted by discordant apparitions, but that would make them sound flimsier and vaguer than the vigorously graphic compositions that they are: not dreamy but, rather, truly dreamlike, which is to say hauntingly specific, brutally elliptical, wily in their resistance to easy explanation.

Prior to his brief flowering, Lewton had been a dabbler in journalism, poetry, and pornography, a writer of pulp novels with titles like

*Where the Cobra Sings* and *The Cossack Sword*, a publicist at MGM, and for eight doubtless grueling years a writer, story editor, and factotum for David Selznick. Afterward, poor health and professional misfortune pretty much sidelined him before he died at forty-six in 1951. From what came before, it would have been impossible to predict the nature and the durability of the work he did at RKO, but the very disparateness of his early career offers some clues to the peculiar qualities of that work. Born as Vladimir Leventon in Yalta in 1904, he and his family came to America five years later to rejoin his mother's younger sister, who as Alla Nazimova had become a Broadway star—the great exponent of Ibsen—and whose subsequent filmmaking career would clear a way for Lewton in the film business.

Lewton's early literary productions veered from the aspirations of Old World high culture to the imperatives of hard-boiled American brashness, from poems written under the pseudonym Toison d'Or to novels exploring tabloid crime cases (*The Fateful Star Murder*) and the misadventures of hard-luck girls drifting into prostitution (*No Bed of Her Own*). A certain neurotic flamboyance seems to have impressed people early on—"Two particular phobias of Lewton's youth," his biographer Edmund G. Bansak notes, "were his fear of cats and his extreme aversion to being touched"—but any artistic ambitions were rapidly subsumed by the demands of commercial work: he was, in his son's words,

> a kind of hack, but he enjoyed the challenge that came with turning hack work into something special. . . . There is a sort of pride in being a whore. He saw a certain honesty in being able to make a living.

Whatever mixture of whorish pride, dandyish rebellion, barely suppressed phobia, aesthetic yearning, and nostalgia for the world of his birthplace might swirl in Lewton's consciousness (his son described him as "a strange combination of gentleness and authoritarianism"), he had acquired through those eight years with Selznick as thorough a command of the practicalities of grand-scale filmmaking as anyone in Hollywood. He had been responsible, with the director Jacques Tourneur, for the memorable revolutionary scenes in the 1935 *A Tale of Two Cities*, and took credit for some of the most vivid details—"the harp, the parrot, and the ancestral portraits being taken out of town"— in the evacuation of Atlanta in *Gone with the Wind*. He had also apparently been pushed to his limits by that most obsessive of moguls: "You can't talk reason," he wrote of Selznick, "to a man who believes that he has made the greatest motion picture of all time, past, present, and future."

THERE IS A quality of happy accident to the inception of his career at RKO. Had it not been for the failure of Orson Welles's *The Magnificent Ambersons*—a debacle that led to executive upheaval at the studio— there might have been no occasion to celebrate Lewton. As it was, the timing was perfect: Lewton wanted to leave Selznick, and RKO's new chief, Charles Koerner, was looking for someone who could help move the studio in a more frankly commercial direction. Universal had just made a huge profit on *The Wolf Man*, and so Koerner invited Lewton to head up a unit dedicated to turning out short, low-budget horror films. Lewton liked to joke that somebody had said he wrote "horrible novels" and the studio had misconstrued it as "horror novels."

An instinctive anti-authoritarian who had learned to play the game had now been entrusted with a good deal of authority, however tightly defined the limits within which it could be exercised. Lewton was still answerable to the studio executives he despised. His budgets were stringent, and the films had to be marketed to an audience assumed by RKO to crave only the most lurid stimulation, in an era whose horror movies were dominated by werewolves, ape-men, brain transplants, and old dark houses of the creakiest kind. Even the titles were often imposed: *Cat People* and *I Walked with a Zombie*, the first two productions, began in fact as nothing but titles, with Lewton obliged to concoct stories to match.

With *Cat People* Lewton demonstrated that he could give his bosses what they wanted—a movie brought in for under $135,000 that grossed some $4 million worldwide—while altogether subverting their notions of what a horror movie should be. Lewton's most obvious breakthrough was to avoid showing what the audience is supposed to be afraid of, on the grounds that what we don't see is more frightening than what we see—and also cheaper to depict in a movie. This approach has largely defined his popular reputation, as evidenced in the titles of Bansak's biography (*Fearing the Dark*) and the documentary that accompanies the DVD set (*Shadows in the Dark*), not to mention the episode of Vincente Minnelli's *The Bad and the Beautiful* (1952) where producer Kirk Douglas applies the same method to the production of *Doom of the Cat Men*. Jane Randolph's long walk through Central Park, stalked by an unseen panther, in which the only scary thing that happens in the end is a bus whooshing harmlessly to an abrupt halt, is the classic instance, the blueprint for what became an unavoidable cliché of horror films.

In fact, whatever effect it may have had on audiences in 1942, *Cat People* now seems one of the least frightening of horror films. What it has instead is a sinuously strung out mood of barely suppressed eroticism and gnawing discontent that develops from the opening instants, when Kent Smith as Oliver Reed—the straightest of straight men, "a good plain Americano" in his own words—meets, at the Central Park zoo, the exotic Simone Simon, as the Serbian émigré artist Irena Dubrovna, who fears she may be one of the diabolical "cat people" driven underground in medieval times. They fall in love and get married, but the marriage cannot be consummated because of her fear that sex will unleash her destructive cat-nature; he sends her to a psychiatrist and then finds consolation with a less troubled girlfriend. The mood created is not of horror so much as the disorientations of exile and the lingering sadness of sexual dissatisfaction.

Everything is in the details: Irena turning on a light in a darkened room as she murmurs, "I like the dark, it's friendly"; her encounter with the unknown catlike woman who stares at her and greets her as a sister (an exchange of glances that lasts only a second but flavors the whole film); the beads of water clinging to Irena's naked back as she crouches forward in a tub with clawlike feet (an image of startling erotic potency for 1942 Hollywood); the giant black statue of the Egyptian god Anubis by which she stands on a museum stairway. Even the most genuinely frightening scene—in which Irena, in (unseen) panther form, stalks her rival, Oliver's girlfriend, in a deserted swimming pool—lingers in mind more for the exhilarating patterns of the lights in the water, an explosion of pure abstraction beautifully realized by the director, Jacques Tourneur, and cinematographer, Nicholas Musuraca.

The huge success of *Cat People* enabled Lewton to keep making, under the guise of B-movie thrillers, movies that are often more like symbolist poems or obscure fetishistic rituals. They are not so much frightening as unnervingly strange and shot through with a palpable sadness. They are almost too beautiful to be scary, except that the beauty that soothes is finally what most unsettles. As Tom Conway, playing a world-weary plantation owner in *I Walked with a Zombie*, remarks to the young nurse who is accompanying him to his island home, across a glistening sea evoked with gorgeously blatant cinematographic fakery: "That luminous water—it takes its gleam from millions of dead bodies, the glitter of putrescence. There's no beauty here, only death and decay."


THE INTENSELY PERSONAL quality of these films is not belied by their being thoroughly collective enterprises. Obsessive and controlling he could certainly be, but there is little sense that he curtailed or distorted the intentions of those he worked with. In Jacques Tourneur, who directed *Cat People*, *I Walked with a Zombie*, and *The Leopard Man*, he found the perfect partner, a film poet who imparted luminous intensity to every moment of those films; but in the other films, directed by Robert Wise and Mark Robson, both originally editors who had worked with Orson Welles, Lewton achieved results as expressive, if less unfailingly inspired.

Quite aside from any question of expressive beauty, one could look at these films purely as instances of great skill marshaled under the most restrictive circumstances. Their brevity (they range in length from sixty-six to seventy-nine minutes), their slender budgets, their reliance on preexisting production materials (costumes and sets from *Gone with the Wind*, *The Magnificent Ambersons*, and *The Bells of St. Mary's* are worked in as needed), above all the requirement that the end product be acceptable in a precisely defined commercial niche (however puzzled horror audiences may have been to find that *Curse of the Cat People* was in fact a delicate fantasy of childhood loneliness): to have satisfied all those conditions and still produced work of such careful detail and defiant individuality was a rare feat. It is not hard to understand the impact produced on contemporary critics like Manny Farber ("They are about the only Hollywood movies in which the writing and direction try to keep in front of rather than behind the audience's intelligence") and James Agee ("I esteem them so highly because for all their unevenness their achievements are so consistently alive, limber, poetic, humane, so eager toward the possibilities of the screen, and so resolutely against the grain of all we have learned to expect from the big studios").

Part of what made Lewton's films stand out was their flaunting of cultural sophistication. *The Seventh Victim* opens with a quote from John Donne ("I run to Death, and Death meets me as fast, / And all my Pleasures are like Yesterday"); *Isle of the Dead* takes its title and its central image from Arnold Böcklin's painting; *The Body Snatcher* weaves in a traditional British ballad of the sort that might have been found on a Folkways release; *Bedlam*, set in eighteenth-century London, reenacts Hogarth's print of Bedlam in the "Rake's Progress" series; *I Walked with a Zombie* is serious in its effort to incorporate calypso music and Haitian ritual, not to mention the way it makes the legacy of slavery a central theme through the recurring visual motif of "Ti Misery," a slave-ship figurehead of Saint Sebastian. Fashion illustrators, psychoanalysts, and Greenwich Village poets are characteristic denizens of Lewton's world, while hints of homosexual interest (the cat woman who accosts Irena, the intellectual radio officer who flirts openly with the hero of *The Ghost Ship*) play around its edges.

A world is acknowledged in which the exotic—rhumba music, ethnic restaurants, Elizabethan poetry, books on psychology—is normal, while the all-American straightness of the office workers in *Cat People* or the Christmas carolers in *Curse of the Cat People* has begun to seem strange. (The backlot New York of *Cat People* and *The Seventh Victim* carries a powerful charge of displaced ordinariness that became diffused when Lewton switched to costume pictures like *The Body Snatcher* and *Bedlam*.)

Finally there is the dialogue, in its day often characterized as surprisingly literate, if not as ponderously literary, but counting for as much as the images in Lewton's cinematic scheme. Words are important here, and the self-conscious verbal flourishes are there to make sure their importance is not missed. In his essay on *The Seventh Victim*, John Ashbery describes "our sense throughout the film that people are saying anything that comes into their heads," but the sort of thing that comes into their heads often seems a message from beyond the confines of the narrative, a prophetic tip that, however solemn or obvious, produces a jarring effect by the unexpectedness with which it is dropped in. "The poor don't cheat one another. We're all poor together." "Caged animals are unpredictable—they're like frustrated human beings." "Authority cannot be questioned." "The people who live only by the law are both wrong and cruel." "The horseman on the pale horse is pestilence; it follows the wars." "Amy, listen to me. Death isn't such a terrible thing." "—What was the matter with him? —I don't know, sir. He didn't want to die."

Yet after we have remarked on their influence on subsequent filmmakers, their technical inventiveness, and the heterogeneity of an allusive range that gives them a collage-like quality, there remains the heart of Lewton's films to be accounted for: the emotional force that makes them a great deal more than the sum of their very diverting parts. In *Icons of Grief*, Alexander Nemerov links that force directly to the war that was raging at a distance when the films were made; the persistent sadness, the inescapable presence of death are an acknowledgment of a grief that the American public would rather avoid facing but to which Lewton, more Russian than American at heart, responds with imagery that reflects the religious icons of his cultural past, imagery that he smuggles into films marketed as quickie thrillers.

Nemerov develops his thesis forcefully and with a rich complement of period detail ranging from Norman Rockwell magazine covers to photographs of dead soldiers in *Life*; he discerns historical necessity in every detail of the way things happen to fall out, so that, for example, the mad boy in *Bedlam*, who is painted gold for the amusement of courtiers and dies of asphyxia in consequence, becomes an emblem of the bomb that had fallen on Hiroshima five days before the scene was shot:

> The close-up of the boy's face . . . is a post-Hiroshima editing choice that seems, all unknowing, to give some imaginative expression to radiation sickness, flash burns, and the bomb's other terrible effects.

Whatever one makes of the farther reaches of this associative logic, *Icons of Grief* is a superbly original (and intricately researched) attempt to define the singularity of this work. Nemerov identifies two crucial and related aspects of Lewton's aesthetic: the unusual importance he allows minor characters and his penchant for figures of iconic immobility "standing statuesque and alone." "This figure," he writes,

> would . . . arrest the flow of the film, suspend the plot, and for just those moments produce the melancholy and all-but-sculptural frozenness of a world that has stopped.

To linger on the icons Nemerov singles out—Simone Simon as the ghostly Irena standing in the snow in *Curse of the Cat People* and singing an old French song to a troubled child; Skelton Knaggs as the mute Finnish sailor in *The Ghost Ship*, sharpening his knife aboard the ill-omened *Altair* as we hear his thoughts in voice-over ("I am cut off from other men, but in my own silence I can hear things they cannot hear"); Darby Jones as the catatonic zombie Carre-Four who guards with staring eyes the path to the *houmfort* in *I Walked with a Zombie*; and Glenn Vernon as *Bedlam*'s Gilded Boy—is to confirm how elegantly he has moved into the core of Lewton's parallel cinematic world, finding out the privileged sacred recesses and translating the oracular pronouncements.

Nemerov makes overt what one might have sensed all along, that Lewton's stories are contrived so as to provide a way out of the story, to be liberated beyond plot into a commemorative domain of stillness and silence, grounded in "a prerational, magical conception of the image." Writing of the somnambulistic gait of two key figures in *I Walked with a Zombie*, he describes how Lewton "tried to slow movement down enough so that, almost impossibly, it too might take on the quality of stillness." Throughout Nemerov captures with exactness the qualities of rhythm and composition that draw one back to these movies, and underscores how deliberately those effects evade the spectator's expectations.

He emphasizes finally the "minor mode" of Lewton's films, their deliberate offhandedness and underplaying of what could easily have been grandiloquent moments. The penitential procession at the end of *The Leopard Man*—a march across the desert to commemorate a massacre of Indians by conquistadors—is powerful precisely because of the extreme concision of the images that record it, so far from big-scale Hollywood bombast. In Lewton's films the unexpected erupts, then vanishes as rapidly—vanishes from sight but not from memory. Here digressions are central, fleeting characters are dominant, and moments of stasis and silence are the heart of the action.

Prolonged contemplation of this toy theater, with its artificial sets and lighting, its densely furnished frames in which small figures are crowded together in artful tableaux, its bric-a-brac of songs, statues, poetic mottoes, and obscure rituals, prompts questions about what audience this performance is really intended for. The odd blankness of many of the principal players, offset by the vividness and grotesquerie of characters who may emerge only for a moment, might be standing in for the spectator. It's as if the leading characters, those naive intruders, were themselves watching a film, and found themselves constantly bewildered by the narrative's gaps and rapid changes of focus. In this world you never know where to look or whom to trust. The cleaning woman on her hands and knees in the lobby of the office building in *Cat People* is somehow as important—the image's composition tells us so—as the panther-threatened leads, and when the police chief in *The Leopard Man* describes an insignificant shoeshine man as "a genius in his own line," the piece of dialogue dangles like an Ariadnean thread to lead out of the labyrinth, as if the whole world were hanging on a shoestring.

*The New York Review of Books*, 2006

# the labyrinth of adulthood

THE CIRCUMSTANCES OF OUR FIRST encounters with movies are often as memorable as the movies themselves. Sometimes the juxtaposition of movie and circumstance seems merely accidental; but there are those films that change us enough that we can identify the first viewing as the precise moment when we became a different person. Carol Reed's *The Fallen Idol* (1948)—which I first saw on afternoon television, at an age close to that of the boy who is its protagonist—remains such a film for me and I daresay for many who saw it at an appropriately early age. What it is like to see *The Fallen Idol* for the first time as an adult it is hard for me to imagine; seen in childhood, it was like a door swung ajar to reveal an adult world not yet suspected, and in the process to alter forever the self-awareness of the child spectator. To come back, years later, to the close-up of Bobby Henrey processing the overheard conversation of his beloved mentor, the butler Baines— "It makes no difference about the boy . . . Of course he doesn't understand"—is like being privileged to relive, over and over, the moment of realizing how thoroughly adults, even the most loved, pursue their own agendas.

Part of the effect has to do with Bobby Henrey himself, whose manifest nonprofessionalism sets him curiously apart from the rest of the very polished proceedings—in a way that deepens the film's sense of missed connections. The film itself exemplifies the extraordinary craftsmanship of British cinema in the late 1940s, both behind the camera and in front of it. Even as a child, I could grasp that there was something remarkable about the intricate surfaces created by Georges Périnal's cinematography and Vincent Korda's set designs and the sometimes harsh spareness of Graham Greene's dialogue and Carol Reed's direction. Ralph Richardson could make plausible the idea of Baines as irresistible idol because, in the fluid exactness of his gestures and line readings, he was in fact irresistible. The two women—Michèle Morgan, as the compassionate, suffering Julie, and Sonia Dresdel, as the terrifying and finally tragic Mrs. Baines—might have been competing deities of two different religions, overpowering images of Pity and Rage respectively.

But in the midst of this world of adult splendor and mystery, Henrey—the boy Phile through whose eyes we see most of what happens and whose gaze, peering dreamily through the railings of a broad winding staircase, is our point of entry into the film—is somehow just a kid. No actor, he has all the genuine awkwardness and inappropriateness of childhood. He talks too loud and at the wrong moments; he inserts himself in places where he shouldn't be; he fails to take hints and winces when he begins to get some sense of what he has been failing to understand. When he throws a scare into Baines by imitating the voice of the butler's dreaded wife, the effect is genuinely obnoxious. What saves his performance-that-isn't-a-performance from being as irritating to the audience as it is at moments to the characters in the film is the way Reed's direction acts for him. The whole cinematic apparatus is enlisted to convey what Phile sees and what spaces he moves through, in the process creating as close an impression of a child's perception as any film has managed.

He is not just any child but the privileged son of a diplomat, inhabiting an embassy of palatial intricacy. We sense the privilege in his physical delicacy and in an arrogance that can be forgiven only because it is so unselfconscious. Privilege here quickly becomes indistinguishable from loneliness and silent suffering. Phile's father speaks to him as to a stranger; his mother, we learn in the first few minutes, has been away for eight months being treated for a serious illness; and the bored and unloved child has been given over to the care of a woman who in her seemingly causeless malevolence embodies every childhood fear. In a world of protocol and businesslike good cheer that would otherwise have been a site for untroubled adventures, Mrs. Baines, unforgettably incarnated by the dark and piercing Dresdel, represents a meanness of spirit that cannot be skirted: "You know what happens to little boys who tell lies?"

She is the killjoy without whom the child's world would be a very pleasant place. At the same time, his growing awareness of her power to intimidate her husband brings out, if only in the joke of mimicking her in order to make Baines jump, a potential for cruelty in Phile, even if afterward he begins to feel ashamed: "I thought it would be funny." Mrs. Baines, it would seem, exists in order to educate Phile in the existence of evil, and his early retort to her—"I hate you"—has an effect as explosive as any physical violence. A state of war has been revealed, and Phile's movements are those of a soldier on a reconnaissance mission, as he darts around the labyrinth of the embassy to evade her vigilance. The shadows and tilted angles turn the embassy into a place of hideouts and potential ambushes, in which Phile's principal occupation is to spy.

Everyone, in fact, spies on everyone. "What's torture?" Phile asks Julie at one point, and the whole film might be taken as a definition of torture at its most civilized. If Phile creeps about to avoid the all-seeing eye of Mrs. Baines, Baines and his girlfriend Julie—when the boy surprises them in the dingy tea shop where they find refuge—likewise behave with Phile as if they were squirming under his monitoring, watching their every word and coming up with bland cover stories to explain their behavior. The charming little boy has become someone who must be lied to, distracted, used as a prop for a secret rendezvous, and there are moments when he begins to look quite odious, a little monster getting in the way of the lovers desperate to be alone together.

In the solipsistic world of childhood, space exists in order for Phile to play in it, and adults exist to assist him in his play, giving him boxes for his pet snake or taking him to the zoo (to see the snakes, of course). He stares out into their world as if it were a spectacle provided for his enjoyment. But the longer and harder he stares, the more his situation becomes that of the child who has wandered by mistake into a movie for grown-ups—a half-understood drama about lovers having an assignation in a tea shop, or about an unhappily married man asking his wife for "his freedom"—whatever that might be. Small wonder, then, that as a nine-year-old watching *The Fallen Idol* on channel 9, I began to feel as if I were watching a movie about myself watching *The Fallen Idol*: a perfect doubling of the spying game whose constant twisting movements make the film a more insidious counterpart to Reed's *The Third Man*.

Everyone, it was explained here, was a double agent, and everyone inevitably the object of others' surveillance. The shifting of viewpoints, from shot to shot or within the same shot, is what *The Fallen Idol* is made of. Graham Greene's vision of betrayal as central human experience found its perfect corollary in Reed's characteristic tilted angles, which here serve as constant, sometimes brutal, reminders that someone else is watching or overhearing. A sense of dread permeates ordinary life; the slightest gesture or most innocuous object can trigger disastrous consequences. As Baines tells Phile when he returns a telltale pocket handkerchief, "It's things like that give secrets away." A few moments later Phile will be trapped into giving away his most important secret, merely through using the wrong pronoun.

Like *The Third Man*, *The Fallen Idol* is a postwar movie in which war is shown to have no end. The battle continues in parlor and kitchen, and what begins in play ends in what to Phile will always look like murder. How could it be an accident, when it happened in an atmosphere of such unbridled murderousness? The death of Mrs. Baines seems the culmination of all the lies and all the spying that turn out to be the very essence of the world that Phile, all unknowing, inhabited; and the horrifying wicked stepmother ends not as perpetrator but victim. It is a mark of what Reed has accomplished here that a character presented from the outset as an emblem of malice acquires by the end a

THE LABYRINTH OF ADULTHOOD

nearly tragic pathos. In becoming aware of the suffering that underlies her apparent wickedness, Phile enters the domain of a different kind of knowledge.

What he will make of that knowledge remains sealed. Reed softened the irremediable somberness of Greene's short story, in which the boy's betrayal of his idol poisoned his whole life, to provide an ending at least potentially happy—the police, by substituting one misunderstanding for another, have averted the worst outcome, and Phile's mother has come home—but there is no telling what Phile will make of a world which he has just begun to see clearly, and with a new wariness. The spatial labyrinth of the embassy in which so much of the movie has been enacted gives way in its final moments to an unseen temporal labyrinth, the anticipation of how all these events will play back in the memory of an adult Phile whose birth we have just witnessed.

The Criterion Collection, 2006

# meditations at the cinema café

1.

I SHARED A podium not long ago with David Thomson. It was one of those very general and open-ended discussions about film—roaming over the past and future of Hollywood, what the audience wants, what the industry needs, the erosion of old standards, the conflict between art and commerce—and at one point Thomson threw out the question: "Is it possible that the movies have lost their magic?" It was the sort of question that someone is likely to throw out in such a discussion, and its meaning has everything to do with the relative age of the person asking it. What magic? Whose magic?

The reference might have been to some lost glamor, the never-to-be-recaptured first glimpse of Bogie and Bacall, or the Gold Diggers of 1933, or Dietrich gazing at Anna May Wong or King Kong at Fay Wray, all the way back to the more primal thrills of Tom Mix and Douglas Fairbanks, until you might find yourself among ghosts, with a bunch of unalerted Parisians ducking behind a table in fear to avoid the Lumières' train arriving at the La Ciotat station in 1898. Looking out at the mostly very young audience, I had to wonder whether for many of them the outer limit of old-time movie magic might be, say, *Star Wars*. Or maybe *Fight Club*.

I'm not sure exactly what Thomson had in mind, because the discussion predictably veered rapidly in another direction, but he may well have been thinking not of the aura of any particular film or era but rather the "magic" alluded to in the title of an old British film, *The Magic Box*, about the invention of cinematography: the primitive sense of awe elicited, in the beginning, in the face of photographs that move. The question then would be whether that awe had given way to habituation and even boredom, to be recalled the way a long-term opium addict thinks back fondly on the by-now-unattainable freshness and novelty of his first pipe. The myth of the first encounter marks the transition from one world to another, and there is no going back.

One might well wonder whether movies at this point are even clearly distinguishable from the mess of paraphernalia that surrounds them—the personal computers, iPods, and cell phones to which their users seem almost biologically attached—especially as movies increasingly figure as one among many forms of information delivered by such devices. To speak of the magic of movies in this context would be a little like invoking the all-too-often-forgotten magic of traffic lights, washing machines, Mister Coffee, and other useful and remarkable inventions.

At that point in the discussion I would have liked to say something about the sheer unearthly strangeness of cinema, about the way it breaks with previous human experience. To get to that it would be necessary to stand once again outside movies as if confronting an alien and unexpected presence. The magic, so called, would be an equal mix of enchantment and trauma. To reconstruct that first encounter, to make it strange again, would mean dismantling habituated responses and becoming a little frightened, a little disoriented, to be taken by surprise all over again, like a caveman dropped down without warning at the laundromat—all this to recover the shock effect of, say, a one-shot movie of a tree filmed against a bare sky, its branches swaying in the wind. Pure beauty, with underlying terror: and if the image were perceived with an ever so slight difference, if the merest suggestion of the phantasmal seemed to hover among the branches, then it would be pure terror with underlying beauty.

Quite aside from the trees and the branches, what you are being given in that primordial moment is a demonstration of power, the power to make things appear out of nothing, and to plunge them back into darkness. Whose power? Maybe that of Dr. Caligari, or Dr. Mabuse, or of that *Unseen Enemy* in Griffith's Biograph short who by aiming a gun through a hole in the wall of the room in which Lillian Gish and her sister are trapped seems to call into play all the latent claustrophobia of the movie screen.

What I had really been led to think about, though, as this question of movie magic briefly surfaced and then subsided, was not so much the historical origin of movies but the origins of my own movie-watching. I was spontaneously dredging up some early memories of the effect of watching home movies with my family. If these were not the first movies I saw (although they may well have been), they were certainly the first whose projection I witnessed. I was aware of the reel mounted on the projector, the light shining through, the beam of light reaching across the darkened room while the family gathered around in what felt very much like a religious ritual, one of those secret Orphic displays shown to initiates in ancient mystery cults. From the moment the lights were turned out the room was transformed into a different space. Everything was designed so that attention would converge irresistibly on the images that moved on the screen: images of the very people watching them, images of the backyard just beyond the window, behind the barrier of drapes, except that here was daylight in the nighttime, springtime in winter, last year still taking place in a world of its own.

I suppose that no subsequent metaphysical conundrum posed by movies—not all the intricate games of appearance and identity that would draw me to *Vertigo* and *Laura* and *The Thief of Bagdad* (the Korda version) and *Ugetsu* and *Lola Montès* and *Solaris* and *Eyes Wide Shut*—nothing would challenge my sense of reality and logic so profoundly as trying to make sense of that machinery and of those images that reconstituted a lost but known reality, again and again. Eventually those random moments—my grandmother standing in front of a flowerbed in early spring, my brothers clowning in a huge pile of autumn leaves, myself gazing with a certain bewilderment at the preparations for some sort of parade—seemed privileged by the mere fact of having been filmed. The limits thus established were brutal: whatever was not filmed disappeared forever.

More than that, these filmed images came to constitute a narrative, as if the order, length, and composition of the individual shots obeyed some inner logic, and everything fell out as it was obscurely meant to. Once anything—the most slight and pointless flailing or intrusion—was put on the screen, it became necessary. Of course, given that my father was unquestionably the auteur of these films, that was more or less the case, although his framing and editing were certainly less rigorous than, say, Fritz Lang's; but I doubt that I had yet attained that much sophistication about aesthetic causes and effects. The movies simply were. They had a life of their own, a distinct visual character stemming from the way the slightly unreal color registered changes in natural lighting.

What could be at once more ordinary and more strange than the intimate weirdness of those simulacra living their lives in an oddly displaced space and time? This was already science fiction, even in a four-year-old's perspective. I could not have foreseen that the strangeness of the difference between the "real" space where I sat watching and the "other" space of my family's doubles on the screen would be compounded incalculably by the passage of time, so that only from a third vantage—in that future where I would later reside and remember—could the full strangeness be gauged by triangulation. Only when the show is over do you start to wonder where you have been all along and experience a belated panic of displacement.

All these are just chance effects. We are in the realm of accident, yet it's just in that realm that this so-called magic makes its presence known: in the accidental juxtaposition, the unintended gesture, the unanticipated angle of perception, above all in the unforeseeable transformations that time's passage works on an object apparently unchanged. Art might then be a matter not of creating but of corralling the magic that would otherwise wander around loose, and perhaps even anticipating how that magic would withstand erosion. At some point—and maybe it's always the central point—what is most deliberate and what is most random appear to converge.

2.

MOVIES ARE OF course neither magical nor accidental in origin. They are the deliberate product of scientific experiment, no less than the railroad or the telegraph. They are a crucial part of the huge prosthetic initiative that began to achieve its goals by the middle of the nineteenth century, the project to extend the reach and capabilities of the human body so as to go faster, to keep going longer, to communicate at great distances, and—through photography—to fix the gaze and make a record of what is seen. The machine sees what I tell it to see and it keeps it for me, makes it permanent. The still camera is already a time machine in that it prolongs a visual perception beyond its moment, and so creates a new kind of moment in which that past instant is both of infinite duration and infinitely open to inspection: somehow made prisoner within the present moment, within the frame that defines it. The mist of romantic poetry by which the imagination is subjugated becomes a concrete fog whose precise structure and luminosity is printed out as firmly and absolutely as the message in a telegram.

A progression of still images moving at railroad speed from one instant to the next produces by the coldest of logic the unreal tree whose branches move in real time. Nothing magical there: if anything it's anti-magic, the definitive de-enchantment of the world, the photographing of time. The movie is a photograph that has acquired the characteristics of the railroad train, moving through time as much as through space, and of the telegraph, allowing contact with the unfolding of distant events in something like real time: not the real time of simultaneity but a real time of duration that becomes indistinguishable from simultaneity, before television emerges to finally erase the distinction.

(D.W. Griffith was already anticipating simultaneous transmission of moving pictures in 1923, but he didn't think it would happen within the next hundred years, not because it would be technically impossible but because the raw unrehearsed footage would be too boring: "In the instantaneous transmission there would be entirely too much waste of the public's time, and that is the important thing—time.")

It is a recording device but also a surveying tool, a device for measurement, a prosthetic device for moving through the world with expanded sensory capacities and expanded memory. It is not surprising that so many of those who took to it were scientific types, technical types: Hitchcock a student at the School of Engineering and Navigation, Hawks a student of mechanical engineering at Cornell, Allan Dwan a student of electrical engineering at Notre Dame, Fritz Lang a student at the College of Technical Sciences at Vienna's Academy of Graphic Arts.

Only after you have built a machine can you find out all that it can tell you, and what effect that telling will have on you. Just as poetry might be defined as the unintended consequence of language as practical communication tool, movie magic might be the unintended consequence of a cinematic apparatus designed to replicate what materiality looks like in action. Nobody could really know in advance what it would be like. I wonder whether we know what it is like even now. Has the surprise indeed worn off or does it persist like a trauma, an unhealed metaphysical affront? Or have we made our peace with that, a peace that might resemble numbness, a taking for granted of the capsule within which we have enclosed ourselves, or which more precisely our immediate ancestors provided us with the means to ceaselessly modify and refit? Can we really locate ourselves within the working out of a scientific experiment that long since went out of control?

In *The Aviator* Martin Scorsese attempts to use every means available to him to describe the fusion of speed, exhilaration, and terror generated by the blurring of distinctions between the machine and the body. The machine is an extension of the body, the body finally an imitator of the machine, and the consciousness that itself designed the machine is caught finally somewhere in the middle, in the no-man's-land that resembles the Western desert in the movie that Howard Hughes watches over and over in his cave-like room. It's not a question of passing judgment on any of this but merely of describing, and the process requires very high rates of compression; this can result in an impression of being hurried along, but that's part of the description.

The movies mutate like a living thing. In some sense they are a living thing, or a piece of one, an artificial extension not only of the living gestures of the photographed but of the living perceptions of the photographer. We change them to suit us better, but there is always the possibility that we change ourselves to suit them better, mutating into ever more perfect movie-watchers: except the movies will at the same time have continued to change into something or some things altogether different, and we will continue not to know precisely where we are.

Movies were in the beginning a way of extracting the world from the world, of scooping out a chunk of the flow of unmediated reality— what Kant did his damnedest to describe as "the swarm of appearances, the rhapsody of perceptions" (maybe that sounds better as *Gewühl der Erscheinungen, Rhapsodie der Wahrnehmungen*)—and turning it into a fixed object. Not only fixed but shrinkable, enlargeable, tintable, spliceable, and repeatable. This now seems to have been an irreversible breach in the previous order of things in the same way that the alphabet once was—the kind of breach that ultimately, a few generations down the road, makes it hard to remember just how things used to be. The alphabet gave us history. I don't think we can be sure yet what movies gave us, perhaps a new improved history that doesn't feel like history at all. It just feels like the place where we hang out.

3.

I HANG OUT sometimes at the Cinema Café on East 60th Street, which is part of a chain whose other branches can be found around New York and for all I know in other towns. Its walls are decorated with blow-ups of movie posters and production stills, and in its front room there are two TV monitors, one of which continuously shows CNN, and the other of which continually shows somewhat randomly selected silent movies. Both movies and news are silent, while a soundtrack is piped in consisting of a mix of the sort of vaguely Franco-Brazilian technopop that could easily be the score for anything from the latest romantic comedy to the latest bulletin on the Weather Channel. The cafe's façade consists entirely of glass doors—open in the warm months—and in that wide frame you can watch the world pass by just as in some 1898 attraction like *Workers Leaving the Lumière Factory*, although because the view is colorful and urban and has, at least when the curtains are pulled back to their widest extent, an aspect ratio somewhat like VistaVision, it more closely resembles the establishing shot in a late Hitchcock film, *The Birds* or *Marnie*, those movies in which the cinematographer Robert Burks achieved a look whose glossy precision locates the image right on the dividing line between the real and the unreal.

The effect is of a spatio-temporal palimpsest, with different layers of reality jostling each other in the same field of vision. Within a frame created by the motionless forms of giant movie posters—*Citizen Kane, Casablanca, Rebel Without a Cause, La Dolce Vita, Doctor Zhivago*—overlapping just enough that I may simultaneously be registering images of Alfred Hitchcock, Laurel and Hardy, Ingrid Bergman, Anita Ekberg, and James Dean—distinct and self-contained realities roll out on the two monitors, both visible at the same time.

To my right the highly stylized rituals of CNN's news reporting constitute another framing device, hemming in whatever story is unfolding—a hostage drama, a press conference by a government spokesman, a Midwestern blizzard—with a movie-like supertitle (ATLANTA COURTROOM TRAGEDY), a crawl of unrelated alternative stories moving along the bottom of the screen, the regular interjection of talking heads, and captions for the hearing-impaired with just enough typos to confirm the simultaneity of the broadcast; there wasn't time to correct anything.

To my left, Buster Keaton clings to the paddle wheel of a steamboat, or Douglas Fairbanks scales the wall of a chateau. And all the while, out of the corner of my eye, there is a perfect opportunity to watch the people of the city walk by oblivious to the fact that they are part of a framed spectacle. The overall effect is of a peculiar kind of aquarium in which some of the fish are somehow more real than others, yet all partake of some degree of reality.

The silent movies take on a peculiar quality of life forms struggling to survive outside their proper environment, dragged out of the darkness where they would thrive into a bright and crowded afternoon. But it's equally clear that they are indeed life forms, squirming with as much vitality as the more or less hieratic talking heads of CNN. Yet they are not just a different kind of spectacle but a different kind of seeing. To be caught up in the flow of *Steamboat Bill, Jr.* or *The Three Musketeers* or *The Immigrant* is to intercept not merely the show on the screen but the exchange of glances on which that show was predicated. These images could never have existed outside their world, and the fact that they are there at all summons up a phantom habitat, with us sitting in for the spectators who have disappeared.

On one such afternoon I looked up to see a movie I didn't recognize. At one blink I classed it as a fairly typical mid-twenties Hollywood product, with scenes of genteel life framed as in a waxworks. Within seconds a recognizable reaction was forming, a compound of nostalgia and campy appreciation of creaky formalities and admiration for the beauty of some of the players. At a second blink the reaction was already changing. In this succession of moments—of well-dressed people moving in and out of drawing rooms, of two women confronting each other in a hallway, of a woman ascending a staircase—there were some that might have been filmed by Murnau. There crept in just that sense of fated and indelible gesture in the most trivial action, so that a stroll into the garden could be a form of desperate mythical flight from some underworld, the same underworld perhaps that all these actors now inhabited: the realm of gray ghosts.

The movie, as it turned out, was Alfred Hitchcock's *Easy Virtue*, a 1927 adaptation of a Noël Coward play, starring Isabel Jeans and Franklin Dyall, and just knowing that induced a certain detachment, the calm of knowing where something fit into a chronological grid.

But how alive they had all been in the moments of uncertainty, as if they had indeed momentarily escaped from whatever purgatory exists for dead movie actors, maybe someplace like the island of living holograms in Adolfo Bioy Casares's novel *The Invention of Morel*. They were walking around in the garden and really enjoying themselves. No one told them what movie they were in.

But it was also as if something had momentarily escaped in me. Some habitual boundary had wavered and I had experienced a purely animal reaction to what was happening on the screen—"Who are those people over there?"—and in the wake of that short burst of adrenaline had had to reestablish that, well, they're not exactly people and they're not exactly over there—although they were certainly somewhere, once. A layer of separation had been peeled away; the effect however was not to tie things closer together but to reveal further distances. I had the impression of receiving messages by mistake.

In the dawn of their invention new machines bestow exciting powers. Two people with cell phones can track each other through the labyrinth of a city, like explorers equipped with walkie-talkies, and then, as each turns a corner, come face-to-face, and it's as perfectly choreographed as Fred Astaire and Cyd Charisse walking in Central Park, or a simulacrum of Central Park, in *The Band Wagon*. In watching this old movie there's a similar convergence—the director equipped with his prosthetic device, his movie-making machine, moves along one line, tracking the world, and my consciousness, equipped with another prosthetic device, the movie-projecting machine, moves along another line, tracking his tracking, and where those lines converge—the third point of a triangle—is the world. The odd difference is that his world exists in another place and time. I have come to the appointed spot, but too late.

It's a matter again of unintended consequences, even in response to something that is most deliberately intended—that is, a Hitchcock movie; or a Fritz Lang movie; or a Murnau movie. Or especially in response to what is most deliberately intended. Only when the machine is wielded with sensitivity to its full capabilities can the limits of the machine be most poignantly apprehended—whether the machine is language or the cinematograph. Unless, perhaps, that exposure of limits was implied by the maker of the work, even if unconsciously: in which case we have the consolation—however much consolation it might be—of no longer being trapped altogether in the realm of accident. We didn't lose our way by mistake; we were guided here, even if it remains true that we can't get out and can't get back to the place from which the signal is emanating.

These points of contact seem like glances exchanged between people in different cars moving in different directions. They are going ever deeper into the past, while we move at accelerating speeds toward spaces we are unable to anticipate, which we will perceive through further refinements of the cinematograph, refinements that we are equally unable to anticipate although not for want of trying. Our descendants can have fun looking at *A.I.*, *Gattaca*, *Blade Runner*, *Total Recall*, and *The Matrix*, trying to figure how we were able so totally to miss the boat on where things were really heading. The strangeness of movies is just one aspect, however fascinating, of the wider strangeness of the life we have been living lately—by lately meaning perhaps since the invention of photography, or of the steam engine, or maybe of the alphabet: especially the alphabet, since movies amount to finding a way to turn everything visible into a form of alphabet, malleable and recombinable.

To look for a resting point within that acceleration is to pile strangeness on top of strangeness, although such a resting point is exactly the peculiar comfort that old movies provide. They provide it more and more, by means of the new machinery that gives us ever more control over them, gives us the power, however limited and illusory, to make time stop and then start again at will. We are permitted, we are strongly encouraged to savor movies as a separate and controllable world.

But just now I prefer to think about the moments when the illusion of separateness and controllability fails, when the real terror of the cinematograph is able to become manifest. Not long ago I had the experience, after a long watch by the deathbed of a loved one, of going to see a movie by Murnau—I had never seen it and knew nothing about it—*Burning Earth*, a rather elaborate melodrama about family conflicts over property rights, and in the middle of the film there was a deathbed scene, brief but extremely vivid, lit by candles as it was in the Old World, looking like an archaic German woodcut come to real and startling life in extremis. And for me it was like the momentary lining up of planets in their separate orbits: the two worlds, of the screen and of life, became one, or rather it became clear again that the screen was nothing more than a form of life: shadowy life, attenuated life, stylized and abstracted life, life perhaps unnaturally preserved, yet coextensive with ours. The desperation of that desire to extend life burns in movies, and maybe we can feel it most vividly in the oldest ones, in the most belated messages.

The poignance is not merely in the fact that the world we see on the screen is no longer ours, but that the very eyes we see with are not ours. It's as if you were to put a rusted helmet on your head and find that you were thereby permitted to look through the eyes of some ancient person, walk through his space, possess his world at one remove. How many hours have I spent allowing my vision to be a surrogate vehicle for the dead eyes of Fritz Lang, allowing him to continue to look? The ideas of authorship, of style, of the *caméra stylo* can hardly begin to do justice to how strange that is. But who can doubt that what is to follow will be stranger? You don't have to be a fan of science fiction if you're already a character of science fiction. It proved too much even for Fritz Lang. In his old age he told an interviewer that he wanted to make a movie about how television had destroyed the imagination of the young.

Then again, turning my head to the right again to catch the latest roundup of events on CNN, it occurs to me that old Fritz may well have had a point.

*Film Comment*, 2006

# all aboard

*THE LADY VANISHES* IS THE film that best exemplifies Hitchcock's often-asserted desire to offer audiences not a slice of life but a slice of cake. Even Claude Chabrol and Eric Rohmer, in their pioneering study of Hitchcock, for once abandoned the search for hidden meanings and—while rating it "an excellent English film, an excellent Hitchcock film"—decided it was one that "requires little commentary," while François Truffaut declared that every time he tried to study the film's trick shots and camera movements he became too absorbed in the plot to notice them. Perhaps they were disarmed by pleasure, *The Lady Vanishes* being as pure a pleasure as the movies have offered. The ever-spirited Miss Froy, not long before she vanishes, remarks that her name "rhymes with *joy*," and indeed the whole film breathes an air of delight like nothing else in Hitchcock. The central situation—the disappearance of a woman whose very existence is subsequently denied by everyone but the protagonist—may seem to provide the perfect matrix for the kind of paranoid melodrama that would proliferate a few years later, in the forties, in films like *Phantom Lady, Gaslight,* and *My Name Is Julia Ross,* but here the dark shadows of conspiracy are countered by a brightness and brilliance of tone almost Mozartean in its equanimity. Most of the time we are too exhilarated to be frightened.

The film arose in a more accidental way than was customary with Hitchcock. In 1937, he was at a turning point in his career. After making his way to the forefront of the British film industry with works like *The Man Who Knew Too Much* (1934) and *The 39 Steps* (1935), he was involved in negotiations with David Selznick that would soon take him to Hollywood. Still under contract to Gaumont British, however, and at loose ends for a script, he reached for a project already developed and in fact nearly filmed a year earlier by the American director Roy William Neill. Though Hitchcock and his wife, Alma Reville, made significant adjustments (notably with regard to the early hotel scenes and the final shoot-out), the script (freely adapted from *The Wheel Spins*, a rather unthrilling thriller by Ethel Lina White) is very much the work of the brilliant screenwriting team of Sidney Gilliat and Frank Launder, to whom especially can be credited the verbal richness of the comedy, whether it's Miss Froy busying herself with "a most intriguing acrostic in *The Needlewoman*" or Basil Radford's Charters expostulating, "After all, people don't go about tying up nuns!" (With Hitchcock gone to America, it would be left to Gilliat and Launder—as writers, directors, and producers—to keep up something of that mix of wit and thrills on the home front.)

The cozy claustrophobia of the film, as it moves from overcrowded hotel to tightly packed train compartment, reflects the circumstances of the budget-conscious British film industry of the time (constraints under which Hitchcock had honed his skills). It was filmed, according to Hitchcock, "on a set ninety feet long. We used one coach; all the rest were transparencies or miniatures." A reassuring sense of smallness of scale is instilled by the opening panorama of a snowbound toy train station in the remote Balkan enclave of Bandrika, "one of Europe's few undiscovered corners"; Hitchcock might still be the little boy whose hobby was collecting train schedules from around the world. A hint of giddiness at the harmlessness of it all assures from the start that we are in a world created by movies—the same world explored by Lubitsch comedies and Astaire and Rogers musicals—in which the worst that can befall are the minor discomforts and embarrassments of travel.

Along with the discomforts comes a muted but pervasive sexual charge, taking a variety of forms: the comic byplay of the blinkered cricket fans Caldicott and Charters (with the wonderful team of Naunton Wayne and Basil Radford unavoidably evoking Laurel and Hardy), forced to stay in the maid's room and unnerved by the least hint of sexuality; the suggestive exchanges of the adulterous couple, Mr. and "Mrs." Todhunter (as the titles coyly put it), whose once passionate affair is already cooling off; the trio of irresistible young English girls, Iris Henderson (Margaret Lockwood) and her friends, who for a moment seem to have stepped out of the chorus line of a Busby Berkeley musical. It needs only the midnight meeting of Iris and the rugged young folklorist Gilbert (Michael Redgrave)—as, in a scene straight out of *Top Hat*, she's kept awake by his reenactment on the floor above of a Balkan wedding dance—to set in motion a robustly amusing comedy of courtship.

The mood is frankly sexy in a way that would never really be matched in Hitchcock's American films, where even the most erotically charged moments (Bergman and Grant's protracted kiss in *Notorious*) seem too carefully planned to allow much room for spontaneity. Lockwood and Redgrave, by contrast, really do seem like young people who have just met and who, despite their bumpy introduction, can't wait to run off together. (When they finally find themselves alone in a cab at the end, the relief is palpable.) The film may be not simply a farewell to England but a farewell to youth, by a director about to turn forty. We never forget that these are young people still somewhat on the margins of the grown-up world, with Lockwood rushing too quickly into well-appointed adulthood by way of marrying the wrong man, and Redgrave lingering perhaps a bit too long in uncommitted footloose world-roving—a forecast perhaps of the Grace Kelly–James Stewart couple in *Rear Window*, but in a younger and less neurotic mode.

It isn't until twenty-four minutes into the film that the first dark note intrudes in the abrupt strangling of an apparently harmless serenader. Thereafter the plot takes over in a stunningly swift exposition. From the moment the heroine—concussed by a fallen planter intended for Miss Froy—comes to in her train compartment to confront her oddly assorted fellow passengers, we are in the grip of a narrative rhythm of incomparable assurance. In a very few minutes we have lived the episode of her tea break with Miss Froy, in which Dame May Whitty reinforces the impression, already created by her earlier scene with the hapless cricket fans the night before, that she is the most perfectly harmless of English ladies, a mildly eccentric governess given to poetic fantasies about snowbound mountains but rigorous when it comes to the preparation of her tea. Since in a moment she is going to vanish, Miss Froy must for a moment dominate everything, and Whitty achieves just that, and even more: she makes us feel an affection for Miss Froy deep enough that her disappearance will seem an unspeakable affront, an assault on Englishness itself in its least threatening form.

The pivotal point is the exchange, back in their compartment, of close-ups of Whitty and Lockwood as the former hums the haunting melody sung first by the strangled balladeer and the latter drifts off into a sleep whose duration is represented by a montage of wheels, wires, and railroad tracks. She will come to for the second time in a radically altered reality, in which nothing can be relied on. The intimacy of that last exchange of glances between the two women has a poignancy that infuses all that follows, the scenes of Lockwood and Redgrave relentlessly searching up and down the train's corridors, the introduction of the psychiatrist Dr. Hartz (Paul Lukas) with his suavely enunciated theories of hallucination, the rapidly shifting scenes of denial and concealment and substitution.

Finally, at nearly the exact midpoint of the film, the momentary reemergence of Miss Froy's name, spelled out on the dusty window of the dining car (an apparition perfectly timed in both its appearances and its disappearance), precipitates a crisis for Lockwood as she realizes that not even Redgrave believes her. It is a moment rich in Hitchcockian resonances. In her despairing outburst—"Why don't you do something before it's too late?"—we catch a glimpse of future and more painfully depicted moments: Teresa Wright in *Shadow of a Doubt* exploding under the pressure of her secret knowledge of her uncle's guilt, Doris Day in *The Man Who Knew Too Much* screaming as she is forced to choose between saving a stranger's life and risking her son's, Vera Miles in *The Wrong Man* slipping into madness in the wake of her husband's wrongful incrimination.

But Margaret Lockwood here is the freshest and least damaged of Hitchcock's heroines, and what comes through is not so much her despair as her determination to get to the bottom of things despite all opposition. Her insistence on the reality of what she has seen is the only sure guide through a labyrinth of false impressions, even as the insidious Dr. Hartz tries to convince her that the vanished Miss Froy is "merely a vivid subjective image." The whole train, for that matter, is a congeries of vivid subjective images, from the magician's rabbits peering up out of a top hat at a violent struggle in the baggage car to the nun in high heels keeping guard over an accident victim wrapped up like a mummy. This Europe of sinister baronesses and grinning conjurers is indeed a runaway train bound for nowhere good.

All along, the film has pitted England against the world, with the English characters not necessarily getting the best of it. The loathsome adulterer Todhunter (Cecil Parker at his most unctuous) is the very picture of moral indifference, and only Whitty and Redgrave show much interest, however condescending, in continental mores. Wayne and Radford, as the cricket fans desperate to get back in time for the match, effortlessly steal the film with their running display of blithe bafflement at all things foreign. But a film that mocks British insularity and hypocrisy ends as a celebration of British pluck and solidarity, as every British character (except for the cowardly appeaser Todhunter, shot down waving a white flag) finally reveals a courageous nature: the sinister nun is really just a good English girl gone astray, and the complacent cricket fans turn out when the chips are down to be dead shots with nerves of steel. Even Dr. Hartz—the most congenial of villains—feels obliged in the end to wish them "jolly good luck." The whole climactic episode is a send-up of *Boy's Own* heroics—except that the blood on Basil Radford's hand is all too real. The dreadful shock on his previously imperturbable face is like a harbinger of the real danger with which the film has finally, unavoidably, made contact.

Back in the days when Hitchcock's American films were usually regarded as a falling off, *The Lady Vanishes* was the film that critics often used as a measuring rod for berating his subsequent output—lamenting the loss of its sharp wit, its free invention, its nimble pace and lighter-than-air frothiness—as if it were a token of the kind of work he might have continued to turn out had he remained in his native land. But given that the year was 1938, it seems unlikely that the mood of *The Lady Vanishes* could easily have been sustained or repeated. This was a bubble of its moment—the assertion of a fairy tale triumph of humor and youthful energy over the darkest forces of Central European evil—realized at the last moment such a bubble was possible. We can watch it over and over just as children can hear the same fairy tale again and again, marveling that such serenity and playfulness could flourish on the brink of an abyss.

The Criterion Collection, 2007

# the guy with the sax:
# a note on *detour*

IT'S THE *ARABIAN NIGHTS* OF dead ends. One nowhere magically
blossoms into another nowhere: just as you thought you were stuck
playing piano for drunks in the Break o' Dawn club, you find yourself
with a three-day beard hitching rides to the West Coast. Just as you
thought you were stuck cadging diner food from the hardcase horse
player who picked you up, you find yourself having to dispose of his
body after he hits his head on a rock. Or maybe he was dead already,
from whatever medical condition those pills in the glove compartment
were for. The ecstasy of *Detour* is its constantly fulfilled promise that
something new and unforeseeable will happen in the next moment: a
stock shot of switchboard operators speeding the hero's phone call to
California, a revelation of a dueling scar, a fantasy of the lost girlfriend
singing in front of a silhouetted horn section. Everything—the speed,
the associative freedom, the intrusions of fantasy and dream into the
banalities of highway and motel, the Ancient Mariner voice-over that
never lets up—speaks of adventure. Except for the fact that everything
has been a dead end to begin with. Al was terminally bitter even before
things went wrong; his relationship with Sue was at a dreary impasse
even before he staked everything on going out to California to see her.
Every imaginable goal was tainted or unworthy or impracticable even
before it was formulated. Finally, forty minutes into this sixty-eight-
minute movie, we get to its innermost realm of mystery, its Shangri-La

or buried kingdom of Kôr: a smoke-filled motel room where two people settle into an afterlife of grating on each other as if they were trapped in some horrible one-act play that can never end. "Every five minutes one of us was wishing we had another bottle, or a radio, or something to read." As a refinement of their punishment, one might imagine one of them picking up a tattered magazine left lying there, a film journal in which an obscure scholar had laboriously catalogued every image from the movie in which they find themselves imprisoned, the juke-box, the rearview mirror, the used car lot, right down to the floral still life over the couch in the room where they are condemned to listen forever to the music on the soundtrack: "I wish that guy with the sax would give up."

*LIT*, 2007

# a northern new jersey
# of the mind

DR. MELFI: "What are you afraid's going to happen?"
TONY: "I don't know! But something. I don't know!"
    —*The Sopranos*, season one, episode one

1.

WATCHING THE LONG good-bye of *The Sopranos* has been a test, and for many of us a proof, of how deep the show's hooks had penetrated. At some point in its long run it came perhaps to be taken for granted. Undeniably, during recent seasons, I had found myself carping about stasis, a hint of aridity, of grogginess. Hadn't all this gone on long enough? Hadn't we spent enough time watching Tony Soprano and the crew conspiring in the back room of Satriale's Pork Store, or trading lacerating verbal jabs at the bar of the Bada Bing club while the strippers in the background went through their changeless paces? How many times could Carmela swallow her misgivings after she and Tony once again quarreled and reconciled? Yet as the seventh and final season rolled out, I found myself inwardly whining—in the tones of an addict as helpless as Christopher Moltisanti's fellow substance abusers in his Twelve-Step group or Dave Scatino, the compulsive gambler lured to his doom in Tony's executive poker game—"Why does it have to end?"

I used to wonder how it would have been to be a reader in the era of serialized fiction, when Dickens could keep a whole culture hanging on for the next installment, and ships arriving in America might be hailed, before anything else, with questions about how things fared with Little Nell. But even *The Old Curiosity Shop* only took a little under a year to unfold. *The Sopranos* began its run in January 1999, extending eventually to eighty-six hour-long episodes. Following it has been like watching a movie that lasted for eight years, with occasional intermission breaks for births, deaths, terrorist incursions, and wars that look to go on much longer than the series. ("You realize we're gonna bomb Iran?" A.J. Soprano asked his father in a late episode.)

At the start *The Sopranos* had the piquancy of a new invention. Television had fostered a claustrophobia of hemmed-in expectations, a culture of flat character types and pat endings. The space into which *The Sopranos* inducted us had the messy picaresque randomness of the real world, yet every detail—every tune heard in passing, every remark overheard at the next table, every artifact glimpsed in the background of a crowded room—glistened as if singled out with obsessive mindfulness. In texture and form it seemed something altogether new to television.

The suggestion originally made to the show's creator, David Chase, was to create a TV version of *The Godfather*, but he chose instead to rework a screenplay he had written years earlier. The concept, baldly recounted, might have seemed a gimmick with limited potential: a lower-tier New Jersey mobster, living an outward life of suburban ease but bedeviled by panic attacks, with great reluctance goes into therapy. In outline—portrait of a mafioso as mid-life family guy harried by growing kids, status-conscious wife, and impossible mother, with criminal associates to provide outrageous laugh lines—it had the makings of a "cutting edge" sitcom, with darker elements (such as the fact that his mother and uncle might be conspiring to have him killed) satirically recalling a *Dallas*-style dynastic soap opera. In execution it rapidly became something consistently rich and surprising, and beautifully unfinished, perhaps unfinishable. It created its own operating principles as it proceeded, while convincing us that this was an actual world we had stumbled on.

There were hints at the outset of a breezily caricatural direction, accenting in broad strokes the disconnect between the nature of the hero's livelihood ("waste management consultant" with a finger in a dozen rackets and scams, from illegal dumping and no-show construction jobs to sports betting and loan-sharking) and the nouveau riche trappings of his family life in West Caldwell, New Jersey (from the crates of Roche Bobois furniture to the elaborate home theater where his wife Carmela would eventually watch *Citizen Kane* on the recommendation of the American Film Institute's "Hundred Best Films" list). But *The Sopranos* moved rapidly beyond easy schemas. Chase's pilot episode, a masterpiece of abbreviated exposition, staked out a teeming alternate world, a northern New Jersey of the mind populated by a score of characters of whom at least fifteen would have major continuing roles, among them Tony's children Meadow and A.J., his malevolent mother Livia and his ineffectual and embittered uncle Corrado (Uncle Junior), and his malcontent protégé Christopher—and each soon took on independent life.

Incarnated by actors then largely unknown to TV audiences, as brilliant a stock company as any ever assembled, they had on first encounter the memorable force of gargoyles. But these were gargoyles with curious depths, able to persuade us they existed even when the camera wasn't running. They spoke a dialogue so compressed and inventive in its mix of tones and jargons that it sounded like a new dialect, a poetically charged speech welded out of obscenities and banalities, misconstrued catchphrases and newly minted messages from the unconscious.

The show undertook to find how many variant aspects of each of these characters could be revealed. We circled around them and studied them from different angles, taking all the time necessary to contemplate these clearly limited yet somehow infinitely mysterious beings. The process could never really be completed except in death—and death would arrive for many. But even after they were gone we would continue to contemplate the precise alchemy of their role in the *Sopranos* scheme of things. Their fate has been to escape from the frame of the show, inhabiting a zone of their own in which their choices continue to perplex, and their individual voices haunt sleepless moments, no matter what the words might be saying.

Most of all I hear the lingering voice of Nancy Marchand, who died after the second season but whose presence shaped the mood of the whole series. As Tony's mother Livia, a monster out of Balzac, manipulative, verbally abusive, endlessly self-pitying ("I wish the Lord would take me"), she provided the foil in comparison with whom Tony could look victimized, a well-meaning adult struggling to cope with an irrational aging parent. I can still hear the grating crescendo with which she delivered the line: "Power? What power? I don't have power, *I'm a shut-in!*" Or the soul-killing tone, as she approached death, of her parting words with her grandson: "It's all a big nothing."

We came to think we knew them like family—if a family was something always unsettling, held together by habit and fear and desperate wishful thinking. The comforting familiarity of a well-loved television presence became, in James Gandolfini's Tony Soprano, a play of beguiling masks luring us only deeper into indeterminacy. To be charmed by him (he made it easy) was to be conned, with a good chance he was equally duped by his own devices. Possibly he meant it wholeheartedly when he told Dr. Melfi: "I'm a good guy basically . . . I love my family." By the time we got to the end we had seen a thousand Tonys—sheepish, serpentine, commanding, calculating, lecherous, self-pitying, savagely sarcastic, tenderly paternal, fatuously self-pleased, teary-eyed over an old radio hit, racked by paranoid mistrust, exploding in feral rage— and seen one switch to another in an instant. Guileless self-revelation was not a possibility, least of all in a psychiatrist's office. He had so many of him to choose from.

Tony's compartmentalized psyche—crosscutting between mob business, family life, and the transcendence he sought variously in Canada geese, peyote visions, or reenactments of World War II on the

History Channel—provided a center so sprawling it could be mistaken for the whole. The mere sight of him padding yet again in white bathrobe toward the refrigerator evoked a disheveled Wotan worthy of a show whose capacity to extend and savor its transitions could seem Wagnerian. But the secret of *The Sopranos* was the exhilarating density and noisiness of its digressions. Around the core group—Tony, his immediate family, his crew—were secondary and tertiary rings of characters with varying lifespans but often equally indelible, some nearly seizing control of an episode or a season (the suave psychopath Richie Aprile, the depressive car dealer Gloria Trillo), others surfacing only for as long, say, as it took them to get beaten half to death for trimming the wrong person's hedges.

The populousness of *The Sopranos* was of a piece with its ample scope and its dizzying mood swings. This territory thick with mobbed-up construction sites and toxic waste dumps turned out, unaccountably, to be a wonderland: not precisely Alice's domain but one likewise filled with magical locations (Bada Bing, Vesuvio's, the pork store), dream states and alternate realities, parodies and non sequiturs, ordinary objects turned menacing or disorienting, and jokes that popped up in the midst of social rituals as arcane as the Queen of Hearts's croquet match. Every episode was saturated with allusions—to movies, songs, history high and low, catchphrases of every creed and cult, the common store of rumor and misinformation—a backbeat of information that might be relevant or meaningless. (Where else would we find a mob guy taking to heart the self-help mantra to "feel the fear and do it anyway"?)

It was a show that came with its own built-in annotation. The philosophical enforcer Paulie Walnuts (Tony Sirico) sentimentalized about taking his mother to see *Man of La Mancha*—"Richard Kiley stared at Ma the whole time he was singing 'The Impossible Dream'"—not long before murdering one of her nursing home friends who caught him stealing her savings from under the mattress. A.J.'s struggle to complete a high school term paper ("The entire point of Melville's *Billy Budd*, it seems to me, is to show how mean humans can be to each other, especially when living in cramped conditions") precipitated a delicately calibrated family symposium on the possible connection of Melville's novel to what Carmela called "this whole gay thing," complete with a reference to Leslie Fiedler and a bad pun from Tony to end the discussion: "He must have been the ship's florist—Billy Bud."

Bad or misconstrued information bounced around in a world defined by random breaks, mostly unlucky. Anything that happened might turn out to be a kind of sucker punch; any exchange could tip into the farcical or the terrifying without warning. We might be tipped out of this world entirely, by way of the wounded Christopher's vision of hell as "The Emerald Piper . . . an Irish bar where it's St. Patrick's Day forever," or Dr. Melfi's dream of Tony's death, accompanied for no evident reason by a chorus of Munchkins from *The Wizard of Oz*, or Tony's prolonged coma-induced alternate existence as a precision optics salesman from Arizona who stumbled into an encounter with Tibetan monks (except that these were *Sopranos*-style Tibetan monks who played rough in defending their turf).

Any throwaway line could encapsulate a scarily decentered world. One night Tony walked into the back room of the Bada Bing and, asked by Silvio what was going on in the main room, replied: "Nothing much. Some asshole slipped on a lime wedge." Gandolfini's little grin at the memory of this offscreen pratfall—a tiny irrepressible twitch of private enjoyment—managed to be at once attractively childish and a window into depths of potential cruelty.

2.

EMOTIONAL BUTTONS WERE pushed with the expertise of a long-time television professional. David Chase had worked in the medium all his adult life—his earlier writing credits included *The Night Stalker*, *The Rockford Files*, and *Northern Exposure*—despite his proclaimed dislike of network television: "I loathe and despise almost every second of it . . . I considered network TV to be propaganda for the corporate state . . . [*Northern Exposure*] was ramming home every week the message that 'life is nothing but great,' 'Americans are great' and 'heartfelt emotion and sharing conquers everything.'" *The Sopranos* thus had something of the quality of a palace coup, a revolution engineered by an insider who, knowing where the fault lines were, could stir an emotional reaction all the better to thwart it, divert it, or turn it into something grotesquely different.

Not all rebellions are youth rebellions. *The Sopranos* seemed to retain at its core some early vision maintained and deepened in secret through a long period of waiting, along with the anger attendant on being forced to wait. Chase—who is Italian American, and who did grow up in northern New Jersey—is a child of the 1960s whose main object of study in college, he has said, was the music of the Rolling Stones. ("I always wanted to be a rock and roll musician much more than I wanted to be anything else.") He has also cited as influences the plays of Shakespeare, O'Neill, and Arthur Miller, and the films of Fellini (*8 ½*) and Polanski (particularly the absurdist crime comedy *Cul-de-Sac*). He has not been shy about broadcasting his artistic allegiances; in episode 2, one character operated Bunuel Brothers Auto Repairs, while another spotted Martin Scorsese walking into a nightclub and shouted out: "*Kundun*! I liked it!"

Chase's having come late to the point of making *The Sopranos* probably accounts for the impulse to make it a show about everything, including everything that television had always left out: most strikingly the toll of age and the limits of the body, explored with a detail that made the show a beauty pageant of the body in decline, with a staggering number of scenes set in hospital rooms, retirement homes, and funeral parlors. Here even gangsters were subject to the most ordinary of physical sufferings and humiliations, and even a mob boss had to worry about his health coverage.

There was always a great deal of plot, and later seasons sometimes moved unavoidably in the direction of soap opera or cliffhanger, but plot was never the governing principle. (Some *Sopranos* fans created a high-speed seven-minute reduction of the show, posted on YouTube, that brilliantly worked in almost every major plot point only to make clear how little the plot finally counted for.) The show was a collage of situations, a mapping of unstable connections. Christopher assassinating a Czech garbage contractor was no more or less important than Carmela eating popcorn while watching *Field of Dreams* with her almost too affable parish priest Father Phil, or Livia listening in barely contained hostility as a nursing home director extolled the benefits of a lecture on the novels of Zora Neale Hurston. A single episode could juxtapose a certain number of disparate elements, and the high pleasure was in the jarring elegance of the juxtaposition.

We were left always on the brink of a resolution—whether of plot, or character analysis, or ultimate significance—that never quite arrived. Instead there were ellipses and asymmetries. A show that in some ways spelled out everything, in language more eloquently obscene than television had permitted, hinged finally on the pauses in between. The effect was above all musical, and each episode was capped with a piece of music—or a chunk of expressive silence—not so much to sum up the proceedings as to provide another ambiguous gloss. Chase pursued, in each episode, the pleasure of a different sort of ending, that of hanging unresolved in a state of rapt frustration, enjoying the patterns as they warily stopped short of coalescing: a paradise of disequilibrium.

3.

CHASE'S NEATEST TRICK was to make a show about the mob—a show that laid out in gratifying detail the workings of scams and hits, political connections and techniques of intimidation, internecine maneuverings and FBI infiltrations—that constantly suggested that the mob was not what the show was really about. By assimilating the mob into everyday life he dissolved it. Tony Soprano was the gangster who lived on the other side of the fence and sat at the next table in the restaurant, mingling in a world quite sufficiently corrupt without him. He was not, in old movie style, the outsider casting a sinister shadow over the American family; he was himself the prime representative of that family. He had grown up on sitcoms and 1970s rock, and there were moments when Tony and Paulie in the back room of Satriale's metamorphosed into Ralph Kramden and Ed Norton at the Raccoon Lodge on *The Honeymooners*, or when Tony, launching one of his racist zingers, seemed a stand-in for Archie Bunker of *All in the Family*.

Tony was a domesticated end point for the romance of gangsterism that looks to be America's most durable contribution to world folklore. It was a romance fed by movies, not just the early classics with Cagney, Robinson, and Muni, but the harsher and less poetic later movies— *The Enforcer* (1951), *The Brothers Rico* (1957), *Johnny Cool* (1963)—in which gangsterism was no longer a violent aberration but the deadly norm, administered by unpitying accountants flanked by expressionless hit men in dark glasses. (Cagney's Public Enemy, a Tony Soprano favorite, looked like a Miltonic rebel angel by comparison.) The cycle culminated in Coppola's *Godfather* films and Scorsese's *Goodfellas*, crucial reference points for *The Sopranos*.

Anyone growing up in postwar America, in the years between the Kefauver hearings of 1951 and the RICO-driven Federal indictments of the mid-1980s, accepted the Mafia as a pervasive if largely invisible presence. You could not penetrate very deeply into American life, certainly not in cities like New York or Chicago, or along a road like the New Jersey Turnpike, without bumping against its edges, if only as rumor or apprehensive surmise. Every now and then, bloody confirmation was provided by a tabloid front page, of Albert Anastasia shot dead in the barbershop of the Park Sheraton in 1957 or Crazy Joey Gallo blown away at Umberto's Clam House in 1972. The ruthlessness and sadism of mobsters (not necessarily Italian but in this era usually assumed to be) provided stories for little boys to frighten other little boys with, and for those frightened boys to convert, perhaps, into secret fantasies of usurpation and revenge.

*The Sopranos* would play on our desire for access to forbidden knowledge, and offer a tour more exhaustive than any movie could offer not only of the secret lives of gangsters, but of their inner lives—if, that is, gangsters turned out to have inner lives. Tony Soprano would be seen from all angles—more thoroughly under surveillance than any federal agent could hope for—as husband, father, brother, lover, employer, analysand. We would see him fumbling for an adequate answer when his teenage daughter asks him if he's in the Mafia, or coping with feelings of depression and inadequacy. Brought thoroughly into his worldview, we would perceive the straight people on the fringes (like Tony's next-door neighbor Dr. Cusamano and his golf buddies, gawking like fans at the gangster in their midst) as the truly alien presences.

Women would humanize him: this faint promise hovered over the early episodes. The domesticated gangster inhabited a world in which, for once, women had equal dramatic weight. It was with his wife, his daughter, his sister, his mother, his analyst, that Tony engaged in his deepest struggles. Two of them—his mother Livia and his odious sister Janice—were at heart killers like himself. His curse was to have been the whelp of Lady Macbeth, with a sister who did nothing to soften that legacy. But wife and daughter and analyst variously held out the possibility of a transformed life, a new way of being. This was revolution: gangster movies consigned women to the roles of trophies, trading chips, or victims, and not uncommonly all three at once (if they were not mothers, characteristically unassimilated to American ways and given to bouts of regretful weeping). The force of these Soprano women made iridescent the masculine monochrome of the gangster genre; surely we must be in the realm of sitcom, or soap opera, or a romantic miniseries like *The Thorn Birds* (although Father Phil made a comically weak substitute for Richard Chamberlain's conflicted priest).

Edie Falco's Carmela, outwardly uncowed, carried the weight of that not quite fulfilled possibility. To be equal to Tony (who, notably, exempted her, along with his daughter, from the violence he was in all other cases prompt to dish out) meant matching him in will and deviousness, on a manifestly unlevel playing field. Edie Falco made Carmela the show's greatest character, as with each line she tested resistances, looking for unsuspected leeway within the well-appointed prison of her domestic life. She would deny that, of course, and she would deny everything, knowing perfectly well what Tony's life was about—yet she could make us believe that it was freedom she was looking for. The great liberating energy of the early seasons was Carmela's oblique and evasive progress toward her potential life, the real self for which all this carefully costumed and made-up performance was a dress rehearsal. If Tony's numerous sexual affairs were always pointedly devoid of interest—since nothing affected him—Carmela's handful of close brushes with desire, exquisitely frustrated, threatened a transformation that would truly devastate this world.

But she was finally the most disappointing character, since in the end she could not win out. Even when, after four seasons, she threw Tony out of the house—because of the girlfriends rather than any of the other misdeeds with whose details she let herself remain happily unacquainted—there seemed nowhere for her to go, aside from a brief affair with an academic administrator who gave her *Madame Bovary* to read before finding her aggressiveness a bit too much after her husband's style. She could have found freedom only by leaving the series altogether; instead, after a decent interval, she accepted Tony's embrace and resigned herself to the resumption of domestic life, a defeated woman. Freedom, in this second phase, meant asserting the intellectual independence to watch a rerun of a Dick Cavett interview with Katharine Hepburn on Turner Classic Movies. Until the end I nurtured the faint notion that Carmela might finally blow Tony's brains out, enraged perhaps to find that out of all the crimes she had closed her eyes to there was one at least that was truly beyond forgiveness—the dreadful execution of the reluctant snitch Adriana, the show's most sympathetic character. But Carmela did not have the stuff of an avenging angel.

It was in those later seasons that the show seemed to become an anguished circling around masculinity itself, as if being a gangster were merely a metaphor for the insoluble dilemma of being male. In describing the separate spheres of men and women, *The Sopranos* had charted an apportionment of male and female roles and powers that was at root almost Islamist in its rigor. Early on we had been shown, for example, how the shamefulness in the mob ethos of a man simply rumored to have a flair for cunnilingus could lead to violence and death.

This was but prelude. By the time we endured, in season six, the long and painful saga of the outing of mob henchman Vito Spatafore, his flight to New England where he attempted to remake his life with a small-town fireman, and his inevitable murder, carried out with a sadism commensurate with the horror "this whole gay thing" provoked in his mob colleagues, the show seemed almost to have exorcised the forceful female presences that once distinguished it. We were to be left with men battering men over the question of who was a man. Faithful to the forces it had set in motion, *The Sopranos* acknowledged that not even in this artificial world could there be any magical exemptions. The triumph of women, capable of turning gangster tragedy into domestic comedy, and representing the miraculous overcoming of ignorant force, had been the engine of the show's stubbornly joyful undertone. Now all that was to be undone, so that we were left in the end with wreckage.

Humor by now was mostly gallows humor. The show had always been some kind of comedy. But that *The Sopranos* was reliably the funniest show on television never alleviated the unease that suffused its most casual transactions. Paulie, the ultimate hard case, was always scary and always funny, with his store of solemn platitudes, dubious health tips, and unexpected flights of theological speculation. (He figured that his multiple sins of murder and mayhem had earned him no more than six thousand years in Purgatory, Purgatory years being in any case very different from ours: "I could do that standing on my head . . . That's like a couple of days here.") The scowling big-haired *consigliere* Silvio Dante (Steve Van Zandt) won us over with his imitation of Al Pacino in *The Godfather Part III* before morphing into the unpitying executioner of Adriana. As if we were marks softened up by easy loans and unsolicited favors from the mob, irresistible wisecracks had greased our passage into one excruciating impasse after another, in a place more closely resembling Hell than Purgatory. Nothing like redemption appeared to be going on there.

4.

BY THE TIME the end approached, the first episodes already belonged to a different era. The songs the Soprano kids listened to were material for oldies stations, and the tea room at the Plaza, where Carmela and Meadow shared their traditional mother-and-daughter luncheon, had slipped into oblivion. We had watched the children grow up, and in the face of James Gandolfini, after nearly a decade under mercilessly intimate surveillance, could observe changes as deep-set and unforgiving as those in the face of a two-term president. *The Sopranos* provided an alternate reality for an era in which such a refuge was much to be prized. The collective brutalities of Tony's crime family and its rivals could hardly compete with what was going on outside. (Tony Soprano's own FBI nemesis was eventually transferred to monitoring al-Qaeda.)

It was disturbing to realize how much we did care about these people. Each of the final episodes was anticipated not so much with pleasure as dread, since each posed the risk of an unacceptable loss, as characters in whom we had invested years of attention were swept away. None of the characters in *The Sopranos* precisely resembled Little Nell, of course. That it was possible to feel so much on behalf of characters often devoid of the least capacity for empathy was a typical *Sopranos* paradox. As if to emphasize that point, the last episodes went out of their way to cast Tony and the rest in an ever more remote and unsympathetic light. The endgame obliged us to be stripped of any remaining illusions. Perhaps, to ease the pain of our disengagement, Chase felt we should be reminded that we had permitted ourselves to love monsters.

With a murder—of his drug-addled protégé Christopher—that erased years of apparent affection, Tony Soprano did his best to dispel any notion that he was capable of sustained moral self-examination, or indeed capable of grasping that the expression of feeling could be anything more than a form of expert mimicry. As for Carmela, she made clear at last her inability to acknowledge the bloodstained realities sustaining her life. The children seemed likewise to surrender listlessly to their fates. The once energetic Columbia graduate Meadow drifted from pre-med toward marriage with another gangster's son—and it already seemed that her burgeoning career in criminal justice could be corrupted by family ties. The perennially troubled A.J. sank deeper into suicidal depression, even if he managed to miscalculate the length of rope necessary to anchor him to the bottom of the family swimming pool. The whole family seemed increasingly like the ghosts of people who hadn't quite died, lingering around the kitchenette that gave them the fitful and uncertain sense of still belonging to the world. After years of reveling in the uncannily lifelike counter-reality of *The Sopranos*, we found ourselves washed up at last in a domain of zombies. The despondent A.J. stared blankly at a television screen—"Whatcha watchin'?" "Nothing."—while the doomed Christopher, unaware he had only moments to live, randomly switched stations on his car radio before settling for the soundtrack of—what else?—*The Departed*.

Once, a long time ago, when psychotherapy still held out redemptive promise, Dr. Melfi had given Tony life-enhancing advice quoted from Carlos Castaneda: "Live every moment as if it were your last dance on earth." Now she was curtly sending him on his way as an untreatable sociopath, convinced finally that "they sharpen their skills as con men on their therapists." Psychoanalysis had provided a theatrical platform for Tony to soliloquize, but now the show kicked away its defining framing device. What began as the story of a potential healing became the description of the last stages of an incurable sickness. The images themselves darkened, as if the sun were removing itself permanently from northern New Jersey. The appropriately apocalyptic literary reference point was Yeats's "The Second Coming"—even if A.J.'s absorption in it led Carmela to protest, in a desperate attempt to restore an equilibrium: "What kind of poem is that to teach college students?"

No imaginable end—Tony killed, dead by mischance, in prison, or in the witness protection program—seemed a satisfying prospect. In the last episode, tantalizingly, event followed event with the promise of freshly evolving situations, just as if the conclusion were not in sight. Perhaps the show would not end at all. In a sense it didn't. To the dismay of many viewers, a black screen—at the moment when Tony may or may not have been fatally shot by a hit man who may or may not have been there, as a jukebox song stopped on the phrase "don't stop"—froze all further narrative development. Or perhaps this was a way of conveying that the show had already ended, perhaps a long time before. After all, was there any kind of ending that we had not already seen? In a sense it had all been nothing but a procession of endings. We could hardly complain that there hadn't been enough of them.

*The New York Review of Books*, 2007

# between heaven and hell

AKIRA KUROSAWA'S PROPENSITY FOR ADAPTING European classics—Dostoyevsky (*The Idiot*), Shakespeare (*Throne of Blood*), Gorky (*The Lower Depths*)—earned him a label, both abroad and at home, as the most "Western" of Japanese directors, even though he never saw himself as other than purely Japanese. Indeed, what could be more Japanese, for a man of Kurosawa's epoch and social class, than to have been brought up on Shakespeare, Balzac, and Dostoyevsky, on Beethoven and Schubert? He was born in 1910, when the Meiji era's enthusiasm for foreign culture had not yet been overwhelmed by rising nationalist tides, the son of a former army officer and school administrator of distinguished samurai descent. It would be more accurate to say that for the young Kurosawa such models had already been so thoroughly assimilated as to form part of his native culture, and far from being exotic transplantations, *Throne of Blood* and *The Lower Depths* are richly detailed explorations of the periods and milieus of Japanese history in which Kurosawa sets them.

His 1963 film *High and Low* represents quite a different project: a contemporary rather than a period film, the adaptation not of a European classic but of an American thriller, Ed McBain's *King's Ransom* (1959), in the era before such thrillers enjoyed much cultural prestige. It is the only time Kurosawa ever worked explicitly with material of American origin (although *Yojimbo* bore a large debt to Dashiell Hammett, then only slightly more prestigious), and he used it not to illuminate a vanished epoch but to produce a map of the Japan of that moment that stretches from the complacent and affluent "heaven" to the needy and nihilistic "hell" of the film's Japanese title, with an efficient police force patrolling the problematic zone where high and low collide.

Kurosawa had treated modern themes before, to be sure. But *High and Low* is more detached in its effect: less romantic in its attitude toward criminality than *Drunken Angel* (1948), less heartrending than *Ikiru* (1952), less savage (though no less contemptuous) than *The Bad Sleep Well* (1960). The tormented young policeman played by Toshiro Mifune in *Stray Dog* (1949) has grown up, perhaps, to be the coolly restrained detective embodied by Tatsuya Nakadai, seeing everything but keeping his judgments to himself until he really can't take it anymore.

To underscore the film's American provenance, Kurosawa gives us early on—in a close-up that intrudes with considerable shock effect into the deep widescreen vistas of the opening interior shots—the unleashed energy of a Japanese boy in a cowboy hat brandishing a toy six-shooter, the pure product of early 1960s imported TV culture. Likewise the central scene at police headquarters, in which the reports of each team are interspersed with visual clips of their investigations, conjures up the American documentary-style police procedurals of the postwar period, such as *The Naked City* or *T-Men*. The modern world in which *High and Low* takes place is unavoidably in some ways an American world—or perhaps the post-American world of a Japan still emerging from years of occupation and accustoming itself to a new era of unbridled economic development bringing with it new kinds of social dislocation.

The choice of material might seem curious. *King's Ransom*, although like most of McBain's books a good swift read, is not even one of the better novels of his "87th Precinct" series, lacking notably the raucous humor and offbeat characterizations that he usually brought to his police station scenes. (McBain, born Salvatore Lombino, was also, as Evan Hunter, the author of *The Blackboard Jungle* and of the screenplay for *The Birds*.) Kurosawa in fact kept little of the novel beyond its gripping premise—a businessman's son is targeted by kidnappers, but they mistakenly abduct his chauffeur's son instead—and claimed to have been impressed chiefly by the audacity of the kidnappers' demand that the businessman nonetheless pay the ransom, a sum that will wipe him out. In *King's Ransom* the driven and arrogant shoe company executive Douglas King refuses to pay the ransom and lucks out anyway, saving both fortune and moral reputation; in *High and Low*, after initial resistance, Kurosawa's protagonist Kingo Gondo (incarnated by Toshiro Mifune in a mode of fury just barely contained) accepts the moral imperative to save the boy and is, although not altogether destroyed, brought considerably down in the world.

From McBain's tight little paperback thriller, Kurosawa fashioned one of his most expansive and symphonic works, a film that immerses itself in the minutiae of the modern metropolis—pay phones, streetcars, garbage disposal centers—while often approaching pure visual abstraction. A single shot in which undercover cops glance at a crooked mirror to watch their suspect ascending a staircase would not be out of place in *The Cabinet of Dr. Caligari*, yet in the context of *High and Low*'s visual design it is not even obtrusive. Kurosawa—whose first training was as an artist—once remarked that at least from *Seven Samurai* on, he "tried to add my sensitivity as a painter to what I hoped was my increasing knowhow as a filmmaker." The exceptional visual density of *High and Low* involves a double perception: every frame can be apprehended in terms of both the weightless, two-dimensional surface of a delicately composed painting and the three-dimensional arena in which heavy bodies move and contend with reckless energy. (When Mifune's Gondo notes, near the beginning, that "shoes carry all your body weight," it only emphasizes the precise sense we always have in Kurosawa of the force displaced in each footfall.)

The director revels in the geometric play permitted by the widescreen ratio. We are positively invited to appreciate his constantly changing designs, as when Gondo opens curtains and a sliding glass door in abrupt horizontal movements analogous to the curiously old-fashioned wipes that were always Kurosawa's signature form of narrative transition. The binding agent is the editing with which Kurosawa, working often with footage captured from multiple angles simultaneously, freely cuts in and out of different spatial planes. There is no more conscious exercise in virtuosity in Kurosawa's oeuvre. The bullet train sequence, in which Gondo throws briefcases filled with ransom money through a bathroom window on the moving train while a police detective frantically films what ensues, runs less than five minutes and is rich enough in visual and rhythmic intricacies for a whole film.

But the bravado technical flourishes are not a matter of gratuitous showing off. The controlled harnessing of energies that might otherwise spin out of control, the pulling together of the disparate material elements he's working with, embody Kurosawa's sense of morally purposeful action. The train sequence is immediately preceded by a scene in which the beleaguered Gondo, reminded of his origins as an ordinary shoemaker, takes out his old tool kit to assist the police in booby-trapping the briefcases with tracking devices, a gesture at once of humility and mastery. *High and Low* takes inventory of the capacities of the director's own tool kit with such concentrated intensity that every moment is in some sense climactic. We move in rapid cuts from one indelible visual formulation to another, each held barely long enough to take in before another replaces it.

THE MOVEMENTS OF Kurosawa's symphony correspond to different locations: Gondo's lavish apartment with its commanding view of Yokohama, the narrow aisles of the bullet train, the sweltering police precinct, the lower depths where Gondo's mansion becomes a reflection in garbage-filled water, and finally the prison where Gondo finally confronts his nemesis. Within these locations (each of which has its own distinct mood and narrative focus) there are openings to further spaces: the inner lining of a shoe exposed to demonstrate its shoddiness; the picture of Mount Fuji over the sea drawn by the kidnapped child (which will rhyme eventually with the actual Fuji half-visible through mist); the 8 mm movie of the retrieval of the ransom; the marks left on a writing pad by a drug addict's frantic message; the illustrative fragments of urban geography interpolated in the precinct sequence; the murky hidden worlds of bars, drug-ridden alleyways, and cheap hotels; and finally—the point of no return—the glass barrier in which criminal and victim each finds the other's face reflected.

The definition of space is not only the method but the subject of *High and Low*. Everything pivots around the spatial relationship between Gondo and the kidnapper: Gondo in his mansion on the hill, the kidnapper looking up from below in his airless shack. Its first third confines itself—in a way that seemed audacious to audiences expecting, perhaps, more of the open-air action of *The Hidden Fortress* or *Yojimbo*—chiefly to the limits of Gondo's luxurious, modern, and, especially by Japanese standards, dazzlingly large living room. As the film begins we are plunged into the final stages of a business meeting abruptly going sour, as the small-minded and rapacious executives of National Shoes fail to bring their colleague Gondo into line with their bid to cheapen the product line and take over the company. A mood of claustrophobia and hostility is established instantly as Gondo brandishes the cheap "new line" shoe sample like a sword and then proceeds to tear it apart with methodical rage. The scene at once invokes and parodies the string of samurai roles that Mifune had just played for Kurosawa.

Mifune's whole performance is imbued with similar gestural allusions. Pacing back and forth in the throes of the business deal by which he plans to effect his own coup d'état at National Shoes, Gondo wields a drink and a telephone as if they were ritual objects bestowing occult power; and later in the film, when he asks the police to remain in the room during a business conference, it's with the barely perceptible imperiousness of an overlord used to being obeyed. (In McBain's novel, the police detest Douglas King and firmly put him in his place; in *High and Low*, Tatsuya Nakadai's Inspector Tokuro and his colleagues come to admire Gondo and serve his interests with devotion.) This subtext explodes into a stunning tableau when the chauffeur Aoki, begging the reluctant Gondo to pay the ransom for his son, finally prostrates himself as if at the feet of a feudal *daimyo*. As Aoki kneels at center screen, Gondo stands at the extreme right, looking downward and away as if under unbearable pressure, while Inspector Tokuro, seated at the other side of the screen and struggling to restrain his discomfort, looks leftward. The scene also occurs in *King's Ransom*—"'Do you want me to get down on my knees, Mr. King? Shall I get on my knees and beg you?' He dropped to his knees, and [police detective] Carella winced and turned away."—but with nothing like the layers of emotional complication that Kurosawa is able to build into a single serene composition.

From samurai to shoe manufacturer: Gondo retains the combative instincts and self-conscious pride of an earlier era while struggling to reconcile himself to life as a company man. Much like Kurosawa (who had left Toho to form his own production company in 1960) fending off the perceived cheapening of Japanese cinema, Gondo touts the virtues of his own individualistic path: "I'll make my own shoes—durable yet stylish—expensive to make, perhaps, but profitable in the long run." With his apparently traditional and compliant wife Reiko (Kyoko Kagawa) at his side, Gondo seems poised to oversee a paean to craft-minded entrepreneurship along the lines of Robert Wise's *Executive Suite*. But with the kidnapper's phone call we are quickly knocked out of that movie—the first of many sudden shifts of focal point.

*High and Low* in a sense is a film with no center, or a film whose center is everywhere: it is concerned with mapping all the human contacts, no matter how tiny or apparently insignificant, that fall within its scope. Gondo may be the samurai hero of his own drama, but in the course of the film he will be seen from many angles, and often he will disappear from view altogether. He has his grand plan to seize control of National Shoes, just as the kidnapper has his grand plan to commit a perfect crime and exact a sky-high ransom. The film's own grand plan is to keep turning the plot around to look at it from other angles, through different eyes.

The real hero might be neither Gondo nor Inspector Tokura but the bald, blunt, bull-like Detective Taguchi, a working-class hero of the oldest school who can barely hold back his contempt for the weaselish executives of National Shoes when they hang Gondo out to dry; or perhaps the chauffeur Aoki, who suffers not only the loss of his child but the intolerable burden of having him restored at his employer's expense, placing him in the position of having received a gift he can never repay and that has destroyed the giver; or perhaps, most appropriately, the kidnapped child Shinichi, who keeps cool enough to record precise impressions of his surroundings and of his kidnapper, and who interrupts the unobservant adults to call their attention to the film's most unexpected visual effect: the pink smoke signaling that the kidnapper is burning the booby-trapped briefcases in which he collected the ransom.

We may even want to bring to the center for a moment the discreet, sometimes almost invisible presence of Gondo's wife Reiko. It is she, after all, who tells him from the outset that "success isn't worth losing your humanity," and whose understated moral suasion directs his ultimate course of action. (Aside from two heroin addicts who both turn up dead, she is the only significant female character in the drama: not surprising, perhaps, from a director who once told Donald Richie that "women simply aren't my specialty.")

THE PINK SMOKE—the only burst of color in a black-and-white film—marks the moment when *High and Low* definitively descends from heaven to hell, the point of entry being a dump that burns "everything that can't be disinfected." This is the juncture when those above finally take notice of the life below them, even if only in the form of burnt evidence. Those below, on the other hand, could always see what was above them. "From down there," as the inspector notes on his arrival in Gondo's apartment, "if he's got a telescope, the kidnapper can see this entire room." The kidnapper, then, has possessed from the beginning the same power as Kurosawa's camera: to command space and find every hiding place within Gondo's seemingly impregnable eyrie. To hide from those eyes even the police are forced to crawl on the floor.

The kidnapper, a medical intern named Ginji Takeuchi (Tsutomu Yamazaki) wears dark glasses, the badge of the lurker who sees without being seen. He does not speak until the last scene of the movie—even then refusing to divulge his story or his real motives. The police hunt for Takeuchi tells us little about him but much about Kurosawa's vision of the nether regions of modern Japan. The luridness of that vision—a confusion of noisy bars with multiracial clienteles and dark side streets swarming with drug addicts who resemble the incarcerated lepers of Fritz Lang's fantasia *The Indian Tomb*—is now, as it was on first release, the least persuasive aspect of *High and Low*. The imagined horrors of that murky inferno simply cannot compete with the clearly delineated nastiness of the National Shoes executive team, for all the expressive beauties of the camerawork that Kurosawa brings to bear.

But the structural force of his conception holds firm right through to that stunning (and much analyzed) confrontation between Gondo and Takeuchi as the latter awaits execution. Nothing is more powerful about this scene than its refusal to provide any disclosure that would explain what we have just been through. What the kidnapper offers finally is not an explanation but a scream of pain. As the guards whisk him out of sight and a dark barrier descends in front of Gondo, the effect is like the typical brusque ending of a Nô play, as ghost or demon vanishes and the chorus intones: "And thereupon the spirit faded and was gone."

In place of some clarification of what all this might mean, then, we are left with Gondo alone facing a blank barrier. He has finally succeeded in being fully alone in a society in which lives impinge relentlessly one on another, and has thereby achieved the solitariness that was the kidnapper's whole identity. Takeuchi is a demon of isolation, defiantly cut loose from those indispensable ties of human contact that are measured throughout every frame of *High and Low* by a constant play of glances and postures. Hierarchies and group identities, and the impulses that can undermine them from within, are charted so clearly that we can draw the invisible lines connecting any character with any other character. From moment to moment they cannot help but show us where they are. The space to which Kurosawa devotes such consummate skill is a space defined by human relations and is thus necessarily a space of constant turmoil, pressure, and struggle, right up to the moment when the barrier slams shut.

The Criterion Collection, 2008

# redoubled obsessions

IN 1929 A FIFTY-YEAR-OLD CONGREGATIONALIST pastor named Lloyd C. Douglas published his first novel. It was a ramshackle sort of book, at its core an undiluted Christian sermon on the life-transforming power of charitable works. But it was a sermon wrapped in the format of a romance novel and spruced up with a veneer of up-to-the-minute pseudoscientific parlance that made Christianity sound like the latest marvel sprung from the imagination of H.G. Wells. (The New Testament was described as "the actual textbook of a science relating to the expansion and development of the human personality.") *Magnificent Obsession* was a mélange of half-baked and drastically under-dramatized subplots, but it began and ended memorably. In the first chapter a feckless young playboy got knocked in the head in a sailing accident and was saved by the use of an inhalator, while unbeknownst to him a great brain surgeon died for want of the same inhalator. In very nearly the last chapter, the same young man, having in the meantime himself become a great brain surgeon in order to atone for the earlier event, employed his skills to save the life and sight of the woman he loves, none other than the young widow of the doctor who died in his place.

However rudimentary Douglas's narrative technique, his book became and remained a bestseller. (It has rarely if ever been out of print.) His condemnation of Jazz Age frivolity arrived in perfect time for the onset of the Great Depression, and his modernized version of the message of the Gospels managed to impart the key to spiritual power—it was a matter of performing service for others while making sure that the service remained a closely held secret—and still wrap up with a satisfying fade-out kiss.

Little wonder that Universal snapped up the movie rights. When John M. Stahl's film was released in 1935, however, Douglas was none too happy with the results. Although the team of screenwriters had retained the beginning and ending, little of what came between had made it to the screen. The writers had done an excellent job of extracting the usable plot points while jettisoning most of the homilies. The great brain surgeon's philosophy of acquiring spiritual power by doing good for others in secret was still there, to be sure, but it had been essentially reduced to a single expository scene, in which young Bobby Merrick (Robert Taylor) was initiated by an avuncular artist, played rather charmingly by Ralph Morgan. To fill the rest of the running time, the writers had fabricated an emotionally wrenching series of narrative twists and turns.

It was from Stahl's movie rather than the novel that Douglas Sirk inherited most of the elements that gave his 1954 remake its aura of excessiveness. This film was a major turning point in Sirk's career: its success sealed his identification with glossy material and led directly to the string of late masterpieces that includes *All That Heaven Allows*, *Written on the Wind*, and *Imitation of Life*, and that would influence so decisively filmmakers from Fassbinder to Todd Haynes. Of all his films, *Magnificent Obsession* stands out for its uniquely over-the-top plotline, and that very outrageousness seems to have prompted a corresponding vigor in Sirk's direction. Instead of toning down the story's emotional extremes, he accepts them and allows their full and somewhat demented force to emerge.

In 1935, it all seemed normal: this was what used to be called "giving it the Hollywood treatment." It wasn't enough for Bobby to be saved at the expense of Doctor Hudson's life; he must also be indirectly responsible for the accident that leaves the doctor's young wife Helen (Irene Dunne) blinded. The whole incomparably weepy second movement— in which Bobby befriends Helen under a false identity, secretly pays for her to be treated by the greatest brain surgeons in Europe, and rescues her from suicidal despair, only to have her run away because she doesn't want his pity—is a pure Hollywood concoction, the culmination and quintessence of early thirties melodrama. The religious elements became mere flavoring for a transcendently morbid love story, and in the process the movie came near to equating Christ's sacrifice for all humanity with Robert Taylor's sacrifice for Irene Dunne.

In some respects, the 1935 version would have looked quite creaky by the early 1950s, not just for the grandiloquence of the weepy bits but for the heavy-handed comic touches with which it was thought necessary to lard the proceedings, from Charles Butterworth's tedious mugging as Betty Furness's dimwitted beau to Arthur Treacher's predictable turn as a silly-ass valet. Sirk would achieve a far more restrained and unified tone, but Stahl's direction did undercut the script's shenanigans with an impressively somber visual design. Seen today, his *Magnificent Obsession* looks like an art deco symphony in which figures standing in a middle distance are framed in cathedral-like fashion by expressive swatches of black, gray, and white.

The central set piece, when Dunne comes near to throwing herself off the balcony of her hotel in despair, only to be retrieved by Taylor's unexpected entrance (we see him first as a reflection in a mirror), is a thing of beauty—equalled but not surpassed by Douglas Sirk's more complex staging of the same episode in his 1954 remake. The final hospital scenes, with their dominant whites and their starkly invoked sign of the cross, achieve an almost overwhelming solemnity of tone, especially in the prolonged horizontal composition of Taylor leaning over Dunne on her hospital bed, an embrace just barely withheld, hovering on the border between life and death. Such were the secret rituals enacted by thirties movie melodramas, no less serious in their purposes for being reliant on such transparently absurd mechanisms.

ACCORDING TO SIRK, *Magnificent Obsession* got remade primarily because Jane Wyman wanted to play the Irene Dunne part. She had the right idea: more subdued and vulnerable than Dunne—who had been unable to entirely suppress her screwball-comedy instincts and managed to seem fairly chipper even when miming blindness—Wyman brought a hint of plausible feeling to a tale that at nearly every point strained credulity. Sirk had no particular stake in the material; he had never seen the Stahl movie, and of the novel he said: "Ross Hunter gave me the book and I tried to read it, but I just couldn't. It is the most confused book you can imagine, it is so abstract in many respects that I couldn't see a picture in it." He worked from an outline of the Stahl version, many scenes of which were faithfully preserved even as the comic dross was weeded out. In the end he spoke with considerable affection of *Magnificent Obsession*'s "combination of kitsch and craziness and trashiness." The movie was in fact one of the great successes of his career, and it firmly established Rock Hudson as the resident dreamboat of the American cinema, just as the earlier version had established Robert Taylor. The ease and sincerity of Hudson's performance help greatly in anchoring the proceedings in some kind of almost-real world.

Sirk was fifty-three when he made the film. He had already had an extraordinary career, but of a kind largely forgotten or unperceived. In the 1920s and 1930s, he had been an important figure in the German theater, working notably with Kurt Weill and Georg Kaiser on their musical drama *The Silver Lake*. (Ultimately, he would go back to stage work after returning to Europe in the 1960s.) He had made nine features with UFA between 1935 and 1937, then got out of Germany and did some work in France and Holland before accepting an invitation to Hollywood in 1939. His early American films—*Summer Storm* (1944), *A Scandal in Paris* (1946), *Lured* (1947)—were notable for their quite literary and European tone, but by 1950 he was a contract director at Universal, working (sometimes dazzlingly, always intelligently) on the full range of available genres: war films, thrillers, farces, musicals, even a Western, the much-underrated *Taza, Son of Cochise* (1954). The best of his first ten films for Universal was *All I Desire* (1953), a black-and-white Barbara Stanwyck vehicle solidly in the "woman's picture" mode, a genre that had dominated the 1940s but was now slipping out of fashion.

With *Magnificent Obsession*, Sirk returned to this genre, but this time with a visual style that was pure fifties: bright, wide, and jammed with the latest in furnishings and consumer goods. He had found the terrain on which he would work for the rest of the decade. Perhaps 1954 was the last time this material could have been filmed with a straight face, and Sirk films it with a ferociously straight face, one might say a demonically straight face. A contemporary audience might receive the picture with peals of knowing laughter as one staggeringly fraught melodramatic moment follows another—I can remember my own jaw dropping in disbelief the first time I saw it—but what is most striking on repeated viewings of *Magnificent Obsession* is the way Sirk keeps strict faith with his materials. He does not distort them—he merely adds layers of nuance and implicit commentary that are perceptible in every composition, every gesture, every intricately swiveling camera movement, every delicately calibrated shift in lighting. (Sirk: "The angles are the director's thoughts. The lighting is his philosophy.")

He puts the story under a microscope where we can study it like Rock Hudson's Bobby Merrick studying the anatomy of the brain, each ridge and lesion made sharply visible. Nothing could be further from the mood of *Magnificent Obsession* than cynical mockery, no matter how acutely conscious the director is that "this is a damned crazy story if there ever was one." Crazy it may be, but so were the situations favored by so many of the playwrights whose work Sirk had staged: Calderón, Kleist, Strindberg, Pirandello. He forces the questions: What if this weren't crazy? What if it were real? What sort of a world would that be, and how different would it be from the one we inhabit?

Here, as in his other films, Sirk's impulse is to disclose—even if only to demonstrate that nothing is more elusive or uncertain than disclosure. But we are given every chance to see: the world is laid open in all its materiality, in color and widescreen if possible, and we are given perfect vantage points from which to appreciate its forms and the behavior of its inhabitants. He even forces our gaze at moments when we might be inclined to look away, brings us in by dint of those melodramatic mechanisms whose workings he grasps so intimately.

The exposition is handled with breathtaking speed—we start in the midst of a widescreen speedboat ride, with Hudson and a female companion heading straight into the camera in full close-up, and the pace scarcely slackens. The tight shot of the companion screaming from the shore as she watches Hudson's boat capsizing is worthy of a horror movie, injecting a note of panic borne out by the catastrophes still in store. Within moments Helen Phillips (Jane Wyman) and her stepdaughter (Barbara Rush) are pulling into the driveway of their spacious lakeside residence, gaily planning the evening's festivities in what looks like a dramatization of an advertising spread from *Life*, but the movie has been moving so breathlessly that we already know about the disastrous news that awaits them. Every forward movement lurches into some further layer of shock or confusion or despair. There is a shot of Wyman, who has just learned of her husband's sudden death, strolling across the lawn toward the lake, her head down, her back to the camera, that encapsulates in a single image the desperate attempt of grief to somehow escape from itself: nature here, instead of consoling, closes in.

The literal collision, not long after, in which Wyman (fleeing Hudson's clumsy attempt at seduction) loses her sight, is prefigured by countless minor intrusions, retreats, collapses, and movements at cross-purposes. As Hudson—recovering from his accident and still in full-blown arrogant playboy mode—has an angry exchange with a resident doctor, their overlapping dialogue is further crisscrossed by the interruptions of radio and cigarette and telephone. At crucial moments, as hints about the late doctor's mysterious activities begin to emerge, scenes are paced and lit like a suspense film. Without belaboring any point too much, Sirk manages to create an atmosphere of near-intolerable stress just barely kept within the bounds of polite behavior, never more than in the sleekly streamlined barroom where isolated customers are pressed on each other as if brutally contesting every spare inch of widescreen space; we linger in this modern hell for not more than a few seconds but it leaves an indelible mark.

Hudson's drunken encounter with the artist Randolph (Otto Kruger), who indoctrinates him with the late surgeon's secret of spiritual power, are imbued with real mystery, as if some occult transference were taking place before our eyes, an effect encouraged by the somewhat Mephistophelian overtones of Kruger's performance. He is made to seem a messenger between worlds, guiding the otherwise bewildered Hudson along invisible fault lines. The words of his dialogue are of less import than the faintly mocking smile that accompanies them, as if he were a higher intelligence condescending to communicate with earthlings. That he is a painter, living among artworks, makes him an ideal Sirkian psychopomp, especially in a film whose central disaster is the loss of sight.

If the film's first half belongs to Hudson and America—a world of beaches and fast cars and brilliant colors—the second belongs to Jane Wyman and the Alpine Europe to which she goes in search of healing. Here the palette darkens, the compositions become more frankly expressionistic, and the local festivities involve a symbolic witch-burning. Helen's inner crisis after she learns that her condition is inoperable—"I know when I wake up in the morning there won't be any dawn"—becomes the emotional center of the film, the full acknowledgment of a suffering without hope of respite. The taut interplay between Wyman and the camera as she moves haltingly through the darkened hotel room toward the balcony and possible suicide—a suicide averted only by the shock of a falling flowerpot—is like condensed opera.

There will be further episodes, as we move inexorably through the contingencies that have been laid down, all the way through to the inevitable life-or-death operation (in a sanitarium pitched in a most artificial desert), the trembling hands, the miraculous restoration of sight. If, at last, the implausibility of the whole enterprise becomes too glaringly apparent—if the simulacrum of reality begins to appear played out—there is the sense that we have, at least, in whatever condition, gotten to the end and whatever promise it has left us with: and there to send us off is Otto Kruger as the artist Randolph, poised above the operating theater like some supernatural stage manager glancing down—whether benevolently or skeptically—at the theater of the world.

The Criterion Collection, 2008

# a persistent immediacy

ERIC ROHMER, WHO TURNED EIGHTY-EIGHT this year, has indicated that *The Romance of Astrea and Celadon* is likely to be his last film. Adapted from an extravagantly long early-seventeenth-century novel, filmed on the cheap in natural settings with young and mostly untried actors, it is in every aspect a film no one else is likely to have thought of making—even if the same could be said of pretty much all Rohmer's films. Back in the 1960s a French producer rejected the script of *My Night at Maud's* as "filmed theater," but even when—after all those *Moral Tales*, *Comedies and Proverbs* and *Tales of the Four Seasons*—some thought they had Rohmer typed, he continued to surprise them with excursions into regional politics (the operetta-like *L'Arbre, le Maire, et la Médiathèque*), the French Revolution seen from a more or less royalist perspective (*The Lady and the Duke*), and the tragic exactions of political loyalties in the 1930s (*Triple Agent*). This time, to judge by the fair number of pitying or scornful reviews that have cropped up on the Internet and elsewhere, many in the audience seem prepared to dismiss *Astrea and Celadon* as an old man's folly.

In his career as a film critic, as one of the strongest voices on behalf of auteurism at *Cahiers du Cinéma*, Rohmer was many times a defender of other such supposed follies. Of an alleged decline in the work of Jean Renoir, for example, he observed: "The history of art offers us no example of an authentic genius who, at the end of his career, had a period of real decline . . . We are prompted to seek evidence of the desire for simplicity that characterized the final works of a Titian, a Rembrandt, a Beethoven, or, closer to us, a Bonnard, a Matisse, or a Stravinsky." He might well have been preparing his own brief in advance. In *Astrea and Celadon* Rohmer seems almost to savor the opportunity of frustrating contemporary expectations with regard to relevance, acting styles, or filmic rhythm. But there is no doubt that he has made precisely the film he wanted to make, a film steeped, indeed, in the "desire for simplicity" but likewise distilling a lifetime of preoccupations—aesthetic, historical, erotic, religious, and, not least, environmental—into a work as beautiful as any he has made.

The *Astrée* of Honoré d'Urfé, from which Rohmer has carved out his 104-minute film, is a novel of some five thousand pages, published between 1607 and 1627 and unfinished at that: a digressive pastoral romance modeled on a Spanish predecessor of the previous century (Montemayor's *Diana*) which itself harked back to the classical models of Heliodorus, Longus, and other ancient novelists. In a France just emerging from the savagery of the Wars of Religion (in which d'Urfé, a career soldier, did his share of plundering and massacring), the book's influence was pervasive. Here was the portrait of a world governed by civilized amorous codes, dedicated to the pleasures of peace and providing models for the shifting circumstances of love and courtship. If *Astrée* ceased to be widely read, it was only because its basic elements had already become part of the ground of modern French literature. In rediscovering d'Urfé, Rohmer explores the roots of his own art, with its tireless parsing of love and jealousy and fidelity.

But it is not that Rohmer wants to recreate the seventeenth century, any more than d'Urfé wanted to recreate the stylized fifth-century Gaul where his novel takes place. The film, an opening title announces, will show us the ancient Gauls as seventeenth-century readers saw them, but that is a matter of props, costumes, and musical interludes, not to mention the cadences and vocabulary of d'Urfé's courtly language, which Rohmer has modernized only sparingly. What he shows us— what the cinema, in his often repeated view, is always showing us—is the world in the present, at least as much of the world as is still capable of displaying an affinity with the world of d'Urfé's imagination. While the novel was set in the plain of Forez in what is now the department of Loire, the film's foreword clarifies that "unfortunately, we were not able to situate this story in the region where the author set it, the plain of Forez being now disfigured by urbanization, the expansion of road-ways, the shrinking of rivers, and the planting of conifers." The film was actually shot at various locations in the Auvergne. Rohmer's environmental protest had the unexpected effect of prompting a lawsuit (eventually dismissed) against his production company by the Conseil Général de la Loire, for denigration of the region.

The narrative salvaged from d'Urfé's interlacing subplots is quite simple. Astrea dismisses her suitor Celadon when she sees him apparently flirting with another shepherdess, even though she loves him and even though it was she herself who had instructed him to pretend affection for the other: one of numerous scenes in Rohmer in which a character spies on someone but completely fails to under-stand what she sees. When she orders Celadon not to show himself to her again unless she tells him to, he throws himself in the river in despair. (The unadorned panning shot of the roiled waters is perhaps the most epic moment in any Rohmer film.) Washed up on a dis-tant shore, he is rescued by Galatea, the somewhat petulant leader of the nymphs who rule the region from a neighboring chateau. She becomes infatuated with him and holds him prisoner; in the mean-time Astrea comes to realize that she has misjudged him and is guilty of sending him to his death.

The further inevitable complications of the intrigue—whose progres-sion is interrupted by a number of rather extended discussions of the relation of the body to the soul and the hidden Trinitarian significance of Gaulish mythology—are resolved by a game of transvestite disguise in which Celadon is finally reunited with his lover by masquerading as the daughter of a helpful local Druid. (The hero's transvestism seems almost a belated acknowledgment of the extent to which Rohmer in film after film has sought to inhabit a female consciousness.)

As thus whittled down, the story comes to resemble in essence one of Rohmer's own cinematic tales: a story of stubborn adherence to a self-imposed delusion and the consequent multiplying of difficulties, in a perplexity that might seemingly have been resolved in a matter of moments. Astrea inflexibly declares that "I never go back on what I say"; Celadon inflexibly chooses to take her at her word. But whether they are to be seen as admirably or foolishly stubborn is left open.

A CONTEMPORARY AUDIENCE would be likely to accept the mechanisms and trappings of this plot only if it were treated in a spirit of burlesque, but that is just what Rohmer has no interest in doing. He takes the material on its own terms, right up to the moment, at once solemn and sublimely silly, when a band of bearded, white-robed Druids gathers in a circle waving branches of mistletoe. It is hardly that he is blind to the ludicrous aspects of d'Urfé's pastoral fantasy, but that he finds so much else there as well, precisely in the heart of what might seem absurd. The wise old Druids and love-sonnets carved on tree trunks, the cartwheeling libertines and lovesick nymphs are just another language to play with, no more unreal than the imaginary scenarios and willful self-deceptions of his contemporary protagonists.

He has not made the film to comment on *L'Astrée*—to find in it a message relevant to the modern condition, or to update its psychology—but to film it: it is there, in the same way that the actors and the French countryside are there. Just as we find unexpected depths in what the camera seizes on in the expressions of the almost too young and beautiful performers, and are perhaps more moved than we might have anticipated by simple shots of a river or a cloud, the literary text opens up like an excavation—not of buried spaces but of buried time. He is not so much "adapting" the text as permitting it to exist again, and then filming what happens.

Even more than in his earlier literary films—*The Marquise of O–* (1976) and *Perceval le Gallois* (1978), both filmed very much "book in hand," as if he had merely let Heinrich von Kleist or Chrétien de

Troyes call the shots—the cinematic language of *Astrea and Celadon* is spare to the point of seeming to vanish altogether. The movement of his Gauls in their landscape not infrequently calls to mind a kind of B-Western, or a kind of home movie—or, more precisely, one of D.W. Griffith's early Biograph shorts. Rohmer has explicitly acknowledged Griffith's influence on the film, as the "great master" of filming in natural settings, an appropriate influence for a film that is a myth of origins. From first to last the mode is blunt presentation, without embellishment of a work that already carries its decoration with it.

The special effects consist of the scenario itself. Three young women in white robes walk along a riverbank. Celadon wakes in darkness, then pulls aside a curtain and recoils in dazzlement from the sunlight. A shrine to love is constructed out of saplings. A tiny cameo portrait of Astrea fills the screen as it is held in an open palm. The images come to us without fanfare, with no extra ingredient to underline their importance. "I make silent movies," Rohmer remarked once, and the comment has never seemed more apt. His approach should not be confused with austerity or minimalism, or still less, as some seem to have concluded, with the incapacity of an aging director. As in his first films, his shots are simply no more detailed or complicated than they need to be. The initial quarrel between the lovers is filmed in a single shot, taking us from tight close-ups to a distance from which we can observe their estrangement, and then following the now isolated Astrea as she runs after Celadon. The sequence's rigorously conceived abstraction can pass just as easily for a casual, almost accidental unfolding; but it is also a cunningly imagined enfolding, wrapping the whole history of the couple into an unbroken spatial continuum, just as in a later shot he will show them enfolded (like an egg in its shell) in a single blanket, hands intertwined, falling slowly and almost without volition into a kiss.

The actors were chosen as much for their physical appearance— "They had to be young and beautiful"—as for their ability to speak the text the way Rohmer intended, and the naive quality of the performances has met with considerable resistance. While admittedly the roguish mugging of Rodolphe Pauly as the capering and inconstant

Hylas takes some getting used to—he seems placed there to establish an upper limit of theatricality, consonant with the philosophy of fickleness that he espouses—the overall tone established by the actors seems exactly right. They do not portray inexperience so much as embody it. The same scenes played with mature actorly authority would not have brought out what Rohmer was looking for: the primary freshness that is the innermost concern of the pastoral. The traces of awkwardness and inhibition in Stéphanie Crayencour as Astrea and Andy Gillet as Celadon express, more fully than the words, the requisite shifting moods of desire and vulnerability and regret. Clearly Rohmer intended that the text be spoken straightforwardly, preferring a relatively flat delivery to any attempt at period grandiloquence or modern psychologizing. It is as if the actors were simply vehicles to let the story tell itself.

But the actors are, finally, the story. Their youth and their physical beauty are what we are being led to contemplate. It may seem perverse (more, perhaps, for younger than for older viewers) for a director in his late eighties to engage in such an openly erotic homage to the joys and pains of youthful love—even filtered through the ceremonies and masquerades of a late Renaissance author—but it is the physical presence of the actors that gives the story its emotional meaning. A bare recounting of the plot would not amount to more than a footnote on the secret link between Graeco-Roman pastoral and the modern novel, even if such secret links—all the ways in which the past leaks into the present—are important to Rohmer. It is only because people—precisely these people, with precisely these eyes and lips and hair—are acting it out that we can be so moved by its preordained narrative turns.

When the nymph Galatea exclaims "God! How beautiful he is!" as she looks down at the sleeping Celadon, she only confirms what the camera has already proven. When Celadon in turn finds Astrea sleeping in the forest and allows himself to gaze at her exposed legs, we are permitted—or, rather, obliged—to share his gaze, the effect redoubled by a voice-over reciting d'Urfé's description of the scene. The narrative is a labyrinth of ritual encounters culminating in the baring of Astrea's breast, as if the whole point of the travails and complications of the benighted lovers were to finally give full value to that ultimate revelation and the embrace it makes inevitable. The mood in the end is at once of sexual happiness and comic exhilaration, with a punchline worthy of the *Moral Tales* or the *Comedies and Proverbs*. The sadness held in check is all in what is not shown: the passing of youth, the passing even of the rural landscapes in which youth has enacted its passions and pursuits, the disappearance of the worlds that humans create in order to have a world they can bear to live in.

The disparate elements of which *Astrea and Celadon* is made are not fused but rather overlaid, a series of transparencies; we see them all at once, but can easily separate them out. There are the seventeenth century of d'Urfé, whose chateaus and paintings provide décor; the fifth-century pastoral Gaul of nymphs and shepherds imagined by him on models provided by classical antiquity, and here represented by paintings depicting such episodes as the judgment of Paris and Psyche spying on the sleeping Eros; the actual trees and hillsides and rivers and clouds of the Auvergne, not background but the very matter of the movie; the actual young men and women reciting d'Urfé's text; the omnipresent birds ceaselessly reciting their own cheeping and twittering text—and, unseen but underlying everything, the camera that records what is going on in front of it in the first years of the twenty-first century, with a blank simplicity that at moments might allow us to believe that Louis Lumière set up the shot at the dawn of cinema.

It is a movie haunted by time, even as it exults in breeze and sunlight. The dead words of a novel whose full text sits mostly unread in the Bibliothèque Nationale are brought to life out of the mouths of the young. The substance if not the subject of a film can only be the succession of present moments that it does not describe but *is*. If this indeed is to be Rohmer's last film, small wonder that he feels obliged to affirm once more that presence which is distinctly what cinema, in a different way than any other art, is about—or at least what his cinema has always been about. The trees are there, the wind is there, the young are there still young; and the words too, even if they were taken from an ancient and perhaps unreadable book, are there too, brought to life not simply by being spoken but by being filmed as they are being spoken.


THE ODDNESS OF film is that it continually forces us to reconsider what terms like "real" and "artificial" might actually mean. In *A Tale of Winter*, a film that despite its almost documentary tonality is only superficially more "realistic" than *Astrea and Celadon*, Rohmer's hapless heroine Félicie, mourning a love lost (or at least seriously misplaced) through an absurd error, is taken to see a performance of Shakespeare's *The Winter's Tale*. She watches as Leontes, shown the statue of his supposedly dead wife Hermione, cries out "It's her!"—and she dissolves in tears. On the way home her intellectual escort, thinking perhaps that the play was beyond her, apologizes condescendingly for its lack of realism. She murmurs, "I don't like what's realistic" (*Je n'aime pas ce qui est semblable*). The film then proceeds toward its own miraculous conclusion, having summed up in that cry of "It's her!" the whole mystery of what the cinema seems at once to offer and to withhold: life caught hold of, life restored.

For all the words in his films, and for all the words he has himself written about films, his own and others, Rohmer manages always to leave the essential unsaid. In countless utterances he has gestured away from anything that can be easily formulated: "In learning how to understand, the modern moviegoer forgot how to see." "[Cinema] does not say things differently but says different things." "My characters' discourse is not necessarily my film's discourse . . . What I say, I do not say with words." In the same way, and despite the relatively high visibility of his films (the greater part of his work has been made available on DVD or video), Rohmer sometimes seems a director who hides in plain sight, a visionary masquerading as a harmless eccentric.

He seemed to have a formula; it was easy to pigeonhole his films as a series of long discussions of, mostly, the dating problems of bourgeois French people, whether philosophy professors, hairdressers, or engineering students. His plots often revolved around the most trivial of misunderstandings between couples, the sort of devices that might once have shored up a vehicle for Astaire and Rogers, or for that matter Elvis Presley. (Imagine *Boyfriends and Girlfriends* remade with musical numbers as *It Happened in Cergy-Pontoise*.) Even if they weren't condemned as "filmed theater" or "like watching paint dry" (Gene Hackman's quip in Arthur Penn's *Night Moves*), Rohmer's films seemed for many to fall into the realm of more or less cozy pleasures. (Pauline Kael, while occasionally praising his craftsmanship, described his films variously as "glib," "complacent," "innocuous," and "minor.") His tendency to work variations on a theme as he moved through successive film cycles, like his predilection for a drastically restrained film grammar, fostered the notion that his work was in some way predictable—much in the self-deceptive way that his characters found their own lives predictable.

Rohmer was born in 1920—he is the eldest of that extraordinary generation of French filmmakers that encompasses Marker, Resnais, Astruc, Varda, Pialat, Rivette, Godard, Chabrol, Demy, Malle, and Truffaut—but he came to filmmaking late, after earlier careers as a provincial high school teacher, a failed novelist, a film critic (and, for a time, editor of *Cahiers du Cinéma*). At *Cahiers* he reverted continually to the directors who had marked him most profoundly: Griffith, Murnau, Hawks, Renoir, and Rossellini (whose *Stromboli* he described as "my Road to Damascus"). With Claude Chabrol he published a study of Hitchcock, brilliant and endlessly suggestive, notorious in its day for attributing to the director themes that then seemed grandiose, such as *le transfert de culpabilité* (the transference of guilt) and *la tentation de la déchéance* (roughly, temptation by downfall). He was nearly forty when he made his first feature in 1959—the greatly underrated and sadly hard to see *The Sign of the Lion*, a small masterpiece about, precisely, *la tentation de la déchéance*. After its total commercial failure he worked as a writer and director of educational TV programs while proceeding slowly with his six-film project, the *Moral Tales,* based on his own unpublished stories, of which he said, "If eventually I did turn them into films, it was because I had not succeeded in writing them."

The unexpected success of *La Collectionneuse* in 1966, followed in 1969 by the international sensation of *My Night at Maud's*, finally gave him the chance to work more regularly; but that regularity was only possible because he made an art of economy. "Often in my films," he has remarked, "the practical and financial choices dovetail quite well with the artistic choices"—choices including the employment of direct sound and natural settings, the absence of special effects, elaborate musical scores, or (except for his literary adaptations) period costuming, and above all the use of small casts of relatively little-known actors enacting stories devoid of complicated action sequences, stories in which the characters, often and at length, talk.

The characters—and this was another trait that made it easy to put Rohmer in a category off by himself—were of a sort that most films ignored or marginalized: they were, in various ways and to various degrees, self-absorbed, self-deluding, caught up in self-defeating habits, petulant, defensive, shy to the point of passive aggression: people who, encountered in life, would be dull or irritating, but who were just as much the heroes of their own lives—and of their films—as the characters portrayed by Cary Grant or Ingrid Bergman. If they lacked glamour, they made up for it with the intensity of their absorption in their own problems. Neither inflating them nor condescending to them, Rohmer simply lured the spectator into becoming implicated in their doings, or more precisely their tellings. The spectator might find the experience either uncomfortably like sitting in a restaurant next to a couple whose conversation is full of gaffes and awkward pauses, or uncomfortably like looking into a mirror.

It was like watching people directing movies of their own lives and led unavoidably to a contemplation of what one's own life might look like if filmed in a similar fashion. There was no need to make up stories because people made them up themselves. Each life was a story, riveting to its protagonist, marked by scenes of emotional outpouring and violent confrontation that, exposed on the screen, were reduced to the tiniest of scales. A brief outburst such as the moment in *The Aviator's Wife* when the hero's older girlfriend broke away from him and ran into the midst of some parked cars, felt, in a Rohmerian context, shockingly violent. Likewise, in the same movie, a series of random encounters and pursuits on a bus and in a park assumed the dimensions of a Hitchcockian chase film in miniature. The characters framed the world around themselves. Human action left to itself appeared to provide its own mise-en-scène, while all the time being observed by a godlike camera indifferently registering contradictions and distinctions. Not that Rohmer really believed in leaving things to chance; it was only that chance had a way of coming to the assistance of his already thoroughly meditated schemes, like the unsolicited gusts of wind that play such an exuberant role in *Astrea and Celadon*.

If there is a paradox in his work, it is the uncanny harmony between an ideal of total control and an aptitude for spontaneous improvisation and chance discovery. Seen from one perspective, his films are tart, sharp, exact, measured, limited, obsessive, the work of a logician, a pedagogue. In another light—or rather in the same light, but from another angle—they are open, airy, rapt, meditative, fundamentally mysterious. A young man (in *Boyfriends and Girlfriends*) recounts a banal fantasy of meeting a girl in the forest; the camera pans, in a rudimentary fashion that makes formal mastery indistinguishable from amateurism, across a cluster of trees, and you almost have the impression that Rohmer made the whole movie so that he could do that shot—except that the impression is not isolated. Such moments occur constantly. The supposed triviality of the situations in his films is the best concealment he could ever have devised for himself.

Taken one at a time, each of his films seems to show with perfect clarity what it is about. We could almost write a book on the kitchens and bedrooms and cafés and offices in which his characters (whom we come to know almost too well) pass their time. Yet seen as a whole— and it is a body of work that insists on being seen as a whole—they exert a lingering sense of open-ended fascination, as if perhaps they were about something altogether different from what we imagined while caught up in the moment-to-moment doings of Frédéric or Delphine or Félicie. Returning to the same film, we find always that it is never the same film twice, and it is never the same detail—whether a shrug or a turn of the head or a reflection in a shop window or an ever so slight forward glide of the camera—that suddenly takes on devastating immediacy. Film being film, the immediacy persists. These are windows that remain open, offering elusive but ineffaceable glimpses of the life within.

*The New York Review of Books,* 2008

# the old frontier

THE FIRST TIME I SAW *The Man Who Shot Liberty Valance*, forty-six years ago, it was in its second if not third run at one of the neighborhood movie theaters that still abounded in New York in the early 1960s. It felt as if it belonged in a theater like that, a little bit faded and off the main drag. *The Man Who Shot Liberty Valance* was born old. With its black-and-white photography and its backlot sets, its aging stars incongruously cast as young men, its stagy turns by John Carradine and Edmond O'Brien, it seemed like a movie from another time. Its use of flashbacks—the revelation made by Tom Doniphon (John Wayne) to Ranse Stoddard (James Stewart) presented as a flashback within the larger flashback of Ranse's narrative that occupies most of the film— only emphasized the fact that the whole movie was a flashback to an age of filmmaking already gone. For young moviegoers the only thing really contemporary about it was the presence of Lee Marvin, who in terms of the John Ford universe seemed like pure rock and roll; and Strother Martin, as his howling half-witted sidekick, was already punk rock. By assembling Marvin, Martin, and Lee Van Cleef as the heavies, Ford had managed to forecast the movies that within a few years would displace his own kind of cinema: *Point Blank, For a Few Dollars More, The Wild Bunch.*

To enter the movie theater to see *Liberty Valance* felt really like stepping out of time, appropriately for a movie that plays so profoundly with time and memory and chronological sequence. It begins with an ending, and for the first quarter hour creates the impression that we have intruded on some private ritual of mourning. The exchange of glances between Marshall Link Appleyard (Andy Devine) and Hallie (Vera Miles) encapsulates a sorrow beyond words. Ford gives us the emotional climax up front, before we can understand anything of what we are seeing, or grasp, for example, the significance of Link's remark: "He didn't carry no handgun, Ranse, he didn't for years." The weight of those opening scenes is so oppressive that what follows seems at first like an escape in the only possible direction—backward, into the past.

(A quick plot summary: A U.S. senator, Ransom Stoddard, and his wife, Hallie, turn up unexpectedly in the Southwestern town of Shinbone. Interviewed by a local newspaper, the senator says they are there to attend the funeral of an obscure local citizen, Tom Doniphon, and when pressed for further explanation he launches into a narrative that constitutes the main body of the film: Ransom Stoddard arrives in Shinbone many years earlier as a young lawyer from the East; on the outskirts of town he is robbed, beaten, and left for dead by a notorious local desperado, Liberty Valance. Rescued by Tom Doniphon and brought to the local restaurant and lodging house, Ransom is reduced to washing dishes. While waiting on tables in an apron one evening, he is confronted by Liberty Valance but avoids further violence through the intervention of Tom. Abhorring the reign of lawlessness in Shinbone, Ransom set up a law office and a school; among his students is the illiterate Hallie, who works at the restaurant, and whom Tom intends to marry. We learn quickly that Liberty Valance is in fact an agent of the big ranchers working against statehood; Ransom takes the side of the settlers and small ranchers campaigning for statehood. He is elected delegate to the territorial convention, but is challenged to a showdown by Valance. He attempts to learn how to use a gun but is clearly outmatched. Although urged to leave town, Ransom faces Valance in the middle of the street; Valance is killed. Ransom goes on to the convention but is unhappy with his new role as "the man who shot Liberty Valance." Tom seeks him out and tells him the truth: it was Tom, not Ransom, who killed Valance, shooting him from an alley at the same time Ransom fired. Tom, who has lost Hallie to Ransom, bitterly insists that Ransom accept the political position that has been thrust on him: "You taught her to read; now give her something to read about." Tom, who has burned down the house he built for Hallie, disappears into obscurity. When Ransom's story is told, the newspaper editor tosses away his notes: "This is the West, sir. When the legend becomes fact, print the legend." On the train back to Washington, Ransom tells Hallie that he wants to retire and move back to Shinbone with her.)


WHEN FORD MADE *Liberty Valance* at sixty-seven, he had already directed over 120 movies, beginning with *The Tornado* in 1917. His health was declining and changes in the film industry were making it ever harder for him to find work; without John Wayne's clout the picture probably wouldn't have gotten made at all. Ford—who over many decades had built up a sort of private polity of actors and technicians in which he reigned supreme—must have sensed that *The Man Who Shot Liberty Valance* might be the last film in which he would be able to exercise the kind of directorial control to which he had grown accustomed.

To ask what Ford's authorial intentions were in this or any other of his films is to pose a question he would likely have found unnecessary. Making movies was what he had been doing since his youth. It was an occupation into which he had fallen for the fortuitous reason that his long-absent older brother Francis had made a career for himself as actor and director. Ford took advantage of the opening and found himself employable as actor and stuntman in an industry just beginning to operate on a much larger scale. (He was one of the Klan riders in D.W. Griffith's *The Birth of a Nation*.) From the moment he began to work as a director, he scarcely had time to contemplate the larger meaning of his chosen profession: he was either immersed in the making of films or (as Joseph McBride describes in his biography *Searching for John Ford*) knocking himself out in alcoholic binges that increasingly became a necessary relief.

Had Ford chosen to make a statement about the meaning of his life—and he was not given to such statements—he would probably have emphasized his years of military service in World War II over his career as a commercial filmmaker. (His military service, as it happens, was chiefly involved with filmmaking.) But even to venture that much is presumptuous; better to say that Ford was a man of pride and unspoken ambition whose essential solitariness expressed itself, paradoxically, in the midst of crowded and tumultuous moviemaking. He made a community—a world—in which he could work and live, and by force of will and talent was largely able to maintain it against outside pressures through the long arc from, say, *The Iron Horse* (1924) to *The Searchers* (1956). When we look at his films as aesthetic objects divorced from the circumstances of their making, we are probably doing what Ford himself had neither the time nor the inclination to do. But it was precisely the quality of his immersion in the process of making them that gives them their peculiar weight. Meaning in Ford—the deep meaning that often contradicts or modifies the apparent meaning of the screenplay—is a byproduct of process.

The script of *The Man Who Shot Liberty Valance* was of his choosing and was the best he had had to work with since Frank Nugent's screenplay for *The Searchers*. In the neatness of its structure it bears comparison to Dudley Nichols's screenplay for Ford's great breakthrough of 1939, *Stagecoach*. There are many connections large and small between *Stagecoach* and *Liberty Valance*, starting with the stagecoach that Ranse Stoddard dusts off just before the main flashback begins. The presence of John Wayne, John Carradine, and Andy Devine stirs memories of the earlier film (indeed, the Andy Devine of *Stagecoach*, with his Mexican wife, might well have aged into the Devine of *Liberty Valance*); John Wayne's Ringo Kid, like Tom Doniphon, has "a cabin half built" for his future bride; Wayne guns down on a dark street a desperado who has just won a poker hand with aces and eights (the "dead man's hand"); and Jack Pennick (the most quietly ubiquitous of Ford's stock company), who was Jack the bartender in *Stagecoach*, is still serving up drinks in *Liberty Valance*.

The Lordsburg of *Stagecoach* is not very different from the Shinbone of *Liberty Valance*. What is different is where the two films end up. In the last scene of *Stagecoach*, the noble outlaw Wayne and the newly reformed prostitute Claire Trevor ride off into the wilderness away from the corruption and moral narrowness of towns, with the full approval of George Bancroft's sheriff: "Well, they're saved from the blessings of civilization!" In *Liberty Valance* no one is saved, because there is no longer a romantic wilderness to ride off into, only a train to Washington, D.C.—the same train that spewed black smoke over the landscape at the beginning of the movie.

In *The Man Who Shot Liberty Valance* Ford had for once, after a string of problematic scripts (*The Horse Soldiers, Sergeant Rutledge, Two Rode Together*), a screenplay that with its tightly meshing arguments and counterarguments suggested a sort of cowboy version of Corneille. In fact, it's a nearly perfect screenplay—at least for Ford. It's hard to imagine what any other director would have made of it, so imbued is every aspect of it, as finally filmed, with the Fordian ambience that by that date had begun to seem quite peculiar, a world unto itself.

From start to finish we are inside the little theater of John Ford. Almost everything feels as if it's taking place indoors, even the street scenes and the stagecoach robbery. Here are no longer any sweeping vistas or epic cavalcades. Instead there is a sort of claustrophobic milling around in the middle distance. The interiors are narrow and (except in the strangely empty "modern" framing sequences) often overcrowded. In its central stretch the movie becomes one jammed set piece after another, much of it in long shot to accommodate all the players. Rather than having wide open spaces fit for heroic action, the characters at times barely have room to turn around. The effect has been compared to the silent *Kammerspiel* films of Murnau or Dreyer, but just as often it harks back to the theatrical tableau setups of

D.W. Griffith, an old-fashioned full-frontal approach of which Ford is entirely conscious. Critics at the time were mostly appalled by the lack of visual splendor. But Ford seems determined to impress us with the ordinariness of the life he depicts. Did any Western ever have so much to say about dishwashing?

It's a film with no digressions, no interludes. So powerful and suggestive is the central schema that every other detail becomes relevant within it, whether the dishwashing—woman's work that brands Ranse Stoddard as ineffectual for undertaking it—or Edmond O'Brien as the newspaper editor Dutton Peabody drunkenly reciting a speech from *Henry V*—the intellectual guarding himself with literature against real-world violence.

Ford's usual choral contingent of drunks, cowards, and stammering bumpkins assembles more or less for the last time to fill out the population of Shinbone. By now their weathered faces seem like part of the landscape. Or rather, in the absence of landscape, it is their faces and voices that become the landscape. The voices are important. For a movie that in retrospect seems to exude an air of stillness, there is a remarkable amount of talk in *Liberty Valance*, and it isn't small talk. We are given a classroom session, an election day political meeting, a territorial convention, each with its share of yelling and speechifying, each an occasion for straight-out rhetorical exhortation from all sides, with even Liberty Valance getting to make a more or less cogent speech laying out the facts of the situation from his narrow but unimpeachably realist viewpoint.

In fact nearly every conversation hinges on a debating point. When Ranse Stoddard asks Liberty Valance and his accomplices what kind of men they are, Valance replies: "What kind of man are you, dude?" A moment later, brandishing his quirt, he announces: "I'll teach you law—Western law!" Everybody is always teaching somebody something. Ranse teaches Hallie to read; Tom teaches Ranse how to shoot a gun.

By the time the movie settles into Ranse's backroom literacy class it might seem to have become mired in the most banal kind of didacticism, with Jeanette Nolan as the Swedish restaurant keeper Mrs. Ericson reciting that "a republic is a state in which the people are the boss" and Woody Strode's Pompey forgetting the phrase "all men are created equal" in the Declaration of Independence so that Ranse can respond: "That's all right, Pompey, a lot of people forget that part." But affirmative as it is—giving Ford, in the civil rights era, a chance to present a racially and ethnically diverse classroom—the scene also quickly gets more complicated as Tom Doniphon barges in to bring word of impending violence. Instantly Ranse loses his authority as a teacher, as the men in the class gather around Tom for his insider's commentary on the situation. Ranse reluctantly breaks up the school in the interest of his students' safety, and we watch in close-up as he erases the sentence on the blackboard: "Education is the basis of law and order." When Tom orders Hallie to go home, it sparks what turns out to be her definitive rebellion against his paternalistic claims on her: "You don't own me!"

This classroom scene is nothing but a series of rapid interjections, some of them purely comic, but in a way it's the most characteristic scene in the movie. The film as a whole may offer proof of Tom Doniphon's initial contention that "you better start packin' a handgun," but it surrounds that contention with layers on layers of words, and it's the words—symbolized by the slogan embedded in the movie's title and burnished by teachers, newspaper editors, and politicians—that finally win out over any original reality.

BY THE TIME Ford made *Liberty Valance* he was practicing an art of compression. He lingers over nothing; there is no time to lavish on second glances. He had always valued speed and spontaneity, and liked to catch actors unprepared before they had a chance to become too attached to their line readings. *The Man Who Shot Liberty Valance* is a film that in memory can seem mournful and languidly contemplative, but on the screen it moves at an urgent clip. There is no voluptuous immersion in the image for its own sake. Scenes that other directors would have milked for suspense or spectacular effect are short and matter-of-fact. Tom's burning of his house, and the release of the horses from the corral to save them from the fire, is recounted in a sequence all the more powerful for being pared to the bone. It burns its way into the movie as if surfacing from some medieval saga or early Swedish silent film, the only moment in *Liberty Valance* that really feels like the outdoors, to signal that the possibility of a wilderness home, the refuge of independent spirits like Tom Doniphon, is going up in flames.

There are moments of repose, even stasis, but they happen very fast and are gone. Certain emblematic shots—the cactus roses blooming amid the burnt-out remnants of Tom's house, the closed coffin framed in the doorway, the cactus rose set on top of the coffin—are inserted as if to remove them from their surroundings and place them outside of time altogether. These moments are stark and sharp and, once gone, never return.

The rest is bustle, a world of unavoidable unruly interaction. Within that bustle there are relatively few moments when characters are alone, but they are crucial: Hallie alone in the classroom after the school has broken up, Ranse alone in the street waiting for Liberty Valance and pausing while he waits to take down what's left of the legal sign that Valance shot up, Tom alone in a dark alleyway after he's killed Valance (although we don't know that yet) and has fully understood that he has lost Hallie to Ranse. Each moment of solitude represents some kind of agonized realization.

In *Liberty Valance* Ford offers only the faintest traces of those communal rituals of song and parade that occupied so much space in his earlier films. Mostly the collective rituals here are political, and they divide as much as they bring together. Aside from the mournful underscoring in the framing scenes, the main body of the film is almost without music except for stray bits of ambient music-making. The only dancing takes place far back in the frame, in one of the most elaborate shots in the film: Tom Doniphon, after the moment described above in the alley, moves forward through the darkness, the camera following him as he emerges into the public square where, outside the cantina, the Mexicans are dancing in celebration of Liberty Valance's death, and Liberty's corpse lies a few yards away on the back of a wagon, the heels hanging down. Tom is in the same frame as the celebration but he takes no part in it.

ALL THESE SCENES and moments and fleeting images find their place within the strong architecture of the central story. That they are not in any way separate from it is the mark of the extraordinarily focused energies of the film. Nothing is allowed to get in the way of the story being told, but somehow everything becomes part of that story. It is a story at once emotionally intimate and chillingly detached, and in that contradiction is the key to an art that, although it seems steeped in nostalgia and sentimentality, is finally marked by an arctic clarity.

For all the talk that goes on, Ford's unraveling of the inner lives of his three central characters is accomplished almost wordlessly, chiefly through the performances he knew how to elicit from actors as different as Vera Miles and Jimmy Stewart and John Wayne. How much we come to know about Hallie, for instance, and how little of it comes from dialogue: her anger at Tom's paternalist condescension; her anger at everything around her, even at Ranse for his awkwardness and unmanly politeness; her love for Ranse that is always a kind of mothering; her final grief that she can share not with her husband but with those she left behind, Devine as Link Appleyard and Strode as Pompey.

At its heart the movie is, as many have observed, the tragedy of Tom Doniphon, and the human dimension of that tragedy is conveyed entirely through what Ford was able to get out of John Wayne. As we see Tom in his first scenes, before Ranse and his law books have changed things forever in Shinbone, he's a man rooted in his world and, as much as he can be, content in it. Through the way Wayne carries himself we understand everything we need to know about that world: his body language becomes a shorthand for the description of a culture. By the end—when Tom barges into the convention hall to have it out with Ranse once and for all—he has become by contrast the Wayne of *The Searchers*, Ethan Edwards in all his bitterness and eternal solitude. The sacrifice he has made can be measured in that physical and emotional metamorphosis.

The scene that follows—in which we finally learn who shot Liberty Valance—is also remarkably short, considering its importance. It's as if Tom can't wait to get out of there. If he has sacrificed his own prospects, his own world, it's perhaps because he wanted Hallie to get what she wanted and perhaps because he really is strong enough (since we already know he's the strongest person in the movie) to realize that any other course of action—to let Ranse die, to let the political status quo continue—would be unworthy of him. If he hadn't, by subjecting Ranse to the hazing ritual in which he spattered his fine clothes with white paint, found out that the lawyer was courageous enough to knock him down, perhaps he wouldn't have considered him worthy of such a sacrifice. But since Ranse passed the test, Tom had to respect him, to help him, and finally to commit a kind of suicide on his behalf. But he doesn't have to like him. The power of the final scene between the two men is in the withholding of the personal affection that is the last thing Tom has left to give. The only way he can preserve any remnant of himself is to walk away leaving Ranse feeling unloved. We wait for the brotherly wink that never comes. Whatever *Liberty Valance* may have to say about American history and society, I have no doubt that this scene also plays out some part of John Ford's story, in a way that he could not have expressed otherwise: a drama less about political foundations than about the intimacies of male loyalties and betrayals.

Instead, by way of an ending, we get the train rolling down the track, winding around and moving deeper into the frame, as if about to disappear into a hole within the image. The famous train that Louis Lumière filmed in 1898 came at the audience, terrifying it with a vision of the future that was upon them. In *The Man Who Shot Liberty Valance* the train leads away, into a future already gone: the future both of the characters in the movie and of John Ford and all the others making the movie. The spectator is left stranded in the past, watching the train move toward the bend.

*The Point*, 2010

# a great book of instances

THERE IS A SEQUENCE AT the end of Frederick Wiseman's *Titicut Follies* (1967)—the next to last—in which a casket is taken from a hearse and carried to a gravesite by a group of inmates of Massachusetts's Bridgewater State Hospital for the criminally insane. They are focused on their task, talking among themselves in low tones as they maneuver the casket into position. Then the priest, Father Mulligan, reads a very brief service (the inmates intoning at the appropriate moment "And let perpetual light shine upon him") concluding with: "Remember, man, that thou art dust, and unto dust thou shalt return. That's all." Priest and inmates quickly depart and for a moment the casket occupies the center of the screen. In that same frame we get a glimpse of everything absent from the rest of the film, air and vegetation and open ground. It is a quietly shocking moment in a film with many more abrasive shocks: we are forced to acknowledge death as a relief. The deceased has made a getaway—after the strip searches, the recollections of child rape, the taunting, the tube feeding, the stony isolation cells—from an almost unbearable existence.

That impression of escape attaches itself as well to the priest's ceremonial language, which (unlike what we have been hearing up to this point) bears no trace of psychiatric jargon and no distortions of mental illness. Before this, we have encountered Father Mulligan in other people's words, as the subject of a joke told at the staff-and-inmate musical show that frames the film and gives it its title, as a character in the disordered rant of the film's most talkative personage, as part of a song improvised by another inmate. We have seen him, a few moments before the cemetery scene, administering last rites. His performance of these rituals carried out countless times before seems no more than perfunctory, yet even in his fairly rushed delivery the phrase "eternal rest" acquires, in the context the film has created, a startling freshness. Here at last is language that is coherent, deliberate, profoundly meaningful, and pristinely devoid of any personal expression. And then it's back to the show: "Sing and dance and take a chance / Until another year, we're through." While guards and inmates take their curtain call, we are given, as throughout the film, constant flickers of expression and gesture hinting at more personal history than any image or any film could possibly encompass.

We are also conscious throughout of the vigor of juxtaposition, the placement of captured images to produce (here far more than in Wiseman's later films) a species of found expressionism. The persistent visual impression—and shot for shot it is one of the most indelible of films, filled with moments that come back unbidden and perhaps unwanted—is often of a very old movie surviving in fragments, some archaic shadow world emanating from a lost corner of Germany or Russia, an apparition from the realm of masks and monsters and white-faced clowns made all the more unsettling by the ghostly theatricality of pom-poms and "Strike Up the Band." The oldness has to do with Bridgewater itself conforming to our sense of an anachronistic dungeon far removed from the modernity of 1967, a place of darkness into which Wiseman has descended with camera and tape recorder in order to bring images out into the light. The present tense of documentary, of the moment captured live, is inflected by a sense of lag or undertow, as if the place itself annulled time.

WISEMAN'S FIRST FILM already has the characteristics of those that followed—the absence of written captions or narration or talking-head

interviews, the structural freedom permitting scenes out of chronological sequence and intercutting of apparently unrelated episodes—but
stands quite distinctly apart in its mood and texture. *Titicut Follies* may
be read somewhat differently now than when it first appeared. It was
made at a moment when representations of madness, and the trope of
the asylum as mirror of the world, pervaded the culture on many different levels, from Ken Kesey's novel *One Flew Over the Cuckoo's Nest*
(1962), and Peter Weiss's play *Marat/Sade* (1963) to movies as various
as Samuel Fuller's *Shock Corridor* (1963) and Philippe de Broca's *King
of Hearts* (1966). This was the heyday of the anti-psychiatry of R.D.
Laing and David Cooper. An audience primed to see headshrinkers
as oppressors had limited sympathy to spare for the psychiatric staff of
Bridgewater. The episode in the yard where inmates discuss the pros
and cons of the Vietnam War—at a time when similar discussions, not
necessarily more cogent or better informed, could be heard in any college dorm or neighborhood bar—needed no prompting to be read as a
transparent commentary on the insanity of the war itself.

Certainly *Titicut Follies* exposes horrors of callousness, casual cruelty, and myopic indifference—and relays suggestions of a decadent
bureaucracy in keeping with the decayed physical condition of the
hospital itself—yet its enduring power and mystery go far beyond the
social impact of any such exposé. The power and mystery have everything to do with the approach Wiseman broached here and has continued to explore, the direct presentation of scenes without preparation
or commentary, leaving the spectator at every point to determine what
is going on and what its significance might be. In many of Wiseman's
later films there is a kind of relief at the outset in not being given names
and dates and arguments to frame our perception: we are allowed to
come upon the world and recognize it. Calmed initially by a sense
of familiarity—as if after all anything we see could only be a further
extension of the world we know—we are at the same time, for the same
reason, nudged into a residual anxious alertness.

Throughout his work there is a sense of being permitted to see with
the eyes of a child or a stranger, knowing little or nothing of where we

are and what has brought us here. We have to rely on visual and aural clues that we learn to read as we once did as a matter of course, and to respond with unanticipated intimacy to people to whom we have not been introduced. We find ourselves assessing them immediately—on the basis perhaps of the most random traits, the shape of a mouth, the movement of a wrist, the style of a shirt—and, again with the child's wariness, feeling out very rapidly who will help or who will hurt, and who might give us some idea of what is going on. When people talk we listen attentively to pick up useful scraps of information or anything that sounds like helpful advice.

Such advice is very hard to find in *Titicut Follies*. Any familiarity here—for most viewers—is likely to be that of a deeply rooted and unpleasant dream, the aura of a dreaded place that everyone can imagine even if they have never been there: a place either without charity or where charity does little apparent good, where one has no freedom and not even a language in which to adequately express that lack, or rather where one's way of using language for such expression becomes itself the reason for further deprivation. The more the patient Vladimir asserts his sanity the more hopeless his case becomes. Yet the more logically the psychiatrists frame their arguments, the more apparent it becomes that they have little hope to offer the patients in their charge. The chain-smoking Dr. Ross, blinking furiously as he questions a child molester or indifferently flicking ashes as he force-feeds a strapped-down inmate, might be a stone-hearted incompetent or a tragically burnt-out case, murmuring essentially to himself the answers that he knows his patients won't absorb anyway. He might even be a man whose deep compassion is well concealed for purposes of self-preservation in a relentlessly chaotic environment where, in Vladimir's words, "all they do is throw cups around . . . It's noisy, they got two television sets which are blaring, machines which are going." The guards and attendants who are there to hold chaos at bay are themselves inextricably caught up in it, and can be seen as condemned to their fate as much as the inmates.

*Titicut Follies* conveys from the outset an overwhelming sense of transgression. I use the word "transgression" with caution, given the film's contentious legal history, merely to register the irresistible sense for the spectator of entering a place off-limits, of being given to see what no outsider was intended to see. Although the hospital is a place of torment, whether by forces external or internal, not everything we see is appalling. But the marginally brighter bits—the birthday party with the trio singing "Have You Ever Been Lonely?", the guard Eddie with his energetic clowning, the kindly volunteer ladies, the nurse moved by her letter from an inmate ("when you get a letter like this . . . it makes you feel as though, well, you at least tried")—tend to be over-shadowed by, notably, the scene early on in which the inmate Jim is taunted by the guards ("You gonna keep that room clean, Jim?") until he explodes in rage. The moments that follow—Jim, naked, stamping up and down in his cell, beating on the barred window—bring us as near as we can be brought into the unreachable space of someone else's locked-in solitude. The shot in which Jim stares toward the camera acknowledges the insuperability of the barrier. We are here beyond any easy question of moral meaning, and well beyond the limits of a notion of privacy that would prevent such a moment ever from being seen. A line has been crossed, and all of Wiseman's work might be seen as a continuing exploration of the implications of that crossing.

TITICUT FOLLIES CAPTURES with exactness how unbearable the progression from one instant to the next becomes for those with noth-ing to occupy them. The doors that close on the inmates lock them into spaces designed for nothing to happen in them. Wiseman's subsequent films are so much about keeping busy: sometimes usefully, sometimes in fulfillment of an obscure and perhaps incomprehensible obligation. The people are all, monks or janitors or security guards or missile-launch instructors, working on something. The inmates in Titicut Follies are precisely those with nothing to do except somehow to get better in a place and under conditions where, it seems, few are likely to. "Why you keeping a man from work?" an African American inmate protests. (A guard asks him if he wants to sell watermelons.) "Where can I work? I'd like to know *where* can I work?" The smallest task ful-filled becomes the minimum definition of a bearable life, even if the task is only to remember the lyrics of "Chinatown, My Chinatown."

Contemplation of the nature of a task and the purpose for which separate tasks converge is a continuing thread in Wiseman's work, as one system after another passes in review. In the process his work as a whole becomes a lexicon of the world. It could be cross-referenced by means of analogous components that repeat from film to film—machines, songs, television programs, animals, priests, janitors, docu-ments, hairstyles—and indexed to serve as a guide to modes of human interaction: a great book of instances. What all those instances would add up to, in any given film and in the work as a whole, remains of course very much an open question. To keep the question open seems to be the constantly reiterated premise, a premise often underscored by the people he films. "Life is rushing by and sometimes we wonder whether we grasp its meaning," says a priest in *Racetrack* (1985). "Why do some people live? What is his aim in life?" asks a neighbor in *Law and Order* (1969) as she watches a wino being rousted from the pave-ment by a couple of policemen.

These are films in which we have emerged from the underworld of *Titicut Follies*, even if the difference is not always obvious. The world aboveground can seem as much of a prison house, as we enter environments that overlap with the imaginative worlds of such postmodern paranoid systems analysts as Gaddis, Mailer, Pynchon, Kubrick. Wiseman's work is, precisely, pared of their exaggeration and caricature, pared likewise of special pleading, but that does not necessarily make it less terrifying. It would not be hard to read *Welfare* (1975) in the light of absurdism—and in case the point were missed, one of the welfare clients, Mr. Hirsch, is there to emphasize it, in a speech that might have been written for a play of his own devising: "I've been waiting for the last hundred and twenty-four days since I got out of the hospital, waiting for something—Godot. But you know what happens, you know what happens in the story of Godot. He never came."

What better arena than the welfare system for an exposition of the madness of bureaucracy, the entrapment of hapless individuals, both clients and workers, in an interminable round of interviews and paper-shuffling, the sense of a just adjudication perpetually deferred? That exposition is made in full, yet such a description would give little idea of the actual character of *Welfare*, a film that finds extraordinary life in the interstices of boredom and obfuscation and maddening frustration. For me it is the great movie about New York in the 1970s—a great tragicomedy of need and deception and resignation and, above all, ceaseless and vigorous argument. Everybody works to make sense of things at every moment, often under extreme pressure.

The disparate episodes spill over with the contradictory meanings imparted to them by their participants. The hapless Mrs. Johnson, trying to cut through walls of red tape, being finally unforgettably counseled by another client: "Valerie, Valerie, Valerie, Valerie, Valerie. You not going to get nowhere up here arguing with him . . . Baby, he only got a certain amount of authority"; the bored young black policeman amusing himself by debating at inordinate length with a racist mugging victim; the complex multiple confrontation, a staggering instance of a mise-en-scène not so much imposed as discovered, of a client, her daughter, an unsympathetic welfare worker, a policeman, and a supervisor: merely to summarize all that is going on in any one of these scenes would be the work of many pages, a whole volume perhaps, and no two observers would agree on what had been observed.

One does not need to have applied for welfare or to have worked for the welfare system to have inhabited some part of this world. We know these benches, these forms, these ritualized question-and-answer sessions, these evasions and confrontations. Even if, say, I only applied for unemployment insurance, or worked in an office where low-level employees were routinely subjected to lie-detector tests, or made photocopies in a shop where just such exhausted people made multiple copies of endlessly refolded official documents, *Welfare* provokes an almost overwhelming sense of immersion in a remembered place.

The power of memory is often called into play by Wiseman's films. One is constantly being jogged into a comparison with other instants, other places, other people, and that recognition enlists us into an active participation. You share a space with what is on the screen, as if you were watching, in Gertrude Stein's phrase, everybody's autobiography. Whatever system is on display is never more than an extension of the one you inhabit. The absence of narration elicits the spectator's own commentary, which becomes part of the film: a provisional working out of where one is in relation to each moment as it passes. You are given not only the opportunity to imagine yourself variously in each role (on both sides of the desk, for instance, in *Welfare*) but can hardly evade that responsibility, and in the process are forced to recognize your own limits and biases. A constant exercise in definition is enforced. You might come to feel uncannily as if the film were looking back at you, taking note of your response to it; and to feel that, after inhabiting it for two or three hours, it had ended by inhabiting you.

In *Titicut Follies* and *Welfare*, as in the rest of Wiseman's films, there is never any pretense that what we see constitutes the main or only story. On the contrary we are thoroughly aware that other scenes could have been shown, that a nearly infinite number of other films could have emerged from within the selected field. The filmmaker exercises the choice of what to look at and how long to sustain that gaze, and in doing so makes us fully conscious of the power inherent in that choice. We are invited to think about the logic of the structures he establishes. The cutting is the (supposedly absent) commentary just as it is the governor of rhythm and duration and narrative form. The films are as much meditations on editing as on what is edited. It is not the least of their genius to have made palpable—indeed breathlessly involving—the notion of film editing as an existential decision.

*Frederick Wiseman* (MOMA), 2010

# the invention of the world

THAT JEAN-LUC GODARD'S *BREATHLESS* SHOULD have reached its fiftieth anniversary is a bit hard to accept, in part because it serves to remind just how much time has passed since I first saw it, within a year of its New York opening. It is also more than a little curious to think that, had I looked back half a century from 1960, when at age twelve I was just getting immersed in movies, I would have been contemplating an inconceivably remote film world whose pathbreaking work was being done by the likes of D.W. Griffith and Louis Feuillade (directors who had not yet even hit their stride). How could so much have changed in that earlier fifty-year span, and so relatively little in the half-century since? *Breathless* still seems very much a live influence; it has remained continuously available, most recently in a pristine Criterion restoration, and will be re-released theatrically to mark the anniversary. That the iconic images of Jean-Paul Belmondo in hat and shades and Jean Seberg in *New York Herald Tribune* T-shirt have never gone away make it easy to pretend it was all the day before yesterday.

For me, as doubtless for many who caught it the first time around, it still feels that way. On a fresh viewing, after a few moments of initial detachment—but then that opening car theft in Marseille was always disorienting—the deeply ingrained associations begin to kick in. I don't so much recollect my first reactions to *Breathless* as find myself involuntarily possessed by them, or rather inextricably embedded in them. I cannot report on *Breathless* as it looks now because it will never lose for me its original mesmeric fascination. To have come upon Seberg and Belmondo exactly as they were may not be quite like getting youth back, but it's the best that movies can do. At the time it seemed to promise an era of wonders to come—unimaginable movies, inventions, pleasures—with Jean-Luc Godard a new name for astonishment. There was perhaps more magic in the anticipation than in all that followed—there generally is. It's impossible to watch it now without thinking, for instance, of the latter history of Jean Seberg, but likewise impossible not to be once again taken over by her just as she takes over her supposedly hardboiled lover, and the movie itself.

That first viewing was followed by many more. *Breathless* became the indispensable text to which anyone who had not already seen it had to be dragged. It became part of the furniture of life; promenades and parties and love scenes (real or attempted) were for a long time all more or less remakes of *Breathless*. Every second of its running time— every stray reference and physical gesture and cinematic device— would be shared and parsed and rehashed. Every peripheral glimpse or overheard fragment of conversation was somehow indispensable. The first time I saw *Breathless* on video—on a tape that looked as if it had been struck from the very print that had made the rounds of Manhattan revival houses in the 1960s—I was amazed to recognize each flaw and scratch. The tiniest peculiarities of film grain were like old friends. (The restored DVD makes the film more blemish-free but at the cost of some cherished associations.)

*Breathless* was the first film I had watched that way, attentive not only to plot or dialogue or deliberately grand composition but to everything that came, however briefly or marginally, into the audiovisual field. Everything seemed potentially important, from a glimpse of wall poster or comic strip to the expression on the face of a passerby on the fringe of the frame. In the same way that every photograph in Robert Frank's *The Americans* (another overwhelming product of that moment) was both offhand and monumental, *Breathless* turned any courtyard or café into a site as resonant as the Eiffel Tower or Notre

Dame. It was not like watching a movie of the world, but rather as if the world itself had forced its way into the movie theater.

I find it easier to reconstruct my own first take on *Breathless* than to grasp, even now, its effect on my elders. To look back to Bosley Crowther's *New York Times* review is to reenter a world that has disappeared: "Sordid is really a mild word for its pile-up of gross indecencies . . . It is emphatically, unrestrainedly vicious, completely devoid of moral tone, concerned mainly with eroticism and the restless drives of a cruel young punk to get along." (He might have been describing, more or less accurately, a drive-in movie of the same period like *The Beat Generation* or *Platinum High School.*) Pauline Kael perceived something not altogether dissimilar, although in subtler terms, finding Belmondo and Seberg "as shallow and empty as the shining young faces you see in sports cars and in suburban supermarkets, and in newspapers after unmotivated, pointless crimes. And you're left with the horrible suspicion that this is a new race, bred in chaos."

If it was a new race, then my contemporaries must be of it. To those of us entering adolescence *Breathless* was more like the trailer for what we hoped our lives would be: hilarious, exhilarating, bracing, and filled with allusions you could happily spend a lifetime tracking down. Reading Dashiell Hammett's *The Glass Key*, one might come upon the same line about not wearing silk socks with tweeds, and, years later, watching Otto Preminger's *Whirlpool*, finally realize it had been the voice of Gene Tierney crying out in that Parisian movie theater: "You don't want to know the truth—you won't let me tell it—you think I'm lying!" These bits of Godardian citation were talismanic street signs, pointing toward hidden alternate worlds: if, as Godard said in a 1961 interview, *Breathless* was more like *Alice in Wonderland* than like *Scarface*, it was a wonderland constructed from pieces of what was then just beginning to be described as "pop culture." The phrase had not yet worn out its welcome.

We took *Breathless* as a manual of how to move through the world in cool balletic fashion, pausing for brief indelible poses, and dropping the occasional gnomic observation after the fashion of Jean-Pierre Melville as the aphoristic novelist Parvulesco. Parvulesco's credo—"To become immortal and then to die"—represented a perfect fusion of Walter Pater's injunction to "burn always with this hard, gemlike flame" and the teen punk epigram of *Knock on Any Door*: "Live fast, die young, and leave a good-looking corpse." If you didn't want to be Belmondo's Michel Poiccard—if, that is, the romance of self-destruction was not altogether tempting—you could always aim for Parvulesco's exquisite contempt.

*Breathless* figured as a series of directives: Wear sunglasses. Smoke cigarettes (as many as required to give every interior an elegantly evanescent haze). Learn French (if only to find out what *dégueulasse* really meant). Go to Paris. Go to the movies, especially the movies of Humphrey Bogart. Behave, when moving among the spaces of the city, as if your movements were continually underscored by the jabbing recurrences of Martial Solal's score. Wear hats indoors. Make faces in the mirror. Play a favorite piece of music with the understated reverence of Belmondo for the Mozart clarinet concerto. Live in discrete, carefully measured takes, leapfrogging from jump cut to jump cut. And aspire to the company of someone just like Jean Seberg, with the hope she would not finally betray you to the police—or, more plausibly, betray you with a rival like the mysteriously creepy *Herald Tribune* editor incarnated by Van Doude.

In the long central scene between Belmondo and Seberg—the scene that in retrospect *was* the movie, all the others merely orbiting around it—we imagined the possibility of love as play. This constant discovering of expressions and gestures, this deployment of hats and posters and quotations from Faulkner in the service of some ineffable higher communication between lovers, was what life was to be about. How many times would we emulate the staring contest in which Seberg gazes at Belmondo "to know what's behind your face"? The answer to her question might well be: nothing, perhaps. We were duly jolted when Belmondo, in response to Faulkner's "Between grief and nothing I will choose grief," opted decisively for nothing: "*Le chagrin c'est idiot, je choisis le néant.*" But if this was nihilism, it was a nihilism that looked very much like fun.

Given the advanced level of game playing going on, all that other business of murder and betrayal and final brutal rejection seemed likewise a game. Each role could be tried on and reversed and changed for another. Back then I don't think I believed for a moment that the Michel who gunned down the cop and mugged the unfortunate fellow in the men's room was the same Michel who clowned so engagingly and was moved by Mozart: any more than I believed that the Patricia who slept her way to journalistic success and ratted on her boyfriend was the same Patricia whose American-accented French was so indescribably irresistible. Each character consisted of a series of moves, perversely changeable, and hardly adding up to anything like a coherent personality. The flitting, whimsical zigzags that Michel and Patricia engaged in with every move looked like supreme freedom, the freedom not to be a character in what Bosley Crowther might have called a "three-dimensional, psychologically nuanced" film. They were free to make themselves up as they went along, and this promised to be no game but the most serious thing in the world.

Movies had always provided materials for improvisational role-playing: that was in fact their chief function. As kids we had played *Lost Patrol* or *King Kong* in the backyard, replaying fantasies brought to us courtesy of Million Dollar Movie—scripts for the imagination, all the more powerful because in pre-video days they had to be reconstructed from memory. If we had learned to stare attentively at movies, it was only in order to retain as much as possible for subsequent use. What seemed to be happening in *Breathless* amounted to a revolution: the people watching the movies had asserted control over them. If Godard became an immediate hero, it was because he had reversed the power relationship of mesmerized viewer to entrancing spectacle.

The wall separating movie from audience had been smashed, right from the moment when Belmondo launched into monologue mode while driving along in his stolen car. It wasn't that he addressed the audience directly (Groucho Marx and Bob Hope and others had done that for comic effect) but that he didn't: he treated the screen as a space in which a private freedom might be indulged. In Godard, the moviegoer had taken over the movie, and where he had gone any of us might follow. The moment-to-moment exchanges of *Breathless* were not exotic or extraordinary in themselves; they became so because they had been filmed—or rather, they existed in the first place in order to be filmed. This was not film as a record of ordinary life but cinematic utopia: a continuous process of inventing the world by turning it into a movie.

*Film Comment,* 2010

# dreamland

THERE IS A PHOTOGRAPH OF Josef von Sternberg from 1937 in which he looks like a character from one of his own films: a turbaned magus with elegantly trimmed beard and moustache, holding a cigarette as he gazes out obliquely, with the hint of an ironic expression too remote to be called a smile. It remains difficult to separate von Sternberg from the mythology that began to form around him early in his career, largely, if not entirely, with his own encouragement. The "von" for instance was not his by birth but was tacked on to his name to add an extra flourish to the credits of a 1924 film (*By Divine Right*) on which he had assisted director Roy William Neill—it wasn't Sternberg's idea, but he embraced it from the start. The aristocratic moniker helped establish his image as another exotic European import, while in fact his roots as a filmmaker were purely American.

He was born in Vienna in 1894, but his family emigrated to America seven years thereafter, and although he did return to Austria between the ages of ten and fourteen, it was in Fort Lee, New Jersey, that he made his first tentative steps into the film business. He came to film almost randomly, as a repairer of damaged celluloid, an appropriately technical job for someone whose technical mastery was evident from his earliest efforts. He worked, virtually from the start, at all aspects of filmmaking, as cutter, cameraman, and screenwriter, and aspired always to combine those functions and more. Of *The Scarlet Empress*

(1934) he would later remark, not untypically: "With one exception, every detail, scenery, paintings, sculptures, costumes, story, photography, every gesture by a player, was dominated by me."

The first film he directed, *The Salvation Hunters* (1925)—a low-budget, independent feature coproduced with the English actor George K. Arthur—caught the attention of Charlie Chaplin and launched von Sternberg into a directorial career that initially seemed to unravel as rapidly as it had taken shape. Signed to MGM, he made a film (*The Exquisite Sinner*) that was then largely reshot by another director; its follow-up, *The Masked Bride*, was abandoned by Sternberg (in Andrew Sarris's account, "he turned his camera toward the ceiling and walked off the set") and finished by someone else. Chaplin then engaged him to make *The Sea Gull* (1926) but, for reasons never fully clarified, suppressed the film after a single public screening (the only print known to survive appears to have been subsequently destroyed for tax reasons). At this early stage Sternberg had already acquired his unshakeable reputation as self-vaunting artist and obsessive and tyrannical taskmaster, driving his actors through endless retakes and striving as he always would for a monopoly of creative control. "If Sternberg set out to inspire general dislike," Kevin Brownlow has written of his reputation among Hollywood colleagues, "he succeeded impressively." (William Powell, after starring in *The Last Command* and *The Drag Net*, had it written into his contract that he was never to be directed by von Sternberg; Joel McCrea walked off the set of *The Scarlet Empress* after a single encounter.)

Von Sternberg's technical know-how made him eminently employable, however, and in 1927 he was entrusted with *Underworld*, a scenario about Chicago gangsters concocted by Ben Hecht, who certainly knew something about the subject. Hecht was aghast at what Sternberg did to his script—only a few elements of the original had been preserved, and Hecht's hard-boiled veneer had given way to a more romantic, not to say operatic, mood—but the film was a massive and unexpected hit, and its success launched an eight-year association with Paramount, by far Sternberg's most productive period. *Underworld* was followed by the masterpieces *The Last Command* and *The Docks of New York* (both 1928), along with two other silent films now lost (*The Drag Net*, 1928, and *The Case of Lena Smith*, 1929).

After his first talkie, *Thunderbolt* (1929), another gangster vehicle with George Bancroft, von Sternberg went to Berlin in 1930, at the invitation of producer Erich Pommer, to make what would become the most famous of all his films, *The Blue Angel*. Its worldwide impact was magnified when von Sternberg brought his discovery Marlene Dietrich to Hollywood and proceeded to make a series of the most obsessively personal films ever made there. But when the popular triumphs *Morocco* (1930) and *Shanghai Express* (1932) were followed by the formally masterful and commercially disastrous *The Scarlet Empress* (1934) and *The Devil Is a Woman* (1935), Paramount was through with him. Afterward, he worked only sporadically and never with the budgets—or the freedom to use them to the limits of his imagination—that he had previously enjoyed.

VON STERNBERG, IN later life, made no great claims for *Underworld*, describing it in his autobiography as "an experiment in photographic violence and montage." He emphasized the concessions he had made to the mass audience (that "homogeneous herd," as he characteristically described it, "united on its lowest level"): "I had provided the work with many an incident to placate the public, not ignoring the moss-covered themes of love and sacrifice. Human kindness was demonstrated by showing a murderer feeding a hungry kitten." Quite aside from his confidently orchestrated central love triangle, the film had other and more novel ingredients. Presumably a large part of what drew the crowds was the profusion of images—pouring out at a rapid tempo von Sternberg was never to surpass—that would become part of the common vocabulary of the gangster genre: a bank window exploding, squad cars moving frantically through dark city streets, loose women parading themselves in underworld lairs, the outlaw hero contemplating a neon sign that proclaims THE CITY IS YOURS, a gangster shot dead in his flower shop, his desperate killer besieged by police in an apartment, the windows shattering from barrages of gunfire as the room fills with smoke.

Rarely again would such images be rendered with the unyielding precision and florid magnificence that von Sternberg brought to them. Charting his characters' movements through shadowy alleys and subterranean nightspots, he turned drab urban spaces into an ominous labyrinth, a mythic place. Audiences may well have been persuaded that they were getting the hard-boiled lowdown on a big city's lower depths, but anything like documentary realism was far from von Sternberg's concerns. It is safe to say that gangsters, and Chicago, and the literary aspirations of Ben Hecht interested him only to the extent that they could form part of that imaginary universe he was only beginning to formulate, and that would masquerade elsewhere as Russia, North Africa, China, Spain, and the South Pacific. Neither quite European nor quite American, he created naturally enough a cinema of exile, taking place everywhere and nowhere. *Underworld* is of a piece with the dream poetry of *Morocco* and *Anatahan* (1953), and was received as such by spectators around the world. In France it was given the resonant title *Les nuits de Chicago*, inspired perhaps by the patch of gorgeous intertitle lyricism that opens the film: "A great city in the dead of night . . . streets lonely, moon-flooded . . . buildings empty as the cliff-dwellings of a forgotten age."

What is apparent from the outset is the extreme concision of von Sternberg's cinematic language. Preambles and subsidiary details interest him not at all. A gangster named Bull Weed (George Bancroft) and an intellectual drunk whose claim of trustworthy silence earns him the nickname Rolls Royce (Clive Brook) encounter each other on the street in the wake of a violent bank robbery. They bond in an exchange of glances that conveys everything we need to know about them: Bull is tough, generous, and stupid; Rolls Royce is capable of loyalty yet endowed with infinite irony. The two male leads represent altogether opposed types, Bancroft a raucous, barreling force of nature, brutal yet open-hearted; Brook (the first of many protagonists one might easily take for a surrogate of the director) a tightly controlled embodiment of brooding intellectual detachment masquerading as sardonic humor.

With barely a pause, we find ourselves off the streets and deep into the nocturnal world of the Dreamland Café. There could hardly be a more appropriate name for this early example of the primal Sternbergian locale, the place where time is suspended so that the most elemental human confrontations and transactions can play themselves out as ritual: the unconscious as nightclub or brothel or casino. He would return to such an interior again and again, in *The Docks of New York*, *The Blue Angel*, *Morocco*, *Blonde Venus* (1932), *The Shanghai Gesture* (1941). It is, as well, the perfect simulacrum of the film studio, where artifice reigns supreme and reality itself becomes malleable through the deployment of artfully fake décor and carefully manipulated lighting. (In his next work, *The Last Command*, the film studio would be the literal setting.)

Following a brief evocation of the scurrying of alley cats, the archetypal woman (never far to seek in his films) enters the visual field— Feathers McCoy, incarnated by Evelyn Brent as a sort of abstract quintessence of the flapper, sheathed in a feather-fringed coat and furthered adorned with a white feather boa that, in a manner typical of von Sternberg, establishes itself as a primary element of the movie. To identify the character with the garment is not simple fetishism (if fetishism is ever simple) but a means of shifting the spectator to the plain of perception where, for von Sternberg, the real narrative action unfolds: the level where cloth and flesh and glint of eye, texture and curvature and depth of shadow, outweigh the plot points that serve merely to direct us toward those effects. This is not to say that he indulges in meaningless abstraction but that he arrives through abstraction at the deep story, the inward story, for which the outer is camouflage. At the heart of the fake is the real.

As Feathers bends at the top of the stairs to adjust her stocking, a loose feather floating down lands at the feet of the disheveled Rolls Royce, employed at sweeping out the place. The way the movement of a single feather is made to dominate our perception establishes once and for all the unique flavor of von Sternberg's film world. This feather, and nothing else, will be the center of the universe for as long as he decrees. The peculiar undulant beauty of its movement, the power of its compressed radiance: such things are not incidentals but essence. In his autobiography he writes: "Light can go straight, penetrate and turn back, be reflected and deflected, gathered and spread, bent as by a soap bubble, made to sparkle and be blocked . . . The journey of rays from that central core to the outposts of blackness is the adventure and drama of light."

The adventure and drama of light is anything but cold. It finds its ultimate expression in those close-ups of faces that are the pivot points of all his films, everything around them serving only to bridge the gaps between one glance and another. If for a time at least he managed to be both supremely self-expressive artist and canny manipulator of popular taste, it was because he could combine in a single image the most obvious meanings and the most infinitely variable shades of ambivalence. The dance of desire and resistance that plays out in the relationship of Feathers and Rolls Royce is played out entirely in a language of glances and gestures that has retained its sense of intimate reality. This place where lovers' eyes meet, or fail to meet—a place potentially of savage cruelty and abject self-punishment, where all possible contradictions of feeling may come into play—is Sternberg's native ground, around which all the rest of his world is constructed out of shadows and nets and paper streamers.

Vision as erotic experience, so basic to how movies work their effect, has rarely been acknowledged so lucidly as in von Sternberg's films. This is perhaps the secret of their enduring freshness: for all the baroque complication and fine-wire work with which they are put together, his worlds have the mercuriality of free-floating desire, even as they penetrate undiscovered reaches of the decadent and grotesque. The great centerpiece of *Underworld*, the criminals' annual ball, is a sodden, bestial mess that is made to seem lighter than air, a delirious carnival of luminosity and exquisitely choreographed chaos. Here as elsewhere in the film, one can become absorbed simply in following the movements of bodies in space, delighting in patterns whose rhythmic beauty exists quite apart from the brutal appetites and uncontrolled rages of the characters.

OF ALL DIRECTORS, Josef von Sternberg most completely took charge of the terms in which his work would be discussed, in statements unsurpassed for unapologetic bluntness: "My pictures are acts of arrogance." "All art is an exploration of an unreal world." "To reality one should prefer the illusion of reality." "Actors are material with which one works." "Marlene is not Marlene, she is me." As curator of his own legend he could easily be seen as passing over into self-parody. *Fun in a Chinese Laundry* (1965), his disdainful, self-aggrandizing autobiography, written in a style that alternates between ponderous irony and purple patches of exotic description, manages simultaneously to elaborate his myth and to undercut it. If his is a cinema of masks, the "I" of this memoir virtually declares itself yet one more mask, and one more calculated to repel than attract.

It is nonetheless one of the best books about the chaotic circumstances under which films are actually made, and ultimately as clear an enunciation of aesthetic principles as any director has formulated. He speaks again and again of the "loose ends" and "slippery factors" inherent in filmmaking, the random expressiveness of anything that comes within range of camera and microphone, an expressiveness that must be curtailed rather than encouraged: "The director writes with the camera whether he wishes to do so or not." His art finally was not one of expansion and profusion but of rigorous compression, eliminating everything that did not pertain to the essence of what he wished to show: "To photograph a human being properly, all that surrounds him must definitely add to him, or it will do nothing but subtract."

Had von Sternberg only made his great silent trilogy—*Underworld*, *The Last Command*, and *The Docks of New York*—he would endure as a supreme example of what it means to write with film. We would miss only the more extreme personal elaborations of the later work:

the seven films with Dietrich (which seem more than ever a single film and a central text of the twentieth century), and the final masterpieces *The Shanghai Gesture* and *Anatahan*, along with a handful of unforgettable scenes in what remains of his version of *Jet Pilot* (1950), a regrettably isolated example of what he could do with color. His high opinion of his own capabilities and his majestic sense of his poetic vocation might indeed seem like intolerable arrogance were they not so undeniably justified.

The Criterion Collection, 2010

# left alone

SEEING LEO MCCAREY'S *MAKE WAY for Tomorrow* for the first time at sixteen I found myself, midway through the picture, in a state of mounting suspense. I was waiting for the moment when it would be spoiled by some loss of nerve or failure of tone—waiting above all for the last-minute change of heart that would precipitate the seemingly inevitable happy ending. This 1937 release, which I caught at a rare screening at the Museum of Modern Art, came as a complete surprise: it did not figure in any film history I knew of and had never turned up on television. I had the privilege of seeing it without the slightest advance notice of what the plot was about, and so was able to experience the full shock of this still shocking film. If, even though overwhelmed, I still failed to rate it as highly as it deserved it was only because the subject matter remained exotic. The fate of the old in a money-driven and ever more youth-centered society was not yet in the forefront of my concerns.

I was more or less of an age with Rhoda, the restless teenager discomfited by having to give up her bedroom for her grandmother; and *Make Way for Tomorrow* is a film that changes not only from scene to scene, and depending on the shifting viewpoints of the various characters, but according to the age of the spectator. That spectator is lucky who, by the time he gets to the age of Bark (Victor Moore) and Lucy (Beulah Bondi), has not lived or witnessed some of these episodes, or has lived them without any residual guilt. The easy judgments of a young viewer give way to an appreciation of how fairly Leo McCarey has treated all his characters. Not even the worst of them—not even the embittered Cora, begrudging her father even a bowl of chicken soup—is turned into a caricature or stock villain. It is precisely that fairness that makes it such a painful film. We come to understand all too well why people fall just shy of doing the courageous or charitable thing.

It is only the element of compassion in McCarey—a compassion even for those who show little of it themselves—that keeps the movie from being as brutally schematic as some Brechtian *Lehrstück* in which impersonal economic forces effortlessly subvert the claims of filial devotion. The toughness is nonetheless impressive. Aged parents lose their home and must rely on the help of their children; those children care for them only begrudgingly; the couple are separated for what is supposed to be only a little while but turns out to be forever. The parents accept their fate as gracefully as they can; the children acknowledge their less than admirable conduct and (it must be presumed) carry on as before. All the touches of human feeling that crop up—the friendship of the Jewish storekeeper Max Rubens, the fleeting moments of fellow feeling evoked in the granddaughter Rhoda and the housekeeper Mamie, the unexpected generosity of the car salesman and the hotel employees at the end—do nothing to alleviate the harshness of the story's bare outline.

It is a movie that insists on being seen more than once for its effects to be grasped. Its beauties reveal themselves most fully when we know the outcome. Many of these beauties have to do with the compression or elision of long stretches of time—or, by contrast, the expansion of instants into eternities. At ninety-two minutes, *Make Way for Tomorrow* feels as long and dense as a novel. It uses everything McCarey knew about pacing—a great deal, since he had learned his craft making hundreds of movies with Laurel and Hardy, Charlie Chase, and other Hal Roach players before moving on to Eddie Cantor, Burns and Allen, W.C. Fields, the Marx Brothers, and Mae West—to chart the intimate rhythms of some of life's most uncomfortable moments. A film about aging becomes more broadly a film about how time is measured, experienced, and valued.

With consummate subtlety McCarey reveals the varying rhythms and time-perceptions of characters within the same scene, the same frame. When Lucy comes to live with George and his family, she disturbs their sense not just of space but of time; she's a drag on the jazz age impatience of Rhoda, an awkward interruption of the carefully calibrated tempo of Anita's bridge party. Likewise, when Bark visits his friend Max, time expands genially; the two men might happily sit there for hours without moving. When Bark returns to his daughter Cora, he is once again a prisoner of her brusque rhythm of automatic denial and exclusion; and when Max comes calling on the ailing Bark, he must force a change to Cora's rhythm just to get through the door.

The movie is bookended by two units of time: the fifty years of Bark and Lucy's marriage and the five hours that in the end are all they have to spend together before separating forever. In between we are given to contemplate a variety of other durations: the three months after which the couple will supposedly be reunited (the three months that for their children are an intolerable period during which their lives must be disrupted); the length of Anita's bridge soirée, with as a subset the length of the feature film (presumably roughly the same length as the one we are watching) that Rhoda is prevailed on to take her grandmother to see, and during which she slips out for a quick rendezvous with her boyfriend; the length, encompassed within that film, of the melodramatic saga of self-sacrifice that we can easily imagine from Lucy's abbreviated summary of it.

THE OPENING SCENE in particular has a tragic force fully perceptible only in retrospect. It provides our sole glimpse of the world about to be broken, or more precisely our introduction to a world already broken, a family fallen apart into incompatible contingents, with only the feckless drunkard Robert preserving a patina of warmth and gaiety.

As the reuniting parents and children tenuously sustain an air of optimism and kind intentions, the premise of the plot—Bark and Lucy's unanticipated financial failure—is laid out with a maximum of concision, the character of each family member unobtrusively sketched. It is the only time we see Bark and Lucy in their own domain, independent figures exuding the weight of a long life lived in one place; and even as we absorb that information we are watching fifty years of stability ineluctably dissolve under the influence of another kind of time: the time in which loans come due before they are ready to be paid.

Evocations of the Old Homestead are a staple of early American film as they were of the American novel and the American stage, but if *Make Way for Tomorrow* begins in a mode that resonates with certain scenes from D.W. Griffith and John Ford and Henry King, it moves very rapidly away from any myth of the united clan. That opening scene allows us to wonder, for example, why Bark and Lucy ended up with so uncharitable a brood. We might notice the barely disguised superiority that Bark feels toward his children, as if he already sees through them: that glimpse prepares us for the sarcastic edge of his last phone call announcing that he and Lucy will not show up for the obligatory farewell dinner intended chiefly to salve the children's consciences. We cannot avoid thinking that if he was irresponsible about money he may have been likewise irresponsible about paying attention to his children, and that Lucy, in showering her offspring with love in the best way she knew, may nonetheless have been a stifling presence they were only too happy to get away from. The very fact that we can ponder such questions indicates the degree to which these characters exist all the way round. We can envision pasts and futures for them, and are constantly pushed toward imagining further scenes beyond the instances shown.

The children emerge from the start as a set of studies in incapacity: Nellie vain and self-absorbed, Robert cheerfully incompetent, Cora nurturing her depression like a slow-acting poison, George applying all his intelligence and sensitivity toward preserving an acceptably harmonious domestic surface even if he has to lacerate his own conscience in the process. We are made aware of how solitary each of them is—an awareness that will only deepen as the film goes on—and aware too of how each changes from moment to moment in response to changing situations. None of the offspring is quite ready for the challenges thrown at them, and they barely conceal their discomfort at being put to the test. Bark and Lucy at the same time are surprised at the newly revealed instability of their world, surprised by the insights it gives them into those they thought they knew. They understand more than their children can stand to give them credit for—the most beautiful shots in the film are the close-ups that reveal that understanding—but what they understand is still partial, still straining to make sense of things. One thinks of the poet George Oppen's phrase: "the old new to age as the young to youth." The power of the long last episode is in its disclosure of two old people continuing to learn about each other until the last moment. Every instant—carefully measured out by railroad timetables and radio announcements—is precious to them because it affords the opportunity to discover a new aspect of each other.

That last episode is also an almost unbearable hymn to freedom, in a movie driven from first to last by harsh necessity, even in an America where luxury hotels occasionally hand out a bit of largesse in the interest of better customer relations and delightful music spreads out over the airwaves as the band leader asks: "Is everybody happy?" We are never allowed to forget the tragedy of a world governed by "the bank." Not one character has any real freedom. The apparent comfort of George and Anita's household is maintained only with difficulty—the bridge evening is not a party but a money-making enterprise. Life is a struggle over minor privileges and small areas of leeway. That the smartest of the children, George, fully appreciates the ultimate vanity of their concerns does not help him to rise above them. He will feel guilt (especially after the painful moment when Lucy reveals he was her favorite child)—more than his less sensitive sisters, more profoundly than his brother who clearly sees himself as an outsider—but not guilty enough to remedy the situation. Guilt is simply the price he is willing to pay for preserving the comforts of a meanly held status quo.

*MAKE WAY FOR Tomorrow* reveals how conscious McCarey's art was while at the same reminding us how rarely he employed it without dilution. Here without question is its undiluted essence, as he well knew. "It was both very humorous and very dramatic," he told *Cahiers du Cinéma* in a 1965 interview. "It's difficult for me to say more about it, but I think it was very lovely to see. . . . If I really have any talent that is where it appears." The humor is crucial for a story that could so easily sink beyond retrieval into the maudlin. The whole film exists along the line where comedy just crosses over into real pain. There is hardly an episode that could not with slight alterations have been a triumph of screwball wit. Imagine how hilarious the bridge party scene could have been, with each moment of social awkwardness and cultural clash played up along the lines of *The Awful Truth*, or into what indelible grotesques Nellie or Cora or Anita could have been transformed.

*Make Way for Tomorrow* stands alone among the films of the period just as it stands alone among McCarey's other films. He would follow it with a magnificent screwball comedy, *The Awful Truth*, and a sublime romantic parable, *Love Affair*, but he would never revert to such unblinking accuracy. The 1930s in American film were an era of unparalleled show-biz rowdiness and gaudy melodramatics, unmatched for behavioral flamboyance and verbal invention. The talkies announced their presence by shouting and showing off. In that context what is most striking about *Make Way* is its refusal to exaggerate. Not once does it go for the revved-up gag line or the milked emotion. The absence of exaggeration is supremely embodied in the performances, especially those of Victor Moore, Beulah Bondi, Thomas Mitchell, Fay Bainter, Maurice Moscovitch, and Louise Beavers. It takes many viewings to take in all the incidental beauties of acting so restrained and truthful.

As Gary Giddins has pointed out, the film is remarkable in its avoidance of any religious allusion, whether verbal or visual. Is it that absence that generates such an unaccustomed sense of the horrific pettiness of everyday life? The piety by which Hollywood expected the miseries of old age to be assuaged is singularly absent, replaced by the memory of passion and an appreciation of the dwindling present moment. The unspoken theme might be what remains after the conventional comforts of faith and family ties have been removed, and the rigor with which that theme is expressed seems to stem from a moment of crisis. Made in the wake of a near-fatal illness and the death of McCarey's father, *Make Way for Tomorrow* is a work of unique contemplative clarity, as if every moment of life were being held up for our mindful inspection.

Single shots could be whole movies: George and Anita contemplating themselves in the mirror could be expanded into a gloomy feature about the future self-recriminations that await them. The weight of gestures and glances is measured with painful precision. The tenderness, for example, with which Rhoda caresses her grandmother in a moment of late-night affection is both a sincere effusion and a meaningless, self-serving reaction. It makes her feel better for a moment, but it does not mean that she will ever make the smallest sacrifice for her grandmother's sake, something of which her grandmother is quite aware. At every moment we are invited to think about how much any given character understands about any other—right up to that last shot in which Lucy is left finally alone, utterly powerless, and perhaps understanding everything.

*Masters of Cinema*, 2010

# dark magic

OUT OF ALL THE EXTRAVAGANT variety of Jean Cocteau's work—the paintings and drawings, the poems, the plays and novels and memoirs, the opera librettos and ballet scenarios—it is likely that his films will have the most enduring influence; and of those films, *Beauty and the Beast* will have the most pervasive effect. When it comes to "fairy tale movies"—if such a genre exists as something other than a profit center for the Disney corporation—there is Cocteau's *Beauty and the Beast* and then there is everything else. It is a safe bet that no one who surrenders to it at an impressionable age ever quite escapes the distinct and disturbing enchantments it sets in motion.

It is perhaps the most self-effacing of Cocteau's works. His flamboyance and wit are placed at the service of the old folkloric tale given its standard form in the eighteenth century by Madame Leprince de Beaumont. Even as he adds his own characteristic complications to the tale—giving the Beast a thoroughly earthly and unenchanted doppelgänger, Avenant, and adding a mythic dimension by means of a secret temple to Diana—he allows the pure force of the narrative to assert itself, as if content for once to figure as a kind of medieval artisan. An artisan among artisans: the film is virtually a showcase for the best in French production design (Christian Bérard), music (Georges Auric), cinematography (Henri Alekan), and costuming (Marcel Escoffier). Yet the net effect is if anything austere rather than lush, a tribute to

Cocteau's unerring sense that here the tale, with its mysterious and inescapable imperatives, is everything.

The film is inescapably tied up with the war during which it was planned. Shooting began four months after the German surrender. The deprivations of the period account for the fact that it was not filmed in color as Cocteau had wished—hard as it is to imagine the movie apart from Alekan's black-and-white palette, with its careful distinction between a deceptively sunny ordinary reality and the Beast's domain of night. The harshness in the background is perceptible in other ways. The storybook setting of a seventeenth-century farmhouse, into which we are ushered by the phrase "once upon a time," is revealed within a few moments as a place of vanity and venality, cowardice and petty-minded squabbling, slaps and insults. It is a fallen world, in which Belle seems to withdraw into a hermetic suffering amid the meanness of her elder sisters, the feckless opportunism of her brother, the moral weakness of her father, and the overtures of Jean Marais's handsome and empty Avenant. The hellishness of this pictorially elegant but reso-lutely unmagical reality, further amplified by the implied rapacity of encircling creditors and moneylenders, makes it an unlikely setting for any conceivable "happy ever after."

By establishing how truly oppressive is the world that Belle and her father inhabit, Cocteau makes all the more uncanny the discovery, by the harried merchant, of a passageway out of it, into the Beast's realm. It is like the breaching of a seam, and we are carried through every part of the process: through misty forest and up deserted staircase, through the great door and, in the most otherworldly of camera movements, down the hall of human arms extending candelabra whose flames spontaneously flare up—a rite of initiation that loses none of its power from learning that it was achieved by filming the action backward, and that it was shot not by Cocteau but by his assistant René Clément. You can play it back time and again without exhausting the sense of shock at having passed through some ordinary invisible portal.

If this is magic it is a shaggy, palpable sort of magic. As a true poet—whether writing verse or otherwise—Cocteau had a hard-earned mistrust of the merely atmospheric, decorative vagueness misnamed "poetic": "My method," he wrote at the outset of his journal of the shooting of *Beauty and the Beast*, "is simple: not to aim at poetry. That must come of its own accord. The mere whispered mention of its name frightens it away." The result, of course, was a film that as much as any other has been praised as lyrical, almost unbearable in its ethereal gorgeousness, a triumph of the imagination—even when it may just as accurately be described as tough-minded, down to earth, ferociously unsentimental. If Cocteau's film continues to breathe, as few have done, the air of the fantastic, it is because we sense at each moment that we are caught up in a process governed by laws, laws that may be difficult to explain or even articulate but that express themselves by the most concrete means: "Fantasy has its own laws, which are like those of perspective. You may not bring what is distant into the foreground, nor render fuzzily what is near." Like a ritual performed in order to produce results, not merely to make the participants feel good, *Beauty and the Beast* moves through its phases undistracted by anything but the business at hand.

Any prettiness is incidental, mere drapery over darker and more archaic imperatives. The underlying structure is nearly pitiless, an intricately intermeshing machinery loaded with hidden traps. Cocteau has a logician's respect for the orders of ritual and the cruel demands of ritual sacrifice. His "magic" has, from certain angles, the paranoid efficiency of a cosmic prison house in which miracles exist but only at a harshly exacted price. The weightless happiness that is the perennial promise of both fairy tales and movies is to be attained at a cost measured out frame by frame, in a story more full of suffering than of wish fulfillment—and in which, indeed, the promise of ecstasy embraced in the moment of final metamorphosis quickly threatens to become a more banal contentment. Even as Belle and her prince (the Beast transformed into the double of the unreliable Avenant) soar into the sky, she seems already to realize that this is not exactly what she wanted. The instant reaction attributed to Greta Garbo captured perfectly the strange disappointment of the "happy" ending: "Give me back my Beast!"

In *Beauty and the Beast*, as previously in *The Blood of a Poet* (1930) and later in *Orpheus* (1950), Cocteau was able to realize the fantastic not as an escape from the real but as an extension of it, its reverse side. He has no interest in Neverlands or Wonderlands. He approaches the paraphernalia of the fairy tale—those enchanted mirrors, keys, gloves—with a technician's dispassion, not taken aback by their existence, any more than by the existence of trees or streams or horses or rose gardens, but always curious about how they function. For Cocteau "movie magic" is not a glib catchphrase. As a science of transformation, cinema becomes true alchemy. The mirror in *Blood of a Poet* that becomes a splashing pool as one passes through it is not an illusion but an achieved reality; in *Orpheus*, the comings and goings between the realms of the living and the dead are rendered in a spirit of documentary observation. If magic requires the use of specialized equipment, for Cocteau that equipment includes the whole somnambulistic repertoire of the movies' night side from Méliès on out. When in watching *Beauty and the Beast* we think at one moment or another of *Nosferatu* or *Metropolis* or *Dracula* or *King Kong*, it is with a sense not that they have been imitated or self-consciously alluded to but as if their effective elements had been incorporated wholesale as needed by the resident shaman.

The magic is sexual throughout—a fantastic but not in the least morbid or phantasmal sex magic. What could be more direct and free of coyness than the image of the Beast drinking water from Belle's hands, although it is so chaste that no censor could ever have assailed it? It is matched by the tactile immediacy of the moment when the grieving beast presses his furry face against the fur coverlet of Belle's empty bed. The irresistible effect of everything that happens after Belle enters the castle is tied to a mood of forbidden intimacy: her slow-motion advance into the Beast's great hall, as she moves past the billowing white curtains and Georges Auric's music bursts out in choral ululations; her passage through the talking door into the privacies of mirror and bed; the night wanderings in which she spies on the Beast in the aftermath of his nocturnal slaughters, while he stares in horror at his smoking hands.

The extraordinarily beautiful shot in which we see the Beast from behind, his head haloed in light, as he ascends the stairs with Belle in his arms, while, on the other side of the screen, light streams through dungeonlike grillwork, conjures with gothic intensity the imminence of a sexual fantasy fulfilled, in a setting made for such fulfillment— a bedroom hidden within a castle hidden within a forest—and with Beauty delivered defenseless into the embrace of a Beast manifestly able to sweep away all resistance. The erotic force of the episode that follows is matched only by the even greater emotional force of the restraint that stops him in his tracks and sends him rushing out of the room saying: "You must not look in my eyes."

It is of course his eyes that we look at, glistening from within the multilayered makeup that cost Marais five hours of application each day, makeup so expressive that Marais's real face seems a blank by comparison. We cannot shake the certainty that an actual creature has been introduced into the world, and the sorrow provoked by his disappearance recurs anew on each viewing. I doubt whether such a solitary and tragic figure has ever been so fully realized in movies, realized not only by Hagop Arakelian's makeup skills and Marais's performance but by the universe that has been created to form a context around him, made out of Cocteau's words, Auric's music, Alekan's images.

As for Belle, she is finally almost as much a cipher as the statue of Diana that breaks the spell by shooting an arrow into the rascally Avenant. When the Beast tells her that "you are the only master here," he underscores the cruelty at the heart of Cocteau's fable. Beauty is indeed the master of all the craftsmanlike skills brought to their highest pitch to realize this singular vision: a Beauty who may offer love or capriciously withhold it, a Beauty who wants only a rose—even if that rose may threaten death to anyone who gives it to her, a Beauty who may after all know herself least of all and therefore never fully grasp her own all-determining power. Only in the mirror-world of art can Beauty and Beast truly cohabit. And even for Cocteau, master of such a range of arts, what art but cinema—the magic mirror itself—could ever realize that cohabitation so persuasively?

The Criterion Collection, 2011

# the variety of filmic experience

IN HIS LAST BOOK WILLIAM James wrote: "One need only shut oneself in a closet and begin to think of the fact of one's being there, of one's queer bodily shape in the darkness (a thing to make children scream at, as Stevenson says), of one's fantastic character and all, to have the wonder steal over the detail as much as over the general fact of being, and to see that it is only familiarity that blunts it. Not only that *anything* should be, but that *this* very thing should be, is mysterious! Philosophy stares, but brings no reasoned solution, for from nothing to being there is no logical bridge." Probably no one is currently contemplating a movie version of *Some Problems of Philosophy*, but Terrence Malick is the rare contemporary filmmaker I can imagine being drawn to the idea—not because he studied with Stanley Cavell at Harvard and has published a translation of Heidegger's *The Essence of Reasons*, but because in all his five films and most especially the latest, *The Tree of Life*, he seems determined to turn narrative movies into vehicles for posing unanswerable metaphysical questions, not in words but in the quite distinct language of cinema.

In the same way that William James applies the tensile force of his logical prose toward the evocation of an imperceptible bridge beyond logic that must, somehow, be there, Malick has continued to muster the resources of film toward embodying what cannot actually be embodied. He wants to make film do what it is least able to do. Not content with showing how the world looks, he wants to show how it is experienced from the inside, even if that inside story can only be suggested through the cunning deployment of *"this* very thing": this door closing, this muttered banality, this drowned body floating in a swimming pool, this wounded dinosaur, this erupting volcano, this suburban backyard, this face averted to avoid looking at another face. What he hopes to arrive at through the splicing together of such elements is something as unresolved as the stares of James's philosophers: a suite of widescreen open questions.

The dialogue track of *The Tree of Life* swarms with questions, right from the start. The drifting, pleading voice-overs that provide the ground bass of *The Tree of Life* are not far in spirit from James's list of "various obscure, abstract, and universal questions which the sciences and life in general suggest but do not solve," any one of which might provide a convenient point of entry to a viewing of Malick's film: "What are 'thoughts,' and what are 'things'? and how are they connected? . . . Is there a common stuff out of which all facts are made? . . . Which is the most real kind of reality? What binds all things into one universe?" The film's portentous epigraph is the grandest question of all, God's challenge to Job—"Where wast thou when I laid the foundations of the earth?"—the ultimate instance of answering a question with a question.

Malick has never shied from grandiosity, and in *The Tree of Life* more than ever before he risks the humorless and overblown. Into what might in other hands have been the small-scale, melancholy tale—too elliptical really to be called a tale—of a not unusually eventful Texas childhood, he has managed to incorporate the creation of the universe, the origins of life on earth, the age of dinosaurs, and the prospect of future dissolution, with musical accompaniment by the massive tonalities of Berlioz's "Requiem Mass." But he has made an audacious and magnificent film.

The extreme variations of scale are no afterthought in Malick's scheme. To show the world in a grain of sand he must first establish what the world is. So he will walk us through the stages and conditions

and outer boundaries of human existence, provide a basic introduction to annihilating and fecundating cosmic forces, move freely back
and forth in time for lingering glances at birth and death and family
and memory as if they were only marginally familiar phenomena, as
if no one had ever done any of this before, in a movie at least—and
indeed who ever did in quite this head-on fashion? He manages to
make childhood (and *The Tree of Life* is beyond anything else a movie
descriptive of childhood) seem a somewhat neglected condition,
deserving of reexamination. He is continually trying out different ways
of representing acts of perception: the perspective of a child looking
up at the adult world, or looking down from some hidden perch, the
abrupt rhythm of a child glancing quickly at some terrifying outburst
of adult anger and then turning away, the sheared-off gaps in editing
that can mark a moment as a fresh eternity disconnected from what
preceded it.

MALICK HAS ALWAYS shown an exact sense of what still remained
to be put on a screen. He is steeped in the work of cinematic anteced-
ents without ever seeming imitative; perhaps only a director with such
a formidable awareness of formal limits could apply himself so deliberately to dissolving or transcending them. His first film, *Badlands*
(1973), a fictionalized version of Charlie Starkweather and Caril Ann
Fugate's 1950s Midwestern murder rampage, was a blast of stylistic
rigor in an era trending more toward laid-back improvisation, each
frame executed with painterly precision, a near-solemn exactness
strangely at odds with the randomness of the protagonists' crime spree.

With its evocation of road movie nihilism, *Badlands* could just
about fit in with other movies of its decade; its successor, *Days of
Heaven* (1978), coming along after *Easy Rider* had given way to *Jaws*,
seemed to be feeling its way toward an entirely different decade, and
not just because of its period setting. The two films were very different in effect: *Badlands* bright and razor-sharp and profoundly opaque,
a perverse marriage of the murderous and childlike; *Days of Heaven*,

set on a farm in the Texas Panhandle, summoning up with a sort of biblical (or at least Dreiserian) splendor and gravity a pre–World War I world of unrelenting harshness and emotional isolation, complete with a plague of locusts.

Perhaps the clue was those locusts: both prophetic figures of devastation and actual creatures, pursuing their lives in intimate close-up within the 70-millimeter frame. To fold the human world into its ecosystem was to imagine a different kind of movie, keyed to different rhythms than the "beats" and "motivations" and "precipitating acts" that had by now become the industrially applied norm. The triangle drama that constituted the story line of Days of Heaven had the rudimentary quality of an early Eugene O'Neill one-acter, stripped even of O'Neill's dialogue. How much did one really care if Richard Gere stabbed Sam Shepard over Brooke Adams? It was a serviceable center, just one of the multiplicity of things going on in the world that Malick mapped with light and framing and jarring juxtaposition, with animals and landscape and weather, and with a narration disconnected just slightly enough from the images to convey the huge gap between words and things, between inner thought and outward event.

There are moments in Days of Heaven when he seems to want not simply to pay homage to Murnau and other silent masters but to become them—not to remake their movies but to make the movies they might have fleetingly imagined, movies with the associative and digressive freedom of a long poem too open-ended for the market to bear. The extended sequence near the end in which three fugitives escape downriver on a raft, the fleeting torch-lit scenes of life on shore conjuring a world of danger and weird beauty, seemed to incarnate Malick's own desire to make the screen itself a medium for escape into some further space, a fluid dimension of his own imagining. In retrospect his films seem like places that one enters rather than stories that one watches.

Malick's reputation would be secure if he had stopped making movies after Badlands and Days of Heaven, and for twenty years he did just that, for reasons not as yet fully chronicled. (Malick has rarely given interviews and is often described in the press as "famously reclusive" or the like.) In *The Thin Red Line* (1998) and *The New World* (2005) he seemed to pick up where he left off, treating large historical subjects (the Guadalcanal campaign and the settling of Jamestown) in a way that subordinated narrative to the eddying convolutions of subjective experience. The narrations that had featured strongly in his first two films now broadened out into a chorus of alternating inner voices almost in the manner of O'Neill's *Strange Interlude*, jettisoning the sharp characterization of the earlier voice-overs for a more trancelike and disembodied tone.

The natural world now more than ever competed with human actors for screen presence. Tight framing gave way to a more exploratory approach, with the camera constantly in motion finding out unexpected pathways, moving among swamps and foliage with desperate freedom. Hyperactive editing found multiple ways to divide scenes into component fragments, to mix up the particles of the world into fresh combinations, to distend or collapse the sense of duration as needed. (Malick's attention to editing accounts to some extent for the long gaps between his films; *The Tree of Life* was three years in the cutting room.) These were not movies that lent themselves to being absorbed in a single viewing. The first encounter was more like an occasion to get a rough sense of structure.

AS MANY HAVE noted, none of Malick's earlier films got nearer to the present than the 1950s. In *The Tree of Life* he has belatedly—he is now in his late sixties—made contact with the contemporary world, which as represented here by the corporate towers of Houston, Texas, seems more a harbinger of some space colony from which all traces of natural ecosystems have been definitively expunged. The towers are the habitat of Sean Penn as an architect ill at ease in his world. The movie itself can be taken as his memory drama, hinging on the death of a younger brother at nineteen; the whole film might be a poem of deep grief diffused over a lifetime.

The remembered eruption of that grief—the faces of the parents as they get the news—is conveyed in sharp disjunctive fragments that give way to Fiona Shaw, as the boy's maternal grandmother, comforting her daughter with a litany of every hackneyed phrase—"life goes on," "you will get over this"—inevitable at such times. The delivery of these catchphrases is too heartfelt to be satirical, but they are strung together a bit too systematically to feel naturalistic. As in all that follows, the effect is of seeing a memory staged, indelible in the realism of its details but edited and compressed over time, the relevant bits run together and the dross filtered out: the world as processed by the mind, with finally only the bright bits magnetized by emotion remaining to flash against darkness.

The time remembered—the time that preceded that catastrophic loss—is the 1950s in a suburb of Waco, Texas. The elusive thread of a story concerns the early life of a boy with two brothers, a devoted but unavoidably intimidating father, and an adored mother. The father, wonderfully played by Brad Pitt, is a complex memory-portrait put together out of broken slivers: his bits of worldly wisdom ("the world's gone to the dogs," "it takes fierce will to get ahead in this world," "the world lives by trickery"), his mass of patents for his profitless inventions, his outbursts of patriarchal rage, his final muted admission of his own inadequacies. He is a frustrated musician and we hear him, or rather Helmut Walcha in his stead, playing Bach's "Toccata and Fugue in G Minor" on a church organ. Since this like everything else is a subjective memory, the amateur plays with the eloquence of a supremely accomplished musician, just as it would have sounded to his children: and the music itself is allowed to become, for the moment, the overpowering presence, the film's characters mere auditors.

Pitt, as patriarch, is master of language: he has more lines than anyone in the film. Jessica Chastain, as the mother who (her voice-over tells us) believes in "the way of grace," is an almost wordless but no less dominant presence, a troublingly sensual font of unlimited love and emotional permission. The quarrels between the parents are glimpsed as if a child were spying on them, or overheard as the same child walks down the street to get away from the scene. Scenes of childhood are played in brief microscopic clips that merge into dream and distorted recollection. An aroma of Freudian family romance pervades the film like a cloud of slightly acrid perfume, and Malick (who has written a screenplay on the case that formed the basis of Breuer and Freud's *Studies in Hysteria*) surrounds early sense-impressions with silences and gaps suggestive of Freud's "screen memory" that conceals another adjacent memory. Every view is partial, every glimpse interrupted.

THE SENSE OF temporal progression melts into the timelessness of the childhood house, as the same domestic interior spaces are seen again and again in different framings, at different hours, at different ages. Malick evokes, almost as a byproduct, an impressionist collage of a 1950s childhood—the mother reading from Kipling's *Jungle Book* at bedtime, the boy drinking water from a garden hose, the children playing in the clouds sprayed from a DDT truck—without heavy reliance on pop hits or news items. But any nostalgic yearning stirred up by his vision of dusky summertime paths is shot through with intimations of pain and uneasiness. The world into which his characters set out, even if it is only the backyard, is a tentative place, every seeming refuge also a potential trap.

The boy Jack, who will grow up to be Sean Penn, and who is played as persuasively as can be imagined by Hunter McCracken, lives through the early storms of rage and guilt and desire with the foreboding of someone to whom something utterly strange and unheard of is happening, whether he is defiantly smashing a window or contemplating the murder of his father as he watches him at work under the jacked-up family car or stealing a bit of lingerie from a woman's drawer and setting it adrift on the water. It occurred to me watching the film that this kind of intense evocation of the barely subdued terrors of childhood is more commonly found in horror movies—*The Shining* or *The Sixth Sense*—but here no gothic melodrama or bursts of violence are needed to convey the tremors under the surface of ordinary life.

In place of the spooky fears of melodrama Malick proposes the existential dread of cosmology. He can't show the life of this boy unless he
shows you his parents; and the time and place where the parents lived;
and the planet on which that era unfolded; and the universe in which that
planet came into existence, and within which it will meet its end. We are
shown wonder upon wonder—the molten inner lives of stars and cells, the
explosive violence of the process out of which life somehow emerged—in
a wordless movie within the movie, although the question of what exactly
is "within" anything else becomes very much a moot point.

The effects designed by Douglas Trumbull (Kubrick's collaborator
on *2001: A Space Odyssey*) and others, fusing the real, the painted, and
the digitally generated, are extraordinary in themselves—a tantalizingly brief glimpse of life in the age of dinosaurs takes precedence for
a few moments over everything else in the film—but more so for the
way their gigantism inflects the whole film, so that the human sense of
proportion geared to our frame and lifespan is juxtaposed with other
scales. But this too is closely bound to the mapping of the mind of
childhood, particularly of a childhood of that era, filled as a matter
of course with imaginings of dinosaurs and exploding stars. A boy
dreams of the universe that dreamt him up in the first place: and it is
no dream at all but the very reality, fluid and tenuous, that we spectators inhabit. The possibility of the disappearance of everything is held
in constant view. "We vanish as a cloud," a minister flatly intones in a
moment plucked out of a church service.

For his ending, or more precisely epilogue, Malick has contrived a
curious allegory of time—a sort of masque, almost—in which all the
characters, at all their different ages, coexist in a single moment. It is a
ritualized restatement of what has already been implicit in every aspect
of *The Tree of Life*: the notion that every moment exists in the present,
whether it is the moment when an asteroid collides into a planet or the
moment when a boy breaks a window, and that the whole of imaginable time can be only one great now.

This is the droning note that underlies the play of color and texture
and metamorphosing forms, the surges of painful emotion that are

understood as natural ripples of a kind with waves and clouds. Made with obsessive precision in all its parts, *The Tree of Life* is nonetheless not a neat movie. Malick is neither neat nor witty nor dry the way one might want so philosophically ambitious a filmmaker to be. But while I would not rush to read a verbal summation by Malick of his philosophical views, I would burn with irresistible curiosity to see the film of any text he might care to adapt, whether it were Spinoza's *Ethics* or the phone book. He does his thinking by means of cinema in its full range of possibilities, and that is at any time a rare spectacle.

*The New York Review of Books*, 2011

# the secret life of objects

WE ENTER OLIVIER ASSAYAS'S *SUMMER HOURS*—it feels almost
like an intrusion—in the middle of movement. Children are hunting
for hidden treasure, under the guidance of an adolescent just at the age
(it's discernible at a glance, in the midst of all the running around) of dis-
tancing herself from their games. We don't know where we are but it isn't
difficult to simply dive into what is offered: the ideal summer afternoon,
in which in a few shots the adventurous geography of childhood is laid
out—its spiraling paths and dizzying hillsides, every point in space an
opening into the unknown—not with an exaggerated sense of wonder
but simply there to be looked at, inhaled, with voluptuous appreciation.

But these moments are already disappearing. A relentless forward
motion is always taking us into the next thing, a different thing. We
are being taken into the kitchen, among the adults. A roast is being put
into the oven with a careful and loving deliberation that is the portrait
of a lifetime. The camera keeps winding ahead: a man is twisting open
a bottle of champagne as he emerges into the outdoors, spraying a cascade of liquid into the intimate midst of a family gathering. Within a
few seconds we seem to know everything. (The exposition is unob-
trusive but absolutely thorough, as minimally exact as one of Ibsen's
opening scenes.)

It's a seventy-fifth birthday celebration for the woman, Hélène
Berthier (Edith Scob), whose three far-flung children are gathered

around her with their spouses and offspring, a woman whose lifelong mission has to been preserve and celebrate the work of her uncle, the painter Paul Berthier, whose upcoming retrospective in San Francisco has been commemorated in a just-published book that the celebrants are now examining and critiquing. The scene is neither frantic nor contemplative. It simply moves quietly but relentlessly forward as things do, always going just a little faster than anyone is ready for. An old photograph, reproduced in the art book, shows the same garden with a different set of people enjoying it in the same fashion. Even as the static image is being held up for comparison with the present moment, that moment is already spinning into something different.

By the end of the first long scene there is a sense of completion, as if everything were all over before it had properly begun. The mother has announced that she will die; the eldest son Frédéric (Charles Berling) has steadfastly resisted that knowledge. There is an immense question, posed at the outset, about what will happen to the beautiful house and the beautiful artworks it contains. Whatever follows has an air of the inevitable; almost everything that happens to these people could have been foreseen. The events with which the film will concern itself might from a certain angle seem a succession of banalities, unrelieved by the slightest melodramatic twist to turn the story on its head; they are simply the sort of things that tend to happen in such cases. Lives unfold, moving toward maturity or moving toward death. (Of course, the specifics of the case are not everyone's idea of ordinariness. The disposition of an inherited art collection worthy of the Musée d'Orsay is not everyone's problem, but it is ordinary to these individuals, because it happens to be their life.)

In the event this succession of banalities is a succession of profound and disturbing surprises. The film is surprising because its characters are constantly surprised: astonished, as people generally are, that the inevitable in fact comes to pass. It is a shock that people should age; a shock that they should die; a shock for parents to appreciate that their children have lives of their own; a shock for children to appreciate, perhaps much later on, that their parents had lives of their own.

In relation to the rest of the film the first scene is the lost treasure: an entirely separate and closed-off film, a portrait of a world whose end is announced by the solitary shot of Hélène sitting alone in the dark after everyone has gone, meditating in silence on her own death. It is the only moment that approaches a fixed and permanent state. She is preparing to enter the realm of the unchanging. The extraordinary compression of what has come before can be gauged by the extent to which we seem to know her. The radiant force of Edith Scob is like nothing else in the film. She is a sort of living ideogram inscribing a meaning that can never quite be reconstituted. She has not merely registered a visual presence whose memory persists specter-like, but, with every darting and delicate gesture and glance, she has described a way of life, an emotional narrative, a system of implied values and relations.

She is already a creature of the past, complete in a way that no one else is. The survivor of a world that no longer exists, we have watched her executing a dignified retreat from what surrounds her, not least from the condescension of her own children to which she responds with her own form of rarefied condescension, as if gazing at them from the plateau of a superior understanding. The rest are all struggling to define themselves, to get a handle on where they stand in relation to things; she is already an achieved definition. She has become a kind of reclusive prophet whose prophecies are sealed up and undeliverable. If she could speak it might be only to make the startling revelation that time exists, and that people come to appreciate the fact only reluctantly, with the fullest knowledge saved for last.

BY THE NEXT scene she has already died, and enough time has passed that the initial grief has subsided. The shock of that reaction is not the film's subject. A slower and more muted process is at work. Her death is not yet completed, and will not be until the very end of the film. The long death of Hélène Berthier encompasses not only her physical disappearance but the disposition of the objects in which she sought to preserve what she loved—objects that to her were not objects at all but extensions of life. Another invisible film lurks behind this one, the story of the ghostly figure of the artist Paul Berthier, Hélène's idol and love object, a figure who has already entered a world of myth that might make the successor state inhabited by his descendants seem washed-out and soulless by comparison. Nothing of him (aside from the faintest and most unreliable of memories) remains but these objects, those he created and those that accrued to him in the flow of a vibrant creative life. But to those who survive they have become problems, enigmas, fetish objects: or, simply, for one of the heirs, a practical solution to the problem of how to afford housing in Beijing.

Her son Frédéric wants to continue Hélène's self-imposed task of preservation, even if it was a task that may have destroyed her life: "There is the residue. There are the objects." We learn quite a lot about these objects in the course of the film: the pair of Corots, the Redon painting, the Degas sculpture shattered long ago in childhood play, the notebooks of Paul Berthier, the Art Nouveau vases, the valuable pieces of furniture. But we are given only the most fleeting glimpses of them, and are never permitted to contemplate them apart from their context. The film is only peripherally about their qualities as objects. Their magnificence, such as it may be, matters only as it is part of what they mean to all those who find themselves involved with them.

This is not to say that the objects are a pretext. If this were a novel, like *Cousin Pons* or *The Spoils of Poynton*, they might be symbols, counters, plot devices. Here, as physical presences, they assume the weight virtually of characters. We witness how different people look at them, handle them, move in relation to them. No novel could achieve anything like the moment when the housekeeper Éloïse brings flowers into the house after Hélène's death and, declaring that "empty vases were like death to her," puts an old vase in the metal sink to fill it with water. We have already learned that, unknown to her, the vase is a work of great value. To see an object of such worth so casually plunked down, and then to experience a sort of humdrum ecstasy as it fills with water—the most ordinary miracle anyone could ask for—speaks, as they say, volumes. It lasts about a second. *Summer Hours* has many of the virtues of a literary work—it is in fact as symmetrically pointed a screenplay as could be imagined, with its important themes sounded discreetly but unmistakably in the dialogue, and with even the most random incident contributing to an overall equipoise—but all that structure and discourse would be for nothing without its expressive soul, which resides in the actors and how they situate themselves in relation to space and time.

The plot of the movie is the fate of the house and the art. Hélène's death is the only catastrophe in a narrative otherwise devoid of deaths, illnesses, or accidents. Frédéric's daughter Sylvie has a brief run-in with the police over a shoplifting incident: that is the sum total of melodramatic incident. The rest, apart from the question of what will become of the inherited artifacts, is a matter of family chitchat: the sister Adrienne is going to get married again and live permanently in New York, the younger brother Jérémie and his wife are going to relocate to Beijing, Frédéric is going to go on trying to come to terms with his evidently not very fulfilling career as an economist and to patch up his relations with the daughter he doesn't seem to spend much time with. Hardly enough plot material for a decent postcard. We go thus far and no farther with these people. We learn the provenance, value, and subsequent destiny of nearly every inherited object but are told just enough about each of these lives to keep at every moment the main thematic line in view. Nonetheless we know them; we see them.

The narrative has clearly imposed limits. The central dilemma about the fate of the art provides the structure of the film itself. It can be taken as a lucidly constructed debate on the meaning and function of art, in which every character participates by every means available, except for those characters (the lawyer, the cop) for whom art is a matter of indifference (and whose indifference is itself part of the argument). While the characters talk about art, they themselves are part of an analogous artistic structure. In the midst of this, pretty much at every instant, other potential story lines come into view that we are free to imagine. The rigors of the screenplay contrast with a sensation of openness, of life spilling out in different directions at every turn.

The intimacy of the playing is such that very few concrete details are needed to get a sense of what these lives are. The laughter of her siblings at Adrienne's announcement of her remarriage is held just long enough to make her start to get annoyed, and then the annoyance is quickly brushed aside. The brothers flare up in anger at each other at the lawyer's office, then joke together at a coffee shop afterward as if nothing had happened. Lisa's presumably long-suffering marriage to the discontented Frédéric is conveyed almost wordlessly in every moment of her performance.

As in his other films but here perhaps more than ever before, Assayas is able to track, unemphatically but decisively, the tiny mood changes of a room full of people through a long scene like the family discussion that culminates in the decision to sell the house. Scenes like this, or the meeting at the lawyer's office, or the quick casual street-corner goodbyes that may well be forever, are recorded with an absolute justice of tone, an ordinariness not satirized or commented on but merely observed, with the occasional bursts of emotion not given any excessive, that is to say movie-ish, weight.

This justice of tone finds its hovering center in an almost accidental protagonist, Charles Berling's Frédéric. We first encounter him hurtling into the midst of the birthday party, not quite getting it right with the uncorking of the champagne, and his subsequent trajectory is indeed that of a man never able to follow through as intended, a man never quite at ease, somehow unfinished, tangled up in his awkward inability to come to the point, his painful mix of sincerity, anger, resentment, self-doubt, self-righteousness. He clings to the house and its artifacts as the only things that tie him to a past to which he is devoted but whose full implications he dodges. The revelation that his mother had a passionate affair with her aging uncle is something he cannot acknowledge; that is to say, he has never fully understood what the art meant in the first place, and he has certainly never cared to realize fully who his mother was. His difficulties in talking with his own children are of a piece with that evasion.

Yet after all he is the only one who really cares about the art, and his constantly self-lacerating existence is nevertheless made to seem more richly interesting than the overseas careerism of his siblings. He at least asks the questions for which he is unable to find anything like satisfying answers. Our knowledge of all these people is partial, but theirs, of themselves and each other, is equally so. Hélène, in her one scene, perhaps sees more than any of them, but her wisdom is already that of a past to which she is the only surviving link, well aware that she herself is on the edge of vanishing. In her absence there is no character to whom anyone might turn for an overarching grasp of the situation in which they are engulfed. Each sees his or her part of it, and these separate spheres join up only in the most transient fashion, usually in moments beyond words. Speech here is an attempt to bridge the gaps, and it is Frédéric who most valiantly and unsuccessfully makes that attempt.

The objects, then, are transmitters of something that no one can precisely define or understand. Compared to the durability of physical materials, feeling is fragile and elusive. In the same frame we see the objects that will persist and the people who will disappear. The frame itself is an object, made possible by a machine. So that this story about the transmission of objects and the transmission of memories becomes a kind of science fiction movie. In this process of objects moving from hand to hand and from generation to generation, the living people can be seen in a certain light as mere accessories. When art becomes for once not background or clue or symptom but the central focus of a story, it turns into something eerie and incomprehensible.

The objects are treasured for their association with memories, but the memories will be lost. Most of them will never even reach the point where they can be transmitted. What we see assures us that the private worlds of each of these characters will remain mostly private, not fully expressed even in their lifetimes. What persists, in living minds, is a fragment of a fragment of a fragment. The objects themselves are more or less stable—they can be shattered but they can also be put back together, as we are shown in the visit to the Musée d'Orsay's restoration wing—but what they are changes over time, even to Hélène. (The restorers at the Orsay, inhabiting a world-within-a-world where art is all, come closest, by sheer obsessive devotion, to beating these odds. They have the otherworldly presence of celestial messengers in a Cocteau film, even if their civilized efforts might seem paltry if looked at alongside the world-consuming devourers at large in other films of Assayas, the pirates of capital of *demonlover* and *Boarding Gate* or the radical nihilists of *Carlos*.)

They are at best signposts, these artifacts, to places no longer there, just as the film itself is a map of disappearances and transmutations. Everything is always dissolving. Along with the dissolution of Hélène's privileged order of intermingled love and art, we are given telegraphic flashes of the dissolution of France into a more flattened-out globalist world represented alike by Jérémie's Chinese career, Adrienne's American marriage and made-in-Japan industrial products, the American-style music at the party.

In the end the art will go to strangers anyway, including the museum-going tourist who barely looks at the art because he's making plans by cell phone to see a movie. Maybe he's off to see some hideously debased product of the torture porn era that Assayas predicted in *demonlover*, or maybe he's off to see *Summer Hours*. The disappearance of the past is not regretted here, only registered. We cannot know if the kids at the big blowout party at the empty house, just before its final sale, are the barbarians of an imminent age of leveling or the harbingers of the next creative spring.

A film, of course, is just another object. Or is it? *Summer Hours* suggests, tacitly, that film might be something a little different: not quite life and not quite art, a perplexing intermediate state with a foot in both worlds, an object constructed out of living moments.

*Olivier Assayas* (Austrian Film Museum), 2012

# the rapture of the silents

BY THE END OF 2011 it became fully apparent that the long-heralded death of film as we have known it was definitively at hand. The age of celluloid was rapidly giving way—had essentially already given way—to an unpredictable digital future. Projectors and 35 millimeter film prints were being replaced in American theaters by hard drives known as DCPs (digital cinema packages). The manufacturing of movie cameras and movie film was slowing to a halt. (Eastman Kodak filed for bankruptcy in January.) Movie studios showed increasing reluctance to strike new prints of old films.

These were clearly only minor portents of much larger changes to come, but it was foreseeable that the whole heritage of films made up until now would soon need to pass through a further technological conversion to be accessible at all, a conversion both very expensive and with little long-term reliability. Economics and past history suggested that a great deal would eventually be lost in the process. You had only to look at the fate of the majority of silent films, lost for many reasons but above all because there was no commercial incentive to preserve them.

As if to acknowledge this most significant sea change in filmmaking, exhibition, and preservation since the end of the silent era—to mark the closure of one era with a toast to the closure of another—the ghost of silent film was summoned up in two of the year's most widely noted releases. Michel Hazanavicius's *The Artist* pulled off the stunt of making an almost entirely silent black-and-white film that took the Oscar for best picture. Martin Scorsese's *Hugo*—Scorsese's first 3-D feature—embedded a retrospective of images created near the dawn of cinema by one of its first great formal inventors.

I approached the Hazanavicius film with a certain dread, half-expecting a confection that would wrap silent movies in an aura of adorable quaintness. But if *The Artist* was pure pastiche, and undeniably cute right down to an audience-charming Jack Russell terrier (who even got to vigorously reenact the ancient *Rescued by Rover* trick of saving his master from imminent disaster), it was made with a care so loving as to be almost didactic in spirit. It might have been conceived as a primer in the appreciation of silent movies—not singular classics like Dovzhenko's *Earth* or Dreyer's *The Passion of Joan of Arc* but the run-of-the-mill movie palace fodder of the mid to late 1920s. Hazanavicius was determined to make the old devices work again, and he succeeded. Audience reaction to *The Artist* tended to mirror a phenomenon I have observed many times at revivals of silent movies: the initial uncertainty, punctuated by nervous laughter, giving way to emotional engagement and finally to a kind of rapture.

*The Artist* translates its meticulous interest in modes of silent storytelling into a source of wonder, wonder perhaps above all that so rudimentary a story line—a fallen screen idol saved by love—should hold the attention. It does after all seem that the mind behaves differently when watching a silent film. With sound, the viewer gets his bearings from what the characters say and what tone they say it in; watching the movie is a kind of eavesdropping. The silents foster a different, nearly prelinguistic mode of apprehension. A peculiar attentiveness results that has something of the intensity of meditation, a wordless and intimate absorption in which the flow goes both ways: the spectator completes the people on the screen, inwardly speaks their words for them rather than listening in.

It is always surprising to experience, yet again, the sense of loss when a silent picture ends, the sudden awareness of how intently one has been staring at the people who have now vanished into air. In that same instant there may also be the awareness of how slender was the story on which that intentness was hung. A movie like *The Kiss* (1929)— Greta Garbo's last silent vehicle, directed by Jacques Feyder—stirs up deep feeling with a plotline of such nullity that it is almost embarrassing to recall. Yet the feeling is real enough, and lingers naggingly.

If Hazanavicius does not rise to the level of Garbo and Feyder, he at least persuasively demonstrates the possibility of such responses. But *The Artist* is finally a movie about the irreversibility of the past. However wonderful the cinematic form it evokes may have been, however wonderful the 1920s may even have been, there is no going back; and so in this film the Douglas Fairbanks–like silent movie idol and his Clara Bow–like jazz baby rival will have to reinvent themselves as all talking–all singing–all dancing stars of the early thirties. We are invited to admire the irreplaceable beauties of the old movies one more time (or more likely, for many viewers, for the first time) before closing the door forever. The movie has the effect of a perfected and unrepeatable gesture. One wonders whether *The Artist* will provide an opening into further explorations for the audiences so taken with it, or whether this will be a case where for many a single film will come to stand for a whole era: a silent movie for people who will never see another one as long as they live.

HUGO, AS MIGHT be expected, turned out to be something very different. For Scorsese the door to the past is never closed. *Hugo* does not so much revisit the past as reveal that it is still alive, elaborately disguised as the present. Brian Selznick's marvelous children's book *The Invention of Hugo Cabret* (2000) provided an intrigue centering around a lost key with the power to animate a mysterious automaton, but the heart of the mystery turned out to be the invention of cinema, or at least the role played in that origin by Georges Méliès with his films of magical trickery. The perennial pursuit, in fantasy tales, of the all-powerful secret becomes in *Hugo* identical with the project of a film archive, and the mystical revelation at the center nothing more or less than the screening of a restored print of Méliès's *A Trip to the Moon* (1902)—and, in the film's most ecstatic indulgence, a recreation of Méliès and his crew in his glass-walled studio, industriously at work making the impossible visible.

By filming the filming of Méliès's films, with the fullest resources of sound and color and wide screen and 3-D, Scorsese instills the illusion that Méliès is still at work, merely availing himself of new tools, as if the whole of cinema continued to exist in one never-ending present. The true magic turns out to be not the illusion conjured up by this metaproduction but the work (carried on over generations) of creating it. The Jules Vernian capsule in which *A Trip to the Moon*'s explorers achieve their voyage would be merely a metaphor for the cinematic capsule that contains all of us and inside which we head toward an unknown destination.

Thus Scorsese averts, just barely, the antiquarian melancholy that otherwise tends to associate itself with the contemplation of silent movies. From the moment they disappeared they have been a metaphor for grandeur turned suddenly obsolete, a metaphor burned into cinematic tradition by way of Billy Wilder's *Sunset Boulevard*. Gloria Swanson's "we had faces" became a gothic epitaph rather than a justified celebration. To linger over the glossies of forgotten silent idols might almost be the definition of obsessive estrangement from the present, the faithful-unto-death adoration of what will never again be marketable. Nita Naldi? Betty Bronson? Lou Tellegen? The sudden and irrevocable outmodedness of the experience of watching silent movies, the notion of those hypnotic gazes being thrown over for the brash noisiness of the living, seems to bring us close to the domain of Edgar Allan Poe or Miss Havisham.

That gothic edge finds an outlet in the work of Guy Maddin, the Canadian filmmaker who in such movies as *The Heart of the World* (2000) and *Brand Upon the Brain!* (2006) has been using the methods and historical associations of silent film as materials for an intimate autobiography, by turns hilarious and frightening and emotionally raw. Maddin proceeds as if his unconscious consisted precisely of an archive of obsolete and sometimes damaged footage whose alternately mesmeric and hysterical acting styles become the most appropriate possible expression for buried psychic archetypes. If *The Artist* evokes the formal elegance of silent film and *Hugo* its heritage of dreamy enchantment, Maddin's films derive an almost shamanistic power from their grasp of what is most eerie about those old images: their power to bring what is demonstrably dead and gone into flickering and still potent life.

MOST PEOPLE, IT is fair to guess, do not find it difficult to ignore silent movies altogether. Beyond the circle of specialized film viewers I rarely encounter an extensive familiarity with silents or much regret at that fact. Outside of film schools there has never been a particularly wide standard repertoire of silent films, because most people don't watch them. A sampling, however brief, of Griffith's huge body of work; Chaplin and Keaton, and Harold Lloyd clinging to the hands of the clock; *The Cabinet of Dr. Caligari, Nosferatu, Battleship Potemkin, Metropolis*; and a smattering of Douglas Fairbanks, Greta Garbo, Lon Chaney, and Louise Brooks would pretty much cover the field. There is after all so much else, far too much of it, to look at. A friend once confided that she "didn't get" how to look at silent films, and before I could offer glib assurance of how easy it is to just sit back and let the images have their way I remembered how many times I too had been stymied or irked when starting down that road.

First of all there was, in the days before digital restoration, the frequent need to contend with inadequate prints whose murky, broken, splotched, or shaky images gave the impression not of a film but of the grossly damaged remnant of a film. But beyond such impediments there were filmic practices that took getting used to: mimed interchanges hard or at least tedious to interpret, plot developments unperceived for want of verbal cues, tableau-like presentations in which shots were held long after the point seemed to have been made, not to mention (especially in American films) wordy intertitles that brought the film to a dead halt while the slowest readers in the audience were given time to absorb them—and, famously, there was the acting, built on a vocabulary of gestures and postures and gazes that had bit by bit become as remote as the Rosetta Stone. There were of course aspects of silent movies that had become archaic even before sound came in. No sooner was an effect achieved than some comic set about burlesquing it. The three and a half decades of silent cinema are a history of mercurially swift absorptions and readjustments.

Anyone who does set out now to explore the silents finds that we are living in a golden age, or at least golden moment, of film restoration and, through DVD and Blu-Ray disks, a golden age of accessibility. (It remains to be seen whether such accessibility will continue to be the case in the wake of the total digital conversion now under way.) An immersion that once required travel to distant archives can now be accomplished on one's couch.

It is a very different sort of viewing experience. These restored and digitized editions are often a transformation of the originals they undertake to reproduce, collating disparate elements and restoring a look of wholeness to torn or decayed images. They are in some instances cleaner than any print ever was. The film speed has been calibrated and adjusted with a precision that would have been unlikely when they were first shown. (At times the images unfold with a voluptuous smoothness and slowness so beautiful and revealing that I cannot help wondering if this is as much a product of the restorer's art as of the filmmaker's.) They are accompanied by modern soundtracks that—sometimes more intrusively and anachronistically than one might wish—tease out fresh implications of feeling and cadence. We watch them in carefully controlled settings of our own choosing, with no hint of the raucous world of vulgar entertainment or mass propaganda into which they were originally beamed.

More significant than these seductive accoutrements is the dramatically expanded repertoire we are now privileged to experience. Newly discovered and restored films rarely or barely discussed in general film histories have been emerging at such a pace that it is hard to keep up. In recent years there has been a stunning procession of rescued films that turn out to be of far more than historic interest: Leonce Perret's *L'Enfant de Paris* (1913), George Loane Tucker's *Traffic in Souls* (1913), Gustavo Serena's *Assunta Spina* (1915), Evgeni Bauer's *The Dying Swan* (1913), Mauritz Stiller's *Sir Arne's Treasure* (1919), Ernst Lubitsch's *Die Bergkatze* (1921), F.W. Murnau's *Phantom* (1922), John Ford's *Hangman's House* (1928), Frank Borzage's *Street Angel* (1928), Franz Osten's *A Throw of Dice* (1929), George Schnéevoigt's *Laila* (1929), Mikhail Kalotozov's *Salt for Svanetia* (1930), Hiroshi Shimizu's *Japanese Girls at the Harbor* (1933).

How could we not have heard about *Laila*, with its extraordinary scenes of wolves chasing a reindeer-driven sled across a sub-Arctic landscape, or *Salt for Svanetia*, with its sublime contemplation of Central Asian isolation and unforgiving folkways? The list may seem long, but it only scratches the surface. There is much more still to come, films already restored and films only recently recovered in archives from Russia to New Zealand. The inevitable decay of nitrate film has apparently not in every case been as swift as feared, and so there are still opportunities to uncover, here and there, what was thought lost forever.

THE SEDUCTION OF silent cinema is the seduction of a form as unique as opera or kabuki, a peculiar way of organizing one's attention. It is a perpetual learning how to see, and a way of coming to the truth of one of Emerson's observations: "The eye is final." But there is the further peculiarity that what you see takes place in a world no longer there. Here are cities since reduced to rubble and rebuilt, stretches of countryside by now turned into interstates and strip malls, glaciated wilderness that has probably succumbed to climate change—and of course the faces of those now long dead, something too easily taken for granted but that haunts movies from the start. The inventors of the medium were already thinking about recording the living as a future consolation for their survivors.

It is a property that will only get stranger. People have had millennia to get used to the idea of the ancientness of written texts; we have not yet seen truly ancient films, having got just a little beyond the century mark. A passenger—a babe in arms—who got off the train at La Ciotat station as the Lumières were filming it in 1895 may well have lived on into the age of television and 3-D. In time, everything before that will seem prehistoric, dating from the era before people could *see* the vanished generations and watch them move in something like real time through a world also in movement.

The reality of their world included of course the desire to escape from that reality by means of the very movies we are watching. Two goals are at work from the beginning of film: to move in as close to the world as possible, and to move as far away from it as possible. They are not always contradictory goals. Even the most banal of natural settings became exotic when filmed; wind-blown trees and eddying waves were primordial special effects. A city street photographed at random, if it was someone else's city, might be as unreal as any studio concoction.

Audiences came not necessarily to relish the fact of existing in 1912 or 1927 but to explore precisely the possibilities denied by that present moment, to look at something else, a distant steppe or the palace of a rajah, the deck of a millionaire's yacht or the interior of a midtown brothel in the midst of a police raid, a world seen from above the clouds or a world entirely taken over by comical acrobats. The abstraction and stylization fostered by silent film were uniquely suited for establishing an obverse zone lying just within the well-named dream palaces, liberated from history and even from logic.

Every film becomes a documentary, even if it is a documentary on the making of illusions. To become aware of the exceptional artistry of the greatest silent filmmakers—of D.W. Griffith or Victor Sjöström or Ernst Lubitsch—is in the same instant to become sensitive to the living material, that is to say people and their habitat, that they are working with. The sense of how the filmmaker is operating in the world cannot be separated from the film. You can read *King Lear* without having to give a thought to Richard Burbage; you cannot watch *The Birth of a Nation* without registering the presence of every member of its large cast and by extension the precise time and place in which they go through their paces.

We feel for them because we see them and in the same moment measure their distance from us. I have not read Selma Lagerlöf's novel *Körkarlen* (*Thy Soul Shall Bear Witness*, 1912), a tale of an alcoholic reprobate redeemed in the manner of Ebenezer Scrooge by ghostly visions, and so cannot judge whether it exerts as powerful an effect as Sjöström's 1921 film version, *The Phantom Carriage*, which the Criterion Collection has issued in a Blu-Ray edition. But whatever the suggestiveness of the fable, the film works on us with the bare palpability of its elements—even of its visual tricks.

The carriage of the title, sent to collect the souls of the dead and driven by the last soul to die on New Year's Eve, is a superimposed image gliding over natural scenes. The dead souls, once extracted from their corpses, are likewise superimpositions wandering through otherwise solid settings. The transparent carriage pauses to collect a vagrant dead of exposure in a marsh. It moves over a rocky coastline to retrieve drowned bodies from a boat half sunk beneath the waves. A simpler trick is unimaginable.

Yet these forlorn images are made even more so by the very impossibility of those transparent forms, as if we were being given a demonstration of what is humanly unattainable. In counterpoint to these supernatural scenes there is the film's other kind of special effect: the human face exposed by lighting designed to bring out expressions of fear, anguish, malicious anger, resigned devotion. Faces look at faces, or toward the empty space that is the audience. Sjöström himself, playing the abusive protagonist in what may, according to an accompanying essay by Paul Mayersberg, be an imitation of his own brutal father, turns himself into the most indelible of visual devices by capturing the demonic glint in his own eyes.

That glint carries across time in the most unnerving way. But it had to be captured in the first place. The authentic artists of silent cinema—and the list gets longer as more films are retrieved—touch us by the deliberateness with which they directed our eyes toward what was there, or rather to what still is there in their work. Such viewing can easily create odd moments of temporal displacement. If 1912 can become the present, 2012 can just as easily become the remote past. Watching the recent and disastrously received Disney release *John Carter* with its digitized frames densely packed with thousands of battling Martians and careening airships, I felt suddenly that I was looking at an artifact of a long-vanished era that devoted itself to such curious spectacles. The people of that time, it seemed, had sought to make images that mutated so rapidly that no single image could be looked at long enough to become fixed in the mind. Had they been looked at that long, it would have become too plain that there was nothing there to see.

A movie like *The Phantom Carriage*, by contrast, was made to be peered into with unwavering attention. Shots were prolonged so that nothing of importance would be lost. Dying faces were photographed as if to bridge the gap between life and death. Silent cinema had perhaps the advantage that the spectator cannot look away. The rapt gaze is the only suitable mode for watching it at all.

*The New York Review of Books*, 2012

# dreaming of water

THE PHRASE "ADVENTURE MOVIE" WAS food, in childhood, for the most pleasurable kind of anticipation. The excitement wasn't really ever about the particular exploits, historical or otherwise, that were ostensibly to be celebrated. It had more to do with the prospect of sweeping movements and eye-popping primary colors—of imposing and ever-changing spatial perspectives—of an immersive experience of rivers and canyons and forests, and the opportunity to wander in half-buried cities or remote encampments. The promise was of dreamlike freedom of movement through a world at once concrete and mysterious, and shaped for unsupervised play. Two quite remarkable American movies that opened this summer, *Beasts of the Southern Wild* and *Moonrise Kingdom*, can be described as adventure movies in the true sense. They breathe an unaccustomed air of freedom and curiosity and what can only be called elation.

Although in other respects as different as can be, they do have certain aspects in common. Each is steeped—*Beasts* throughout, *Kingdom* at its climax—in the element of water at its mostly violently uncontrolled. Each lays claim, with an explorer's attentiveness, to a geographic domain closed off to the outside world. And each is filtered through the consciousness of young leading characters: a six-year-old girl in *Beasts*, a pair of twelve-year-old runaways in *Kingdom*. The filmmakers have not gone to children for the sake of their bewildered innocence but for their ferocious clarity of intention and for radiant intelligence not yet reined in or habituated to sullen conformity.

TO SAY THAT *Beasts of the Southern Wild* was filmed in southern Louisiana understates the case—it seems like an enormous construction made from pieces of southern Louisiana, and inhabited by the people found there by the film's director, Benh Zeitlin, a New Yorker who has been living in New Orleans since 2008. Yet this is no documentary but a work of purest fantasy, set in a world just adjacent to the real and operating with all the liberties of folklore.

We are somewhere south of New Orleans, beyond the levee, on a perpetually endangered floodplain settlement called the Bathtub, a sort of multiracial Eden sustaining itself on wildlife and debris: a loosely linked bayou community below the radar and off the grid. Here the water seeps into everything. We are outside history, outside sociology, caught up straight away in the territories toward which Huck Finn lit out or in the swamp at the end of the mind, a messy profusion of fiddle music and moonshine. They are wild people living among wild things, unconstrained by laws or walls, reliant on ancient prophecies and herbal cures, at home with the water that may overwhelm them at any moment. It hardly matters whether we are in paradise or perdition. Perhaps it is perdition transmuted by sheer cussedness into paradise. In the floating life of the imaginary, opposites merge with an easy profundity; it's just what the imaginary is made for.

The waterlogged environment gives Zeitlin a wraparound, ever present metaphor for the way his film permeates barriers. We soak it up, or dissolve into it. From the start there are rumors of impending flood, apocalyptically couched, as a teacher tattooed with archaic images of aurochs tells her young charges: "Any day now the fabric of the universe is coming unraveled." In short order we endure storm and deluge, move forward into a future of poisoned waters and prehistoric beasts resurrected from melting icecaps, and return at last to the primal swamp as part of an enduring remnant in a drowned world. They are us, these survivors, because what Katrina and other hurricanes did to the Gulf Coast can be taken as a foreshadowing of worse to come. The movie is a sort of primitivist-futurist extravaganza made by hand with the fragments of actual disaster. Yet the note sounded throughout is not the terror of catastrophe—although we see the marks of catastrophe on every hand as we glide past submerged and damaged habitations—but the slim exhilarating margin of survival, the dance on the last bare edge of dry ground. (The film, it should be noted—it is Zeitlin's first feature—was conceived during his long recuperation from a near-fatal car accident.)

In movies the imaginary tends to be expensive, so independent live-action films generally work with what is already in place and steer clear of the realms of large-scale fantasy. Our dream worlds are elaborated for us by corporate entities with the necessary means. *Beasts of the Southern Wild* represents a kind of protest against this state of affairs, an assertion of the right to build one's own make-believe world, with available tools however rudimentary, rather than submitting to the pre-imagined products of Disney, Marvel, Pixar, and the rest. It's a film made cheaply, and I would imagine sometimes dangerously, with amateur actors and dwellings furnished with the detritus of floods and storms. It makes up its mythology analogously to the way a child might make up a history of the world, with the gaps and unexpected detours and lurching transitions intact.

The child here is Quvenzhané Wallis, an African American girl who was discovered in a Louisiana elementary school and was six years old when the film was made. It's hard to imagine what the movie might have been without her. She plays Hushpuppy, whose mother "swam away" (sometimes returning as a disembodied voice) and whose father (played in mingled tones of ferocity and tenderness by a New Orleans baker, Dwight Henry) appears to be dying. Hushpuppy in a sense is the whole movie. What we see is her understanding of how things are—if her father goes missing, it can only be that "Daddy woulda turned into a tree or a bug," and if she listens to animals they tell her what's on their minds—and it can only be as persuasive as she is.

Everything is mediated through her, on the one hand the unlimited turbulence of the phenomenal world (including the contradictory behavior of a father who in one scene rejects her and in another showers her with love) and the other hand a child of almost preternatural seriousness and focused energy. The story, as we piece it together, is the perennial fable of the child who must save her father, her community, her world. Accomplishing this involves no magic formula but the mere assertion of will in the face of all terrors, like her father who as the storm descends on them fires a rifle into the raging skies in defiance.

Wallis's tiny presence is commanding—intense, unflinching, incapable of meek submission—and her manner is far from the winsome ways of most child actors. She is given some large philosophical statements to pronounce—"The entire universe depended on everything fitting together just right"—and by her stance establishes herself as one of those indispensable things on which the universe depends. She is a believable hero because with our own eyes we can see her perform the heroic feat of sustaining an epic film, and in the end accept that her assured glance can indeed (in an image that recalls the world of Maurice Sendak) make predatory beasts kneel before her.

Apply real-world logic and this watery alternate world is in danger of dissolving, like a dream colliding with morning light. When, near the halfway point, a rescue team from the modern world arrives by helicopter to evacuate the residents of the Bathtub and carry them off to a crowded disaster relief center, the movie itself comes uneasily close to losing its delicate balancing of the real and the unreal by a sudden intrusion of inevitable skeptical questions. The rescuers figure as a malevolent intrusive force even though we haven't been given a clear reason to see them that way. It may well be that flood victims suffering from the effects of exposure and hunger would want nothing more than to escape from the shelter where they are receiving food and medical care in order to return to their flooded homes, but Zeitlin does not do much of anything to show why.

A shot of Hushpuppy in the disaster center wearing an anachronistic *Little House on the Prairie*-style dress evokes the notion of the wild

child "civilized" by well-meaning missionaries, and the center's ambience is that of an overcrowded and understaffed clinic operating under
very disadvantageous circumstances. But the moments when she and
the other Bathtub residents flee together from the shelter, racing across
a parking lot toward the bus that will take them back home—as if they
had been liberated and were on their way to the Promised Land—
are the least effectively realized in the movie. We can all recollect
the much-reported horrors of the Superdome where survivors were
crammed together after Katrina, and Zeitlin may be relying on such
recollections, but nothing we see here seems as horrific as it's evidently
meant to be. The shelter has to stand in for the modern world that is
otherwise absent from the film, the soulless land only glimpsed from a
distance on the other side of the levee.

In the end the film finds a more congenial disaster center in the
lake boat that Hushpuppy and some of the other children board in a
search for food, with a skipper likewise given to philosophical musings—"This boat'll take you exactly where you need to be"—and with a
turntable that plays only one record, Fats Waller's "Until the Real Thing
Comes Along," spinning over and over for whores and boatmen as if it
were the last record on earth, an oldie dredged up from the flood. This
boat of dreams seems almost designed to conjure up the most authentically dreamlike of American movies, Charles Laughton's *The Night of
the Hunter*, an equally water-soaked work of the imagination.

I wonder if anyone has undertaken a study of Water and Movies.
It is a subject of almost infinite application, starting from the earliest registering of the movement of waves and rivulets by cinematic
pioneers. Water is the most privileged element in film because it exercises cinematic power merely by being filmed. The bodies of water
that have served as crucial staging grounds would make a catalogue of
the most intense moments in cinema, from the waterfall with which
Buster Keaton contended in *Our Hospitality* to the lotus pool where
June Duprez caught sight of John Justin's reflection in Alexander
Korda's *The Thief of Bagdad*, from the misty lake across which Kinuyo
Tanaka and her children were unwittingly ferried toward misfortune

in Mizoguchi's *Sansho the Bailiff* to the bay from which James Stewart rescued Kim Novak in Hitchcock's *Vertigo*, and on out to the ocean where the doomed hero of Murnau's *Tabu* sank beneath the waves. In all that profusion there are some few films where the watery element so predominates as to create a kind of pool for the mind: Jean Vigo's *L'Atalante* was one such, *Beasts of the Southern Wild* is another.

WATER IS VERY much present in Wes Anderson's *Moonrise Kingdom*, but here the central operating figure is not anarchic bayou but New England coastal island. It is an island bounded by ocean and with wilderness at its core, but kept within some kind of discipline by the forces of social organization that occupy strategic points: lawyers, a police officer, scoutmasters who maintain their troops in good military order, not to mention the visiting representative of a child welfare agency. The anarchy here is in the hearts of two precocious and socially maladroit twelve-year-olds, Sam (Jared Gilman) and Suzy (Kara Hayward), who find each other against all odds—at an amateur performance of Benjamin Britten's opera *Noye's Fludde*—and carry out a carefully planned getaway into the heart of the island, seeking out the sort of cove that fugitive children dream of: a calm refuge where no adult forces can ever intrude. (The dream of escape pervades Anderson's films; his first movie, *Bottle Rocket*, opens with Luke Wilson clambering down a rope of bedsheets to get away from a psychiatric clinic, and a similar rope comes into play in *Moonrise Kingdom*.)

The movie charts the collision of their desire to evade the world and the world's insistence on finding them and bringing them under some kind of control—not necessarily out of love (Sam is an unwanted orphan, and Suzy's parents have other problems on their mind), but in automatic response to the scandalousness of their insistence on being free and independent and, finally, married to each other. There are other adults too, among them the local police chief played by Bruce Willis and the scoutmaster beautifully realized by Edward Norton, more capable of a sympathy that seeps into the film through the tersest of exchanges. Suzy and Sam are at the center of a profuse cast of characters, each of whom has some crucial note to sound and many of whom undergo unexpected evolutions that add continually to the richness of the film's texture.

Such a bald summary already does injustice to the intricacies of Anderson's narrative structures, which are as cunningly laid out as Sam and Suzy's plan of escape. There is a carefully calibrated arrangement and disarrangement of maps and schedules and chronological schemata as the film develops, a narrative trickery both entertaining in itself and filled with the secretive pleasures of childish game-playing with its hideouts and disguises and encoded maps. Anderson's obsession with hermetic structures mirrors that of his characters, who carefully contain themselves within constructed worlds, whether it's the sprawling labyrinth of a home inhabited by Suzy's lawyer-parents (Bill Murray and Frances McDormand) or the frontier stockade that serves as the headquarters of the Khaki Scouts of North America.

All human habitations in Anderson's films tend to have the quality of grotesque and unnatural excrescences, all the more so here in contrast to the wooded crags and rocky streams of the inner island. Sam, a misfit despised by his fellow scouts and disowned by his foster parents, is a master of camping skills adept with map and compass. Crossing a field in coonskin cap as he steals away from Camp Ivanhoe—while on the soundtrack Hank Williams sings the tragic ballad of the lovelorn wooden Indian "Kaw-Liga"—he seems like the perfect embodiment of the values imparted by, say, Fess Parker as Davy Crockett, except that he has arrived too late. Suzy, who alternates between immersion in young adult novels about magical orphans and violent outbursts against her parents and her schoolmates, carries the modern world (the movie is set in 1965) with her in the form of a portable record player and a single Françoise Hardy recording. (The alternation, throughout the film, of the music of Benjamin Britten, Hank Williams, and Françoise Hardy, along with a stirring original score by Alexandre Desplat, is not incidental but central to its meanings.)

Sam and Suzy are inventing the world as they go along, word by word and gesture by gesture. Wes Anderson's anti-naturalism here becomes precisely the only convincingly naturalistic way to express the love story he has imagined. The stylized dialogue in which his characters tend to address each other—and which some viewers have always found wincingly mannered—has never seemed more appropriate than as a lingua franca for alienated twelve-year-olds who on top of everything else must invent a way to communicate with each other. Each brings a certain amount of special knowledge and a certain number of sacred childhood objects to the process, and the extraordinary care with which they negotiate these transfers of information is a measure of how deep their commitment has already gone.

Their tentative dance down by the cove to the music of the portable record player is a scene of tenderhearted and melancholy intelligence, all the more so for being at the center of what is after all a comedy, and at times a broad one. The boisterousness of the film's finale, with its sieges and rescues, its lightning bolts and flash floods, relieves what would otherwise be an almost unbearably sad evocation of what is least preservable about youthful experience: not so much that "loss of innocence" that is such a hackneyed motif of modern American culture (and for which summer camps have always been a favored location), but the awakening of the first radiance of mature intelligence in a world liable to be indifferent or hostile to it, an intelligence that can conceive everything and realize only the tiniest fragment of it.

The respect that Anderson has for his young characters is the essence of *Moonrise Kingdom*, a film that finds a path through material that in other hands would more likely have sunk into a morass of sentimentality. But then pathfinding is the film's central action. Sam earns his coonskin cap by turning the island's creeks and woods into a heroic landscape. The inevitable question is what world or life he could possibly be in training for. None that exists, any more than the worlds of which Suzy reads in her beloved fantasy novels. The books and their cover art are artifacts created for the film, like so many of the objects in Anderson's films. He shares with Jacques Tati and with few contemporaries I can think of the desire to build everything, even the most ordinary objects, afresh. To make a world where everything looks newly made is part of the great adventurousness of his work, and in *Moonrise Kingdom* the effect, by juxtaposition, is to make even the rocks and creeks look new. It is perhaps the only setting in which Sam and Suzy could begin to articulate their goal: "to go on adventures and not get stuck in one place."

*The New York Review of Books*, 2012

# a drifter and his master

LANCASTER DODD—THE CHARACTER PLAYED with such mesmerizing assurance by Philip Seymour Hoffman in Paul Thomas Anderson's *The Master*—is not to be confused with L. Ron Hubbard. That much should be said at the outset, given that the Scientology connection has served as a convenient tag for what Anderson's new film is about. The notion was certainly intriguing, but anyone familiar with Anderson's work might have guessed that some kind of straightforward docudrama was not in the offing. Perhaps one day there will indeed be a biopic that grapples with the convoluted and much-contested details of Hubbard's scarcely credible career as spiritual entrepreneur—one might imagine a mode anywhere from satiric grotesque to Machiavellian analytics to impassioned polemic—but *The Master* is not that film, full though it is of hints in such directions.

It is something more interesting: a freestanding work of the imagination, a contemplative fiction. Anderson has taken whatever he needed from the early history of Scientology, drawing freely on its vocabulary, doctrines, and methods, and from much else besides, to create an intimate epic of irrational need, an inner history of cultish transactions reconfigured as a sorrowful and distinctively American poem. It is such a decisive accomplishment that it casts fresh light on Anderson's previous films—*Hard Eight* (1996), *Boogie Nights* (1997), *Magnolia* (1999), *Punch-Drunk Love* (2002), and *There Will Be Blood* (2007)—a body of work whose coherence and astonishing ambition is clearer than ever.

STOLEN GLIMPSES, CAPTIVE SHADOWS

"The pure products of America go crazy": William Carlos Williams's indelible line might serve as a motto not only for this film but for all of Anderson's work to date. The Cause (Dodd's quasi-religion, analogous to Dianetics) is shown to be just such a pure product, the kind of destination that couldn't exist if enough people didn't desperately need to go there. When movies have attempted to show the inner life of cults and newfangled religions, they have generally sought to convey how strange they are. Anderson by contrast shows how strange they are not.

America has after all long since been the great breeding ground of self-help cults and apocalyptic sects and secret initiations, of home-brewed universal panaceas and fresh-minted pseudoscientific jargon, of occult communal bondings and shunnings. In the perspective of *The Master*, these are not denials but extensions and variations of American life. When Freddie Quell, the traumatized veteran incarnated unforgettably by Joaquin Phoenix, throws in his lot with the Cause, it is not as if he is fleeing from normality into an eerie shadow world. Whether inside or outside the movement, the world as he finds it is equally chaotic and unrelenting.

This is where we live, and it is a country of deep loneliness—that same loneliness that permeates all of Anderson's films, and against which his characters are forever forming themselves into protective families or parodies of families, a population of paternalistic strangers, adoptive sons, surrogate mothers, fake cousins. All his films, different as each has been, have found their way to the heart of a peculiarly American disconnectedness. The freedom to be left alone turns into desperate drift: a desperation measured, often, in hyperactivity and baroque elaboration, as if keeping frantically busy could stave off a lurking sense of emptiness. From the start his films seemed to need to prove themselves with every composition, every line of dialogue, every cut, every music cue. The aggressiveness of style was a declaration of ambition; intending to astonish, the filmmaker made himself so visible that he was one of the characters, another creature of compulsive energy looking for a way to manifest itself.

Often the energy found an outlet in violence, not action-movie fun-fair violence, nor the systematic, "rational" violence of police and criminals, but the violence of pointless, often self-destructive, explosive outbursts—Adam Sandler destroying windows and bathrooms in fits of rage in *Punch-Drunk Love* or Paul Dano making an unprovoked assault on his father in *There Will Be Blood*—the outlet of a blind frustration that can't wait another second. It made for a curious counterpart to the obvious and extraordinary care taken over visible and audible detail, a care that bespoke a profound devotion to the medium itself. The medium, more than the medium's history: Anderson does not lard his films with sly references or affectionate homages to old movies, and pitches his films a bit beyond the comfort zone where one can be reassured that, after all, it's just a movie.

THE INSISTENCE ON a sense of discomfort was not apparent at the outset. When I saw *Boogie Nights* for the first time (having missed Anderson's already masterful debut, *Hard Eight*, the year before) it seemed like the work of a drive-in Balzac, an exuberantly entertaining multicharacter analysis of a whole social swath—the unmistakable late-seventies brew of disco, porn, and cocaine as experienced in the San Fernando Valley in an era corresponding to the filmmaker's childhood—popping from the screen in an indescribable mixture of farce, melodrama, and all too real grotesquerie. Anderson's ability to switch emotional registers kept the film from settling into predictable patterns of redemptive resolution. His great set-pieces (a couple of long party scenes, the crazily protracted episode involving the failed rip-off of a coke dealer) had a lifelike sprawl and choppiness, and the performances he got out of then unfamiliar actors like John C. Reilly, Julianne Moore, Don Cheadle, Philip Baker Hall, and Philip Seymour Hoffman kept things from sliding into caricature or easy pathos.

Anderson's voracious appetite for small details, textures, gestures, verbal styles, the distinguishing marks of every period and neighborhood and clique, made him look like some kind of realist, an impressionist describer of the most fleeting varieties of social interaction, a history painter for a culture where epochs are measured in decades. It was hard to know what to expect from such a filmmaker, and *Magnolia* came as something of a surprise. It looked at first like an only slightly exaggerated cross-section of the present moment, tracking the random intersections of disparate lives and seemingly intending to pour into the mix everything he knew of that world (it was again the San Fernando Valley). He stirred up woozy subcurrents of shame, resentment, guilty desire, estrangement, embarrassment, and every variety of self-torment in an open-ended narrative drawing in drug addiction, cancer, child molestation, commercialized misogyny, and the exploitation of quiz kids, all set to a mournful strain of indie rock balladry and converging on the moment when each character, in isolation, started singing along with the same song.

At that point Anderson began to seem less history painter than expressionist allegorist, describing a permanent present that was also a permanent crisis, with emblematic characters who might have stepped out of a play by Strindberg or Georg Kaiser: the Dying Father, the Angry Son, the Guilty Wife, the Genius Child, roles sometimes embodied by more than one character, and all enlisted in a graph of helpless human neediness. Unappeasable neediness, with its attendant compulsions and necessary delusions, was the pervasive condition in which *Magnolia* was steeped. No individual could be more than a link in that chain of dependencies.

It was and was clearly intended to be too much, breaking the framework of any possible plotline and finally breaking the framework of the real altogether with a downpour of frogs. But if this was expressionism, it was an expressionism that needed scarcely more for its effects than the actual materials of a culture beyond caricature—that, and the presence of actors from whom Anderson elicits performances of astonishing urgency and exactness. It is fair to say that even if you did not care at all about the story or the photography or the music in his films, you could very happily watch them just to look at what the actors are doing from moment to moment: as when, in *Magnolia*, John C. Reilly, as the squarest and politest cop ever, gradually edged around to imposing his authority on an uncooperative tenant; or Philip Baker Hall, as the terminally ill host of a TV quiz show, gave one last example of long-practiced, almost brain-dead professional glibness. But after *Magnolia* it was hard not to wonder where Anderson was heading—perhaps into some stratospheric zone of New Age revelation?

That possibility always seems to lurk. Prophetic figures loom up: there was the founder of the Church of the Third Revelation in *There Will Be Blood*, and now the world-healing message of Lancaster Dodd. Something about the inescapable tactile presence of everything in Anderson's movies seems to elicit such responses. They are grounded in the most oppressively solid and specific of materials—whether the nightmarish hotel and warehouse interiors of the gargoylish and sometimes terrifying comedy *Punch-Drunk Love* or the monumental oil-drilling apparatus of the ultimately claustrophobic epic *There Will Be Blood*—only for all that sense of solidity to melt (in Marx's phrase) into air.

The milieus on which Anderson focuses—the porn film business, the early oil industry, and now the rise of a modern religious franchise—can all be seen as attempts to reconfigure the real, to bring it into line with the claims of the most extravagant desire, and it is that attempt that magnifies to the utmost the sense that the world is not merely implausible but fundamentally unbelievable. When Lancaster Dodd, addressing a roomful of potential converts, suggests that "perhaps what we think we know of this world is false information," he could, for that one moment at least, be speaking for Anderson.

THESE ARE MILIEUS where irrationality, supplemented where necessary by blunt force, trumps any conceivable logical objection. Logicians are in any case on the sidelines in *The Master*. The psychiatrists who try to unravel Freddie Quell's personality difficulties are no more effective than the skeptic who tries to engage Lancaster Dodd in debate at a Park Avenue reception. (The latter gets an offscreen beating, administered by Freddie, for his troubles.) This is, precisely, a world in which there is no one in a position to object, no one to intervene. *The*

*Master*, like Anderson's earlier films but even more deliberately, kicks away any possibility of a stable mooring, a safe observation point that would enable one to put things in a more reassuring perspective.

This is accomplished right from the start in the series of scenes sketching Freddie Quell's history from his discharge from the navy at the end of World War II—his careening flight through circumstances beyond his control—up to the moment when, by stealing aboard a yacht in California, he enters by happenstance the sphere of Lancaster Dodd and the Cause. All the rest of the film is a meticulous and sometimes agonizing parsing of the consequences of that encounter.

Freddie is an inarticulate isolato of Melvillean proportions, an inchoate chunk of jagged impulse and unfailingly awkward affect whose most purposeful activity is concocting moonshine—expertly and at any opportunity—out of any substances at hand, toxic or otherwise. Freddie is the inadaptable individual who defies labels and therapies, the son of an alcoholic father and a psychotic mother, veteran of unspecified wartime experiences that have brought him to the attention of army psychiatrists. He's a mass of tics and sexual compulsions who improvises his life from second to second. As played by Joaquin Phoenix—"played" seems too light a word—he inhabits his body as if it were ill-fitting armor he'd been saddled with. The intelligence that beams from his eyes seems absolutely disconnected from every aspect of his being and his life. He looks as if he'd been broken apart and put back together wrong. Even his face has a life of its own, his mouth twisting at odd angles to register arcane conflicts and resistances.

Freddie barely endures the world; he knocks its props aside trying to fumble for what he needs. To see him dressed up for work as a department-store photographer—his short-lived postwar profession—is to see a suit wrapped around a turbulence only momentarily containing itself. For reasons barely comprehensible he assaults a customer in the department store; we see him next harvesting crops; when a coworker collapses from drinking Freddie's home brew, he flees across an open field. These scenes last only a few minutes, but a Frank Norris or Theodore Dreiser would have found matter for hundreds of pages of exposition in them. The processing of soldiers after the war, scenes in the psycho ward with their tests and helpful pep talks, the differing realities of upscale department stores and migrant workers' camps: we are given them almost wordlessly, in what seems like no time.

The density of Anderson's workmanship allows for maximum compression. *The Master* is shot in 65 millimeter—the first American feature in the format since Kenneth Branagh's *Hamlet* in 1996, and conceivably the last—and the film stock's saturated colors and fine details give each shot the depth and solidity of an actual and often hauntingly beautiful world. The briefest shots—and Freddie's early history is related in such shots—seem fully inhabited, fully realized. The department store episode by itself conjures up with extraordinary fidelity the texture and coloration of postwar magazine photography out of the pages of *Life* and *Vogue*, with all the elusive desires it promised to fulfill. Within that episode, a few quick samples of the garishly unreal lighting for Freddie's photographic portraits provide a panorama of the 1950s American family at its most guilelessly grotesque: not so much a judgment on the American family as a measure of how distant Freddie is from any such domestic life. Such photographic shorthand has always been a mark of Anderson's films, but here it is more seamlessly integrated than ever before, making not for flash effects but an abundance of expressiveness in all the corners, more meanings than one even has time to take in.

The expressiveness is compounded almost continuously by Jonny Greenwood's score with its mix of dissonant tonalities and period music, the two sometimes overlapping as when Greenwood's harsh astringencies are superimposed over Noro Morales's recording of "Sweet Sue": it is an almost literalist way of indicating the distance between the music in Freddie's head and the welcoming sound of Lancaster Dodd's shipboard party. Music is an overwhelming presence in all of Anderson's films, from the disco-saturated soundtrack of *Boogie Nights* to the abrasive tones of Greenwood's earlier score for *There Will Be Blood*— never anything like background music, more like a through-composed parallel track of sustained urgency, participating in the drama rather than commenting on it, not least when (in *The Master*) the orchestra abruptly shuts itself off to allow Philip Seymour Hoffman to sing an a cappella rendition of "On a Slow Boat to China" in which the film's accumulated emotional weight finds a bizarre outlet.

THAT EVERYTHING SHOULD come down to one man singing an old standard to another man across a desktop is a fulfillment of a confrontation that gives the film its center—a center for a film about, precisely, decenteredness and drift. The multiple story lines of earlier Anderson films give way to the dyad of Freddie Quell and Lancaster Dodd circling around each other in a slow dance of attraction and repulsion. The simplification of structure yields an operatic power, with all superfluous details elided and the drama grounded in these two figures.

From the moment Freddie is brought in to meet the Master, the film settles in to contemplate every nuance of their intersection. The conception of character here is not narrowly pointed but capacious. Personalities are treated as landscapes, or forms of brooding music: harboring all sorts of odd crevices and fissures, and capable of no end of abrupt unforeseen mutations. Joaquin Phoenix and Philip Seymour Hoffman are two incompatible worlds uneasily orbiting around each other. Freddie submits to Dodd's "processing," confessing to secret sins and longings, while Dodd enthusiastically laps up Freddie's home brew. Eventually Freddie will do Dodd's enforcing for him, while Dodd pretends to reprimand him for it. Neither can begin to explain what is going on.

Hoffman's Dodd is an astonishing piece of work. I have seen many cinematic attempts to portray charismatic cultish leaders, but have rarely until now seen a convincing representation of such a leader's ability to control the atmosphere around him. Dodd has a deceptive lightness, a bounce, that is downright endearing. At the outset Hoffman seems to be channeling Charles Foster Kane at his most glibly charming, a tack that feels totally right: What better model of mercurial seductiveness could there be, for a man of Dodd's era and Dodd's ambitions, than the young Orson Welles? It's as if he had appropriated that personal manner just as he might appropriate a catchphrase or a method.

Dodd has the gift of sucking up everyone's energy and playing it back as if it were his gift to them, all the while visibly delighting in the process, surprising himself with his own capacity to enchant and control. He is mischievous, buoyed up by the powers of improvisation that might enable him, for example—in a scene that can be read as Freddie's grasp of the group dynamics that lie just under the surface—to persuade a roomful of women of all ages to strip for him, in an atmosphere of sing-along merriment. Dodd's delight, of course, as we are shown in the scene that immediately follows, has as its mirror image his behind-the-scenes aspect of sexual misery and paranoid mistrust, kept in check by his wife Peggy (the Master's secret master, wonderfully realized by Amy Adams) and occasionally—increasingly, one can assume—finding expression in unscheduled explosions of rage.

The internal structures and activities of the Cause are given to us in luminous fragments, out of the corner of the eye. There is no backstory to explain where Dodd came from or how all this got started. The shorthand is quite sufficient, the actors compressing whole histories of lostness and drift and subservience into the tersest exchanges, or sometimes just by the way they stand or sit doing nothing while receiving instruction. We never see the acolytes talking to each other, and we are made to sense the utter lack of mutual love, the simmering meanness in this supposed community.

Dodd's church is a desert of the heart, and it is entirely appropriate that we should end in the Arizona desert for the gathering where he will reconfirm his authority. Laura Dern, as the follower who welcomes Dodd and company into her Philadelphia home, conveys with frightening precision a well-schooled charm that one can easily imagine cracking into a thousand pieces, whether we are watching her rapturously expounding Dodd's technique of time travel under his approving gaze, or being belatedly exposed to the Master's wrathful face when she ventures an inappropriate question about a passage in his newest book.

When his public face is securely in place, Dodd is never not entertaining. Freddie Quell by contrast is never entertaining: he has no public face. The closest he comes to having one is in the role of the inexpressive cult member handing out leaflets on the street to passersby who quicken their step as they enter his vicinity. In Freddie, Dodd sees the perfect guinea pig whom he can transmute into the perfect loyalist, but from the start there is more than that. At their lowest ebb—thrown in adjoining cells of a Philadelphia jail after Dodd is arrested for fraud and Freddie assaults a policeman in his defense—Freddie demolishes the toilet and smashes his head against the bunk while Dodd watches him impassively, finally haranguing him: "I'm the only one that likes you!" At bottom there is a kind of doomed schoolyard craving for a friendship—a fusion, really—of which both are equally incapable. Dodd needs to absorb everything into himself; Freddie is the unassimilable being who resists being absorbed by anyone or anything.

Dodd is another of those figures of controlling intelligence and elusive motivation (Philip Baker Hall in *Hard Eight*, Burt Reynolds in *Boogie Nights*, Daniel Day-Lewis in *There Will Be Blood*) who haunt Anderson's films, and who enact the drama of the attempted dominion (perhaps protective, perhaps manipulative) of the bright over the not so bright. That Dodd finally elicits sympathy does not make him any less monstrous. He comes close to giving a tragic dignity to the con man who can con everyone—even himself—but not the one he most wants to con. Freddie may be the most faithful of foot soldiers, prompt to beat up anyone who challenges Dodd's authority, but he has a stubborn core of truthfulness that make him immune to the ultimate loyalty of actually believing. He may not prefer the solitariness to which his rejection of the Cause condemns him, but it is what he has inherited: the uncomfortable freedom to go out into the world with no resources, no plan, and no master.

# andrew sarris, 1928–2012

THE ARRIVAL IN MY LIFE of *Film Culture* 28 in the spring of 1963, with Andrew Sarris's preliminary sorting out of American movie directors that became the basis for his greatly expanded *The American Cinema* (published in 1968), was one of those before and after moments. It's hard even to reconstruct what it was like to have the past of American film suddenly spread out, a map of a country known previously only through rumor and fragmentary glimpses. Not just a map: a map accompanied with pointed commentary by a guide at once passionate and endlessly curious. It was all so exotic then. The very titles of the movies seemed like a strange kind of recovered poetry. But it was our own past, a lost world of universal neighborhood experience that had been occulted and buried. He pointed out things that I didn't know existed and argued persuasively for their importance. Rarely had there been such a cascade of information and insights and urgently communicated judgments.

It wasn't necessary to agree with those judgments. If Pauline Kael's reviews tended to be monologues, asking nothing beyond mute assent, Sarris didn't merely leave open the possibility of dialogue: he positively insisted on it. To read him was to converse. He even argued with himself (sometimes literally in dialogue form), taking pleasure in revisiting and revising his earlier opinions. For a young auteurist zealot this was sometimes hard to grasp; I remember reeling at his rejection of

*Marnie* in 1964 as at some unlooked-for apostasy. In time the frankness with which he laid out his reactions to what he saw would seem the rarest kind of critical honesty.

No doubt he loved lists, but there was a deep emotion that shaped those lists. Looking back at "Notes on the Auteur Theory in 1962" I find his list of auteurs—beginning "Ophuls, Renoir, Mizoguchi, Hitchcock, Chaplin, Ford, Welles, Dreyer, Rossellini, Murnau"—and it seems like shorthand for a catalogue of mystical experience. If Sarris became the critic I read and reread more than any other, it was perhaps for the sense that at the center of his writing was a reverence for film history—his kind of film history—as a poem of light that could never quite yield up all its secrets, a poem whose variations were infinite and whose traces might be found in the most unexpected places.

*Film Comment* blog, 2012

# acknowledgments

THESE PIECES APPEARED ORIGINALLY IN *The New York Review of Books*, *Bookforum*, *Film Comment*, *Artforum*, *Black Clock*, *LIT*, *The Point*, *Frederick Wiseman* (ed. Joshua Siegel, © MOMA, 2010), and *Olivier Assayas* (ed. Kent Jones, Austrian Film Museum, 2012). A number were written to accompany DVD and Blu-Ray discs released as part of the Criterion Collection, and one for Masters of Cinema (UK).

I am grateful to all the editors who initiated, encouraged, and assisted the writing, and to all those who showed me movies, told me about movies, and argued with me about movies. Although none of the pieces has been drastically revised, I have occasionally taken the opportunity to compress, clarify, correct, or omit.

# index